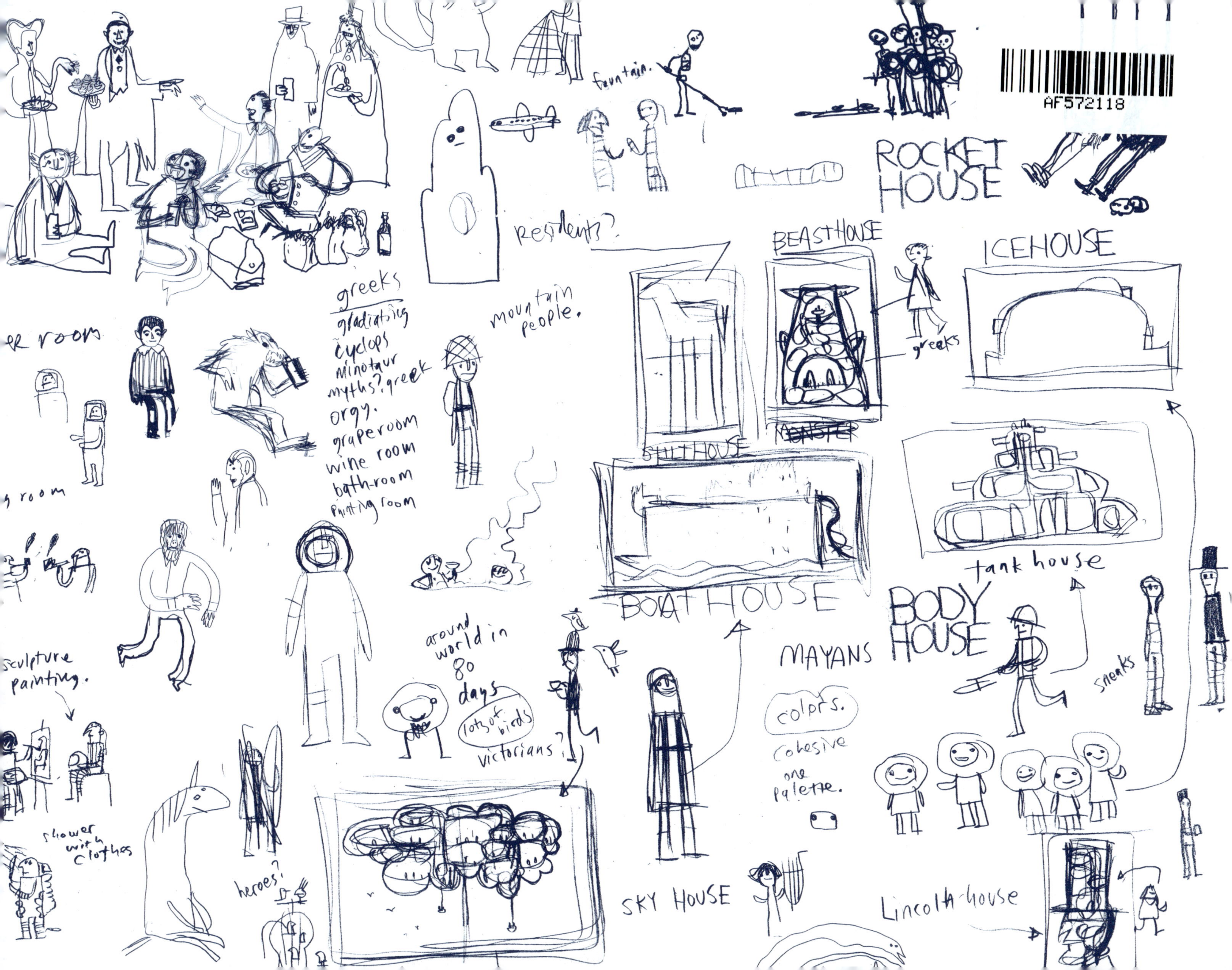

fountain.
AF572118
ROCKET HOUSE
residents?
BEASTHOUSE
ICEHOUSE
greeks
gladiating
cyclops
minotaur
myths? greek
orgy.
graperoom
wine room
bath-room
Painting room
mountain people.
greeks
STILTHOUSE
BOAT HOUSE
tank house
BODY HOUSE
MAYANS
sneaks
colors.
cohesive
one palette.
around world in 80 days
lots of birds
victorians?
sculpture painting.
shower with clothes
heroes?
SKY HOUSE
Lincoln house

AMAZING EVERYTHING

the art of scott c.

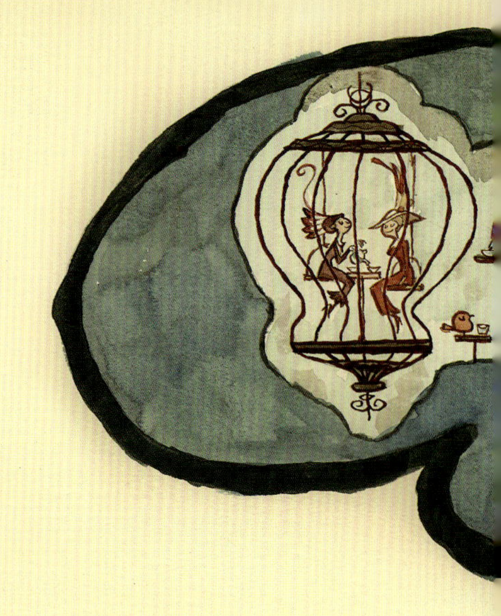

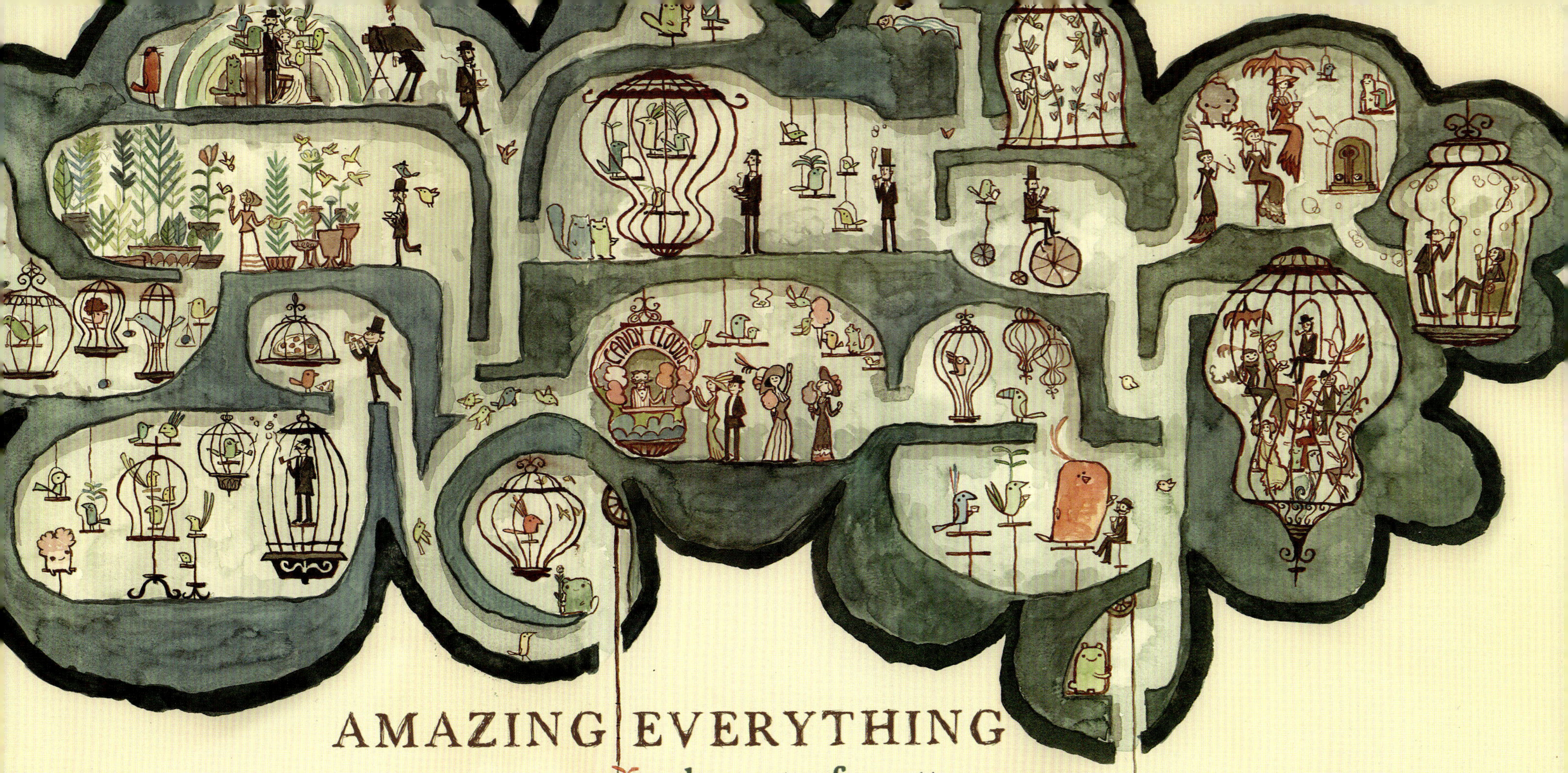

AMAZING EVERYTHING

the art of scott c.

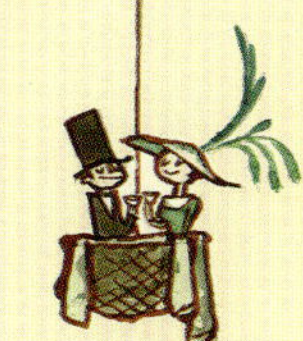

by scott campbell

foreword by jack black

INSIGHT EDITIONS

San Rafael, California

Library of Congress Cataloging-in-Publication Data available.

ISBN: 9-781-60887-047-9

Design by Maurene Goo

Photos of puppets and Scott courtesy of *Comrade Magazine*
Photography by Love Ablan (loveablan.com)
Puppets created by Russ Walko

REPLANTED PAPER

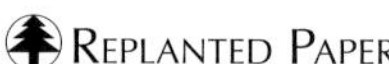

Insight Editions, in association with Roots of Peace, will plant two trees for each tree used in the manufacturing of this book. Roots of Peace is an internationally renowned humanitarian organization dedicated to eradicating land mines worldwide and converting war-torn lands into productive farms and wildlife habitats. Together, we will plant two million fruit and nut trees in Afghanistan and provide farmers there with the skills and support necessary for sustainable land use.

Manufactured in China by Insight Editions

10 9 8 7 6 5 4 3 2 1

INSIGHT EDITIONS
PO Box 3088, San Rafael, CA 94912
www.insighteditions.com

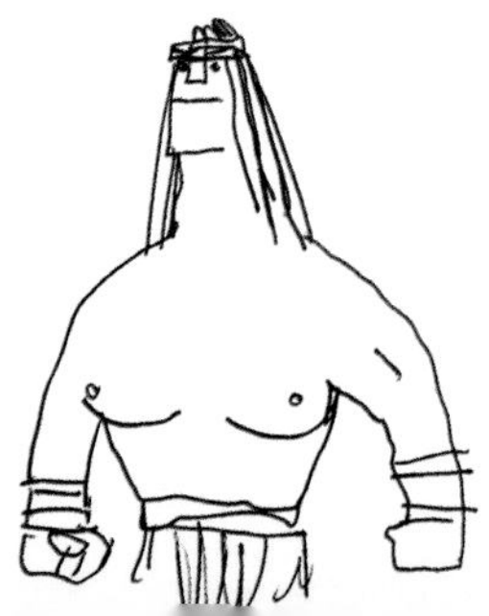

pages 2–3: CLOUD HOUSE | watercolor | 44" x 30" | 2009
right: BATTLE OF THE SERPENTS | watercolor | 11" x 14" | 2006
left: HUNTING FROM ABOVE | watercolor | 5" x 7" | 2009
page 6: BARBARIAN HOUSE | watercolor | 7" x 5" | 2009

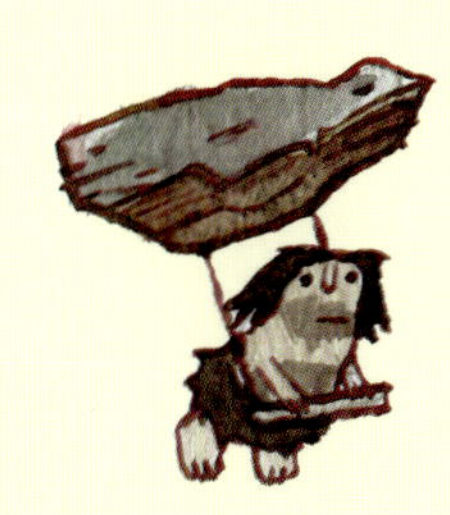
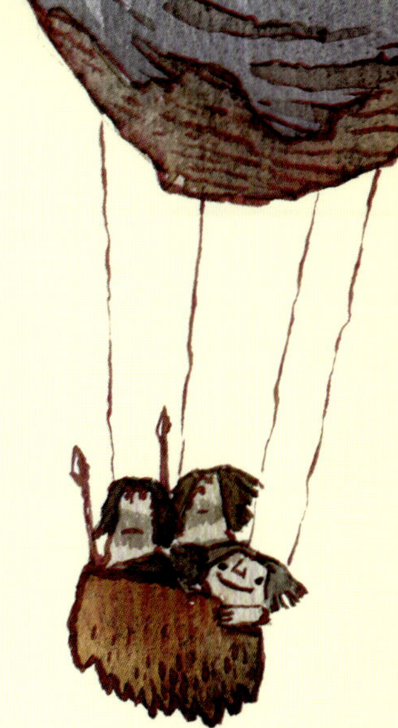

contents

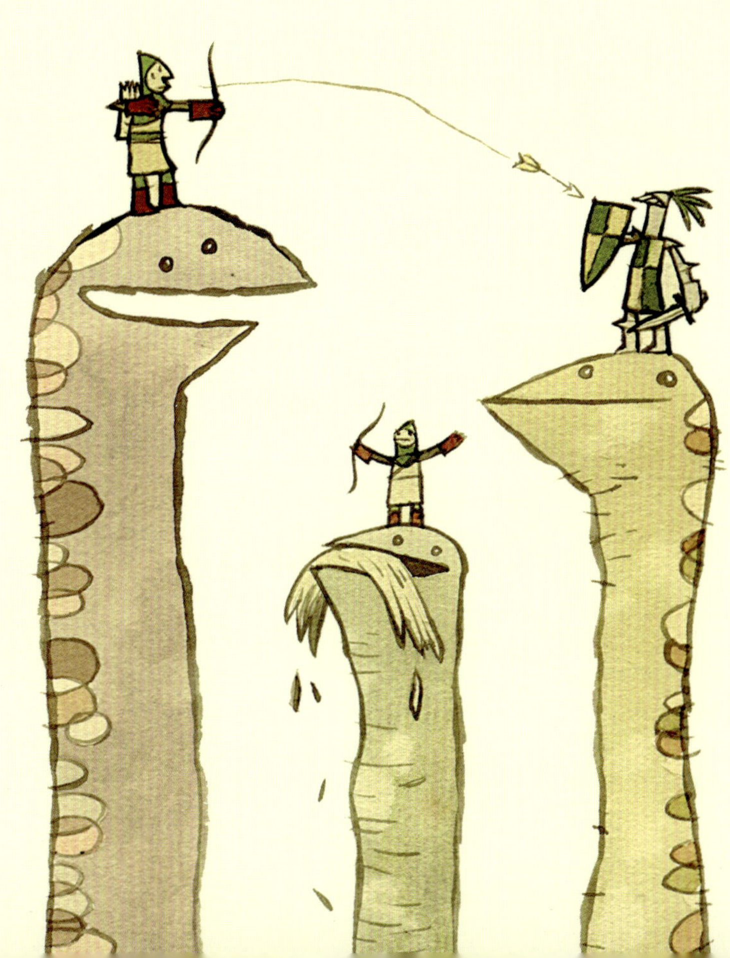

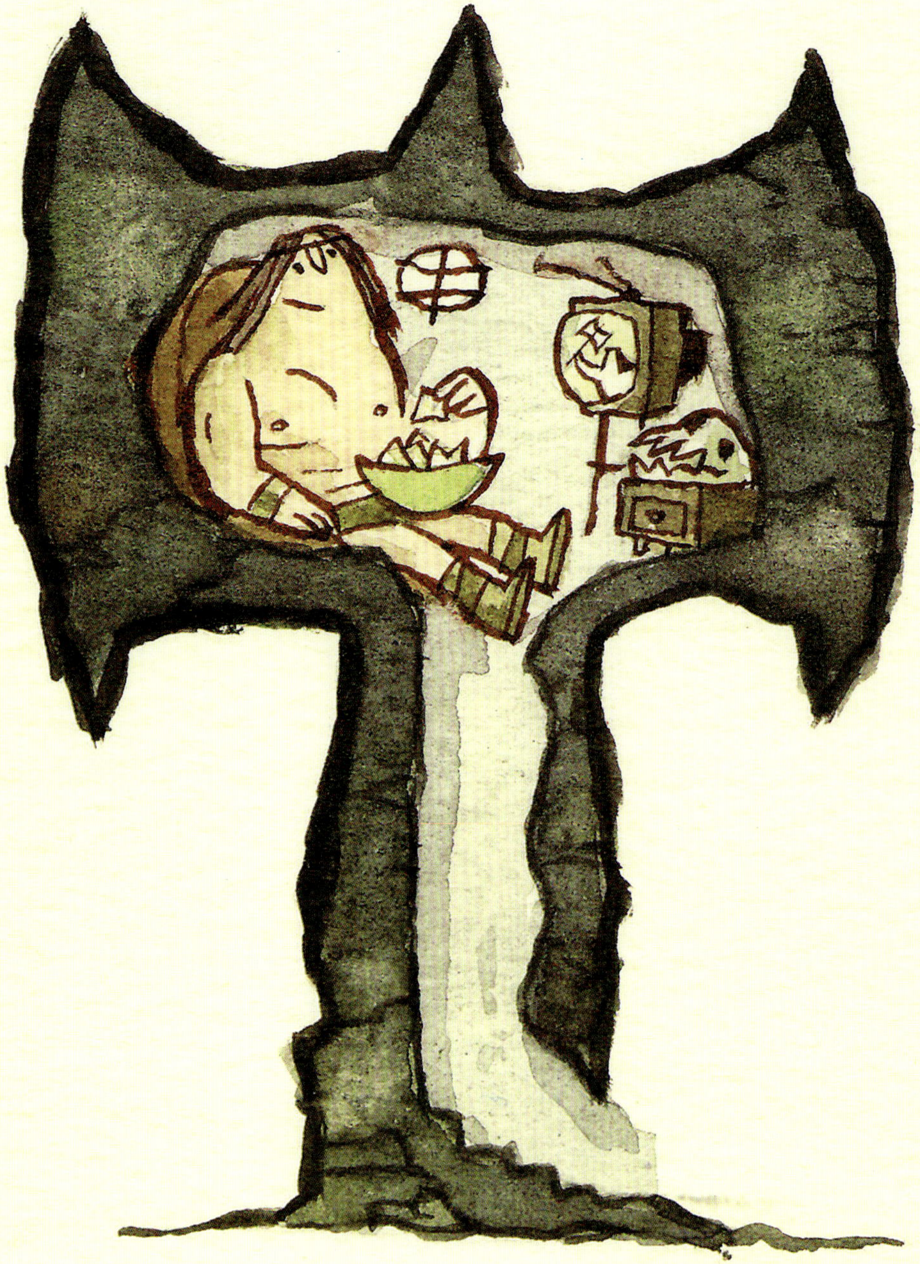

Foreword

i loves me some scott c.

his paintings are all like precious little gems.

so cleverly conceived and skillfully executed.

touching and hilarious.

and timeless.

sometimes he'll bust out some roaring '20s magic.

then the next thing you know, he's painting a kick-ass '80s metal-era masterpiece.

i've seen about seven other artists blatantly try to bite his style.

but no one can replicate his technique,

or clone his unique perspective.

so bite on *this* poseurs.

and enjoy this tasty collection of sweet and shiny gem stones.

scotty c. reigns supreme!

~jack black

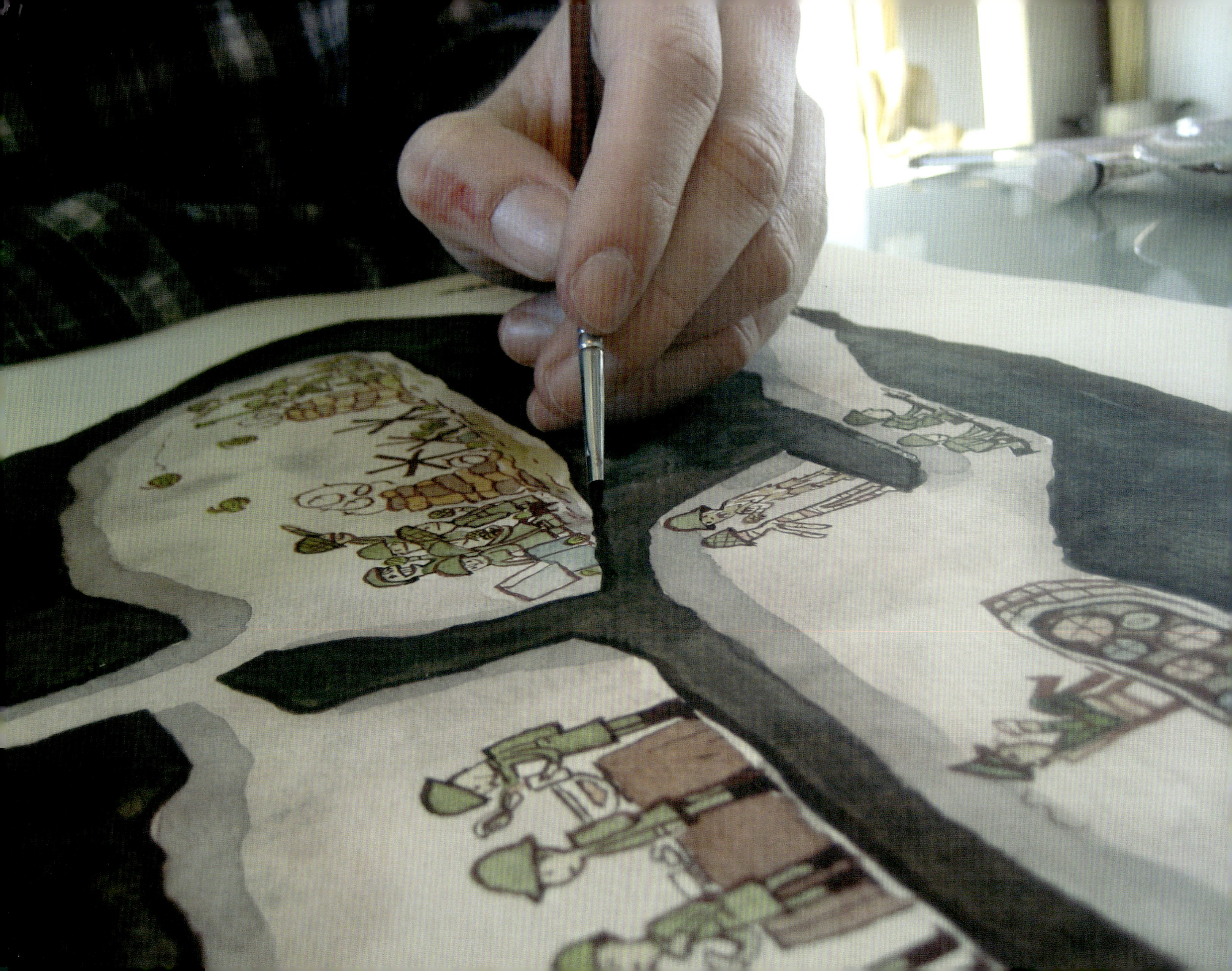

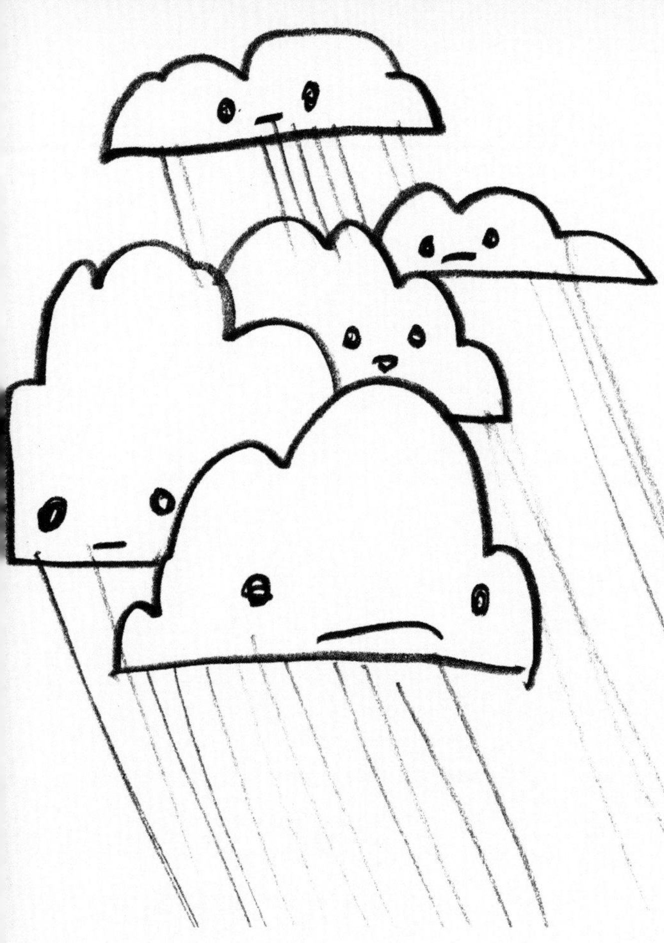

INTRODUCTION

I WOULD LIKE TO TELL YOU A STORY, MY FRIENDS.

The subject of this story is me, but it is also about friendship, hugging, and drawing.

My favorite thing to draw in preschool was potato dudes fighting. I drew these guys on all my school projects. When I saw my mother's disappointment in me as we looked through my first folder of work, I felt I needed to find deeper meaning in my drawings. Potato dudes fighting had served their purpose. I must find the truth.

I looked to my coloring books and comics. My Spider-Man and Incredible Hulk books inspired me to draw Spider-Man and the Incredible Hulk. My Star Wars books inspired me to trace them and bring the drawings to school to charade like I had drawn them. I was a young poseur.

In first grade, I entered my first young authors' fair with an epic novel titled *Mike and His Adventure*, a long and meandering story that seemed to have no end; it was merely a vessel for me to draw dragons and fighting, and my next few young authors' books would get longer and more meandering and never-ending. In second grade, I entered the contest to redesign the logo for the school mascot, the Dilworth Dragon. I entered ten designs—half of them traced from books I had at home—because that increased my odds, and I was flabbergasted when I did not win. I vowed to become the master of drawing dragons.

In third grade, most of my art projects would hit a point where I would ask the question, "Shall I add that last thing that shall put this piece over the top? This is a fine stitching of a dragon, but shall I add that last thing? The sword in its belly with blood pouring out?" Most of the time, I chose to add that last touch. That year, I lost the title of Best Artist to my rival, Nathan, who was master of drawing robots. I resolved then to pay more attention to what that finishing touch might be, and whether it was necessary. I realized I must get more serious about my art.

By sixth grade, I already had under my belt a number of books and comics I had drawn with my brother: a G.I. Joe book, a Star Wars book, a book about a fortune-teller, a Doctor Who book, a Hardy Boys book, a Family Circus book, a book about a make-believe team of heroes called the "X-Tremes," and many more. I was very much into origin stories. My brother and I collected the crap out of comics, and we played D&D quite poorly with

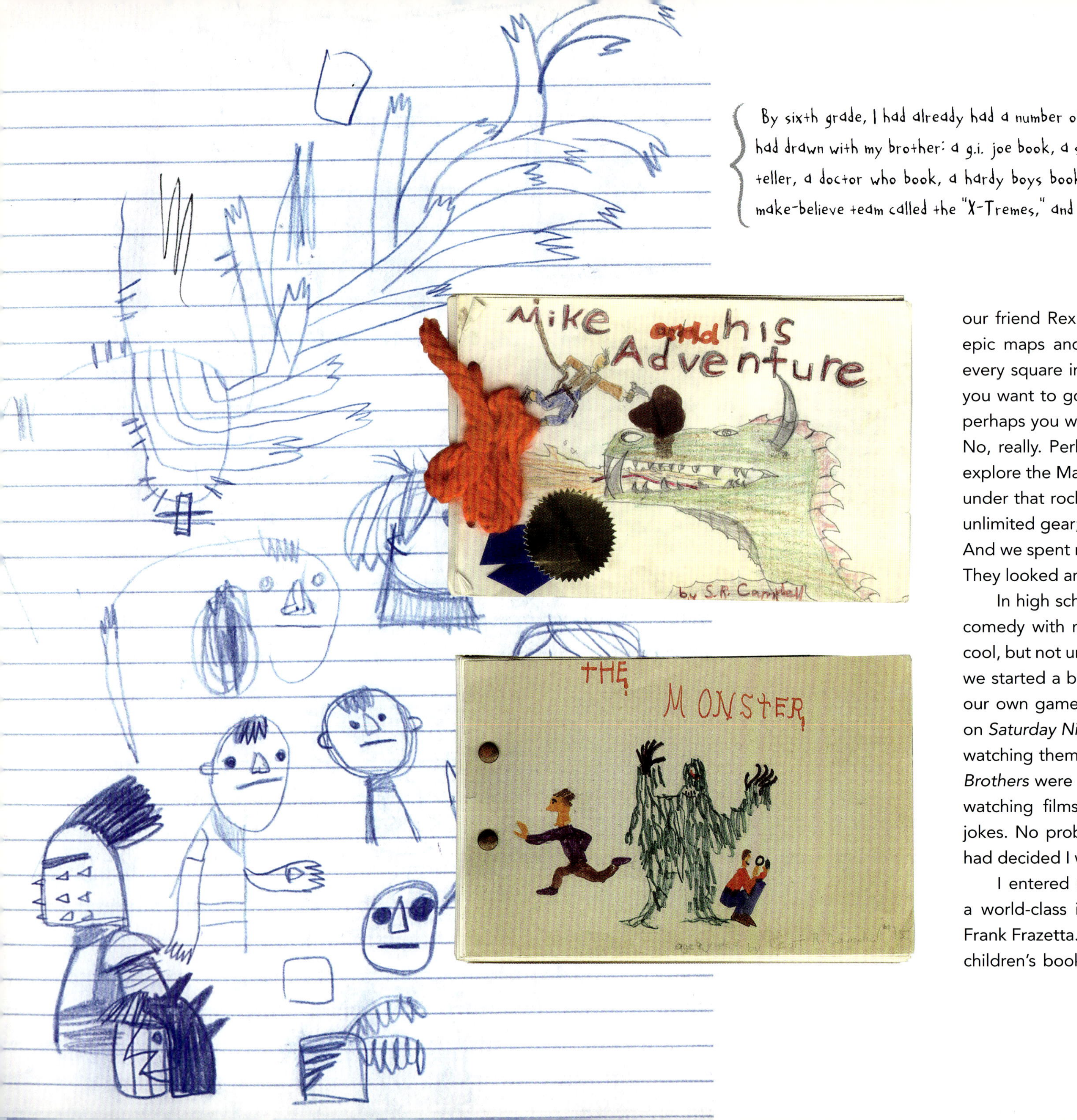

{ By sixth grade, I had already had a number of books and comics under my belt, that I had drawn with my brother: a g.i. joe book, a star wars book, a book about a fortune-teller, a doctor who book, a hardy boys book, a family circus book, a book about a make-believe team called the "X-Tremes," and many more. I was very into origin stories. }

our friend Rex. As the Dungeon Master, I would draw epic maps and force my brother and Rex to explore every square inch of them on their adventure: "I know you want to go to the Canyon of the Lost Temple, but perhaps you would like to explore the Marshlands first. No, really. Perhaps the Marshlands. I think you should explore the Marshlands. Go to the Marshlands and look under that rock." But in return, I allowed them to carry unlimited gear; everything they found, they could carry. And we spent much of our time drawing our characters. They looked amazing covered in all that gear.

In high school, I ventured deeper into the world of comedy with my three friends. We were floaters—not cool, but not uncool. Social limbo. But come senior year, we started a band and became quite cool. We created our own games and movies. I decided I wanted to be on *Saturday Night Live,* and I recorded all the episodes, watching them constantly. *Strange Brew* and *The Blues Brothers* were also in heavy rotation. I had no problem watching films repeatedly in order to memorize the jokes. No problem at all. By the end of high school, I had decided I would like to draw *X-Men* for a living.

I entered school to study illustration and become a world-class illustrator like John Singer Sargent and Frank Frazetta. I focused on comic book illustration and children's book illustration. I studied the human figure

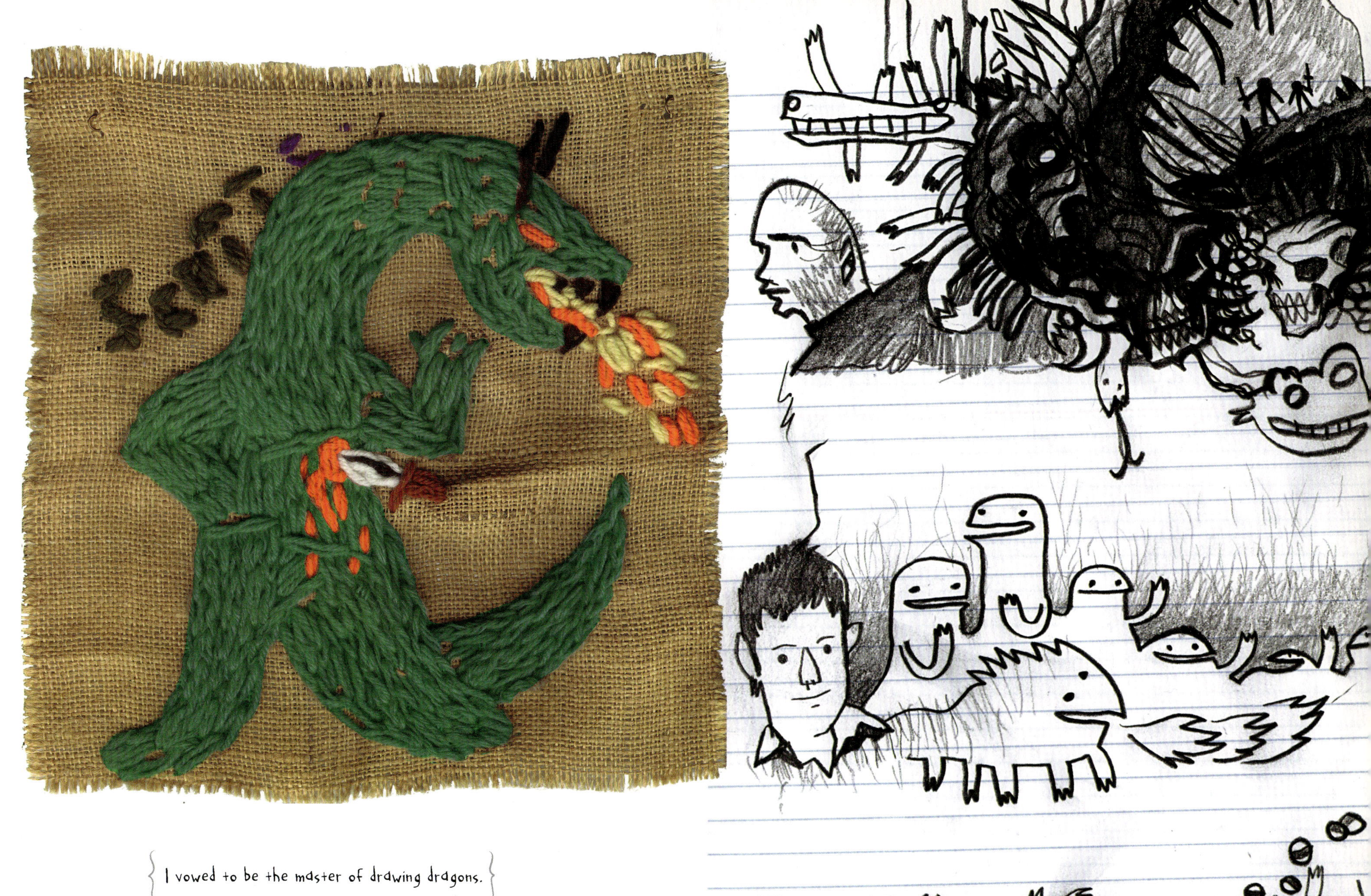

{ I vowed to be the master of drawing dragons. }

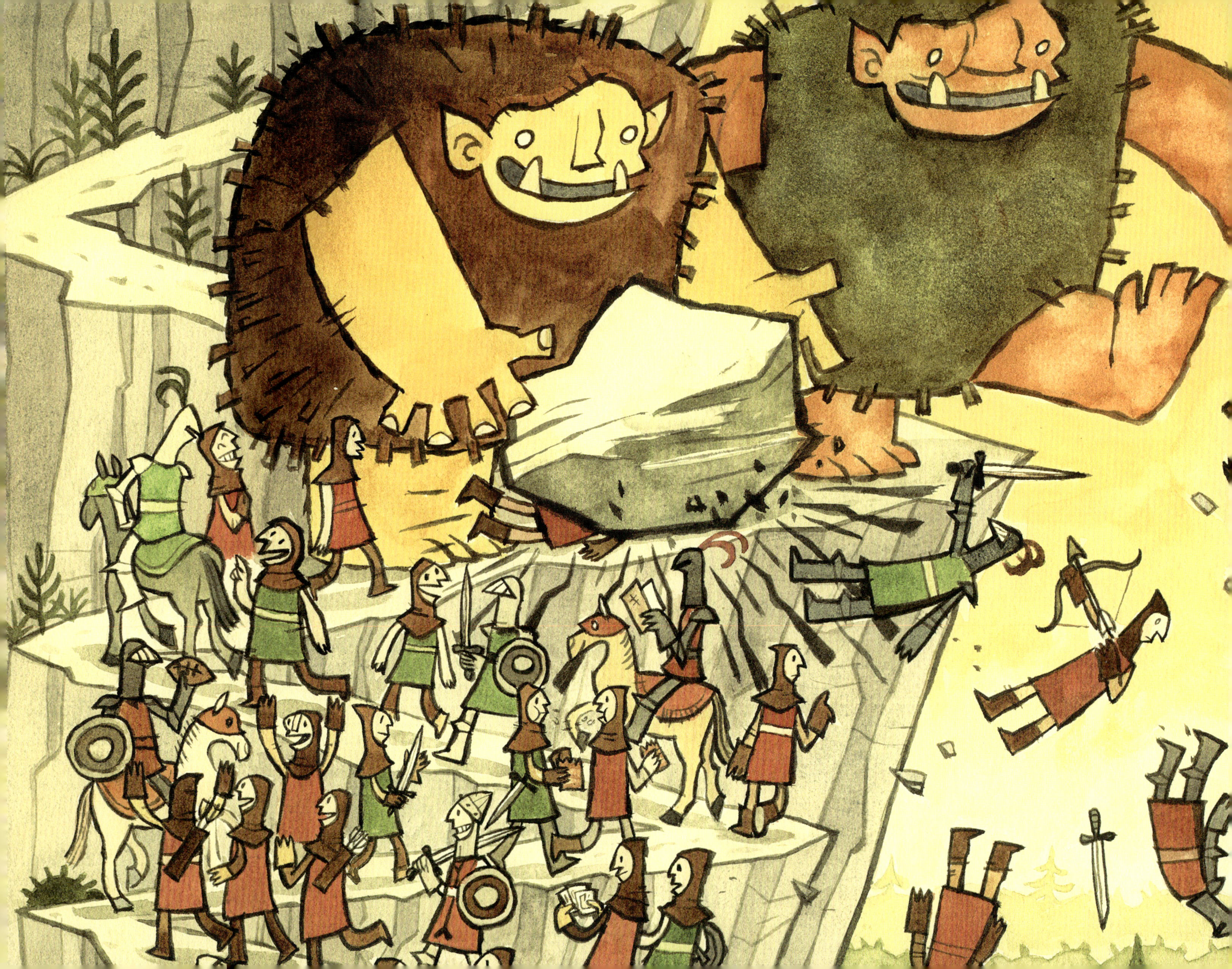

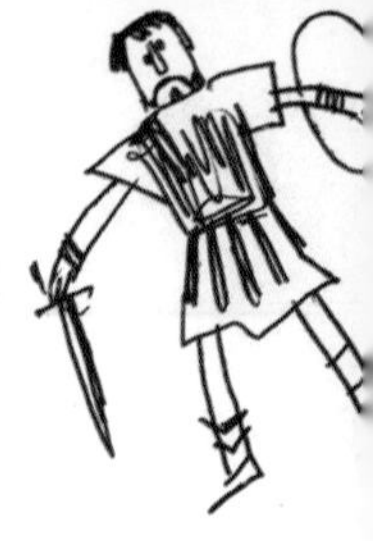

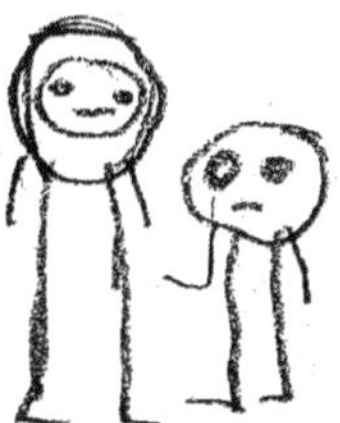

and vowed once again to be the best at drawing people. I was determined to be a people-drawing master and to impress everyone with my amazing skills. But in art school, I made some new friends who exposed me to new types of art. I had previously condemned abstract and conceptual art because I did not understand it. But my friend Paul introduced me to artists like Paul Klee and Jean-Michel Basquiat and comics like *Eightball* and *Yikes*. And I was taken with how they interpret the world.

After college, I was a lost soul—I knew not where to go with my bag of skills—so I often returned to school to hassle my teachers on what I should do. I spent much of my time at a pizza place showing people to their tables. I was very good at showing people amazing spots to sit. A friend from art school got a job at LucasArts and learned how to animate on video games. I had no desire to work in video games, but I had a desire to work on Star Wars. Oh, what a desire I had for Star Wars. I went to Lucas Learning to draw Star Wars games for children, and I became quite happy.

However, there was a little bit of a vacuum in my life after college. There was no longer the camaraderie of artists bouncing their ideas off one another. I feel that it is important to have this sort of community influence in order to stay motivated and grow with one's art. Two separate groups came out of this need for community. One was a group of friends who consisted of painters, musicians, graphic artists, poets, chefs, and puppeteers. We called ourselves MMAC and gathered to share our projects with one another and throw art shows to share them with the people. The comedy/storytelling side of things came from another, smaller group of friends who gathered to make comics together. We called ourselves Hickee and began to visit comic conventions with our self-published comics. It helped us to have goals like art shows and comic conventions to keep productive. It was at one of these art shows that my friend Tim Schafer first felt that his newly conceived game *Psychonauts* might look sweet in my cartoony style. And so I went forth to join him and Double Fine Productions as art director.

So I made comics, threw art shows, and made video games. That was the trifecta. That kept me active, my friends.

But there was something I struggled with—something all my artist friends seemed to have that I did not: They had a reason to create. They had something to say with their art. A message to give everyone. What message did I have? I painted these characters, but they said nothing to me. They looked weird and had strange heads and eyes and sometimes held strange things in their hands and stood in front of some clever pattern. But why was I painting? What did I want to tell people? Was I enjoying the journey of these paintings? Not really. Was I telling tormented stories and commenting about the world around me?

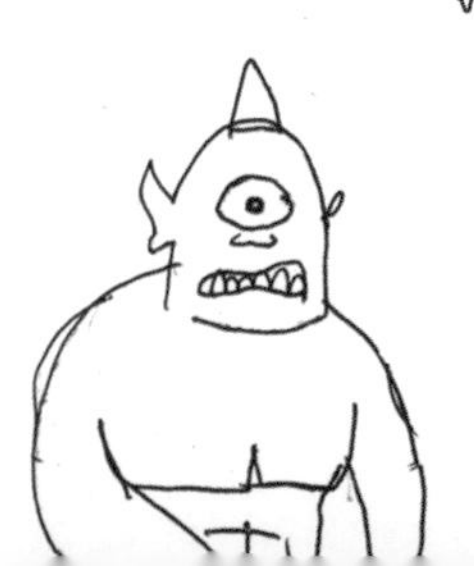

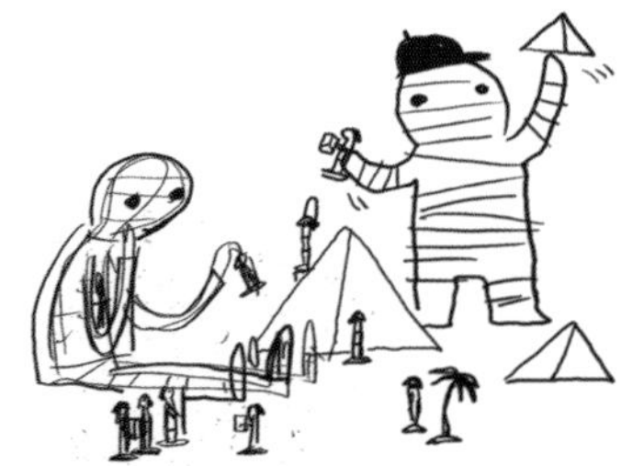

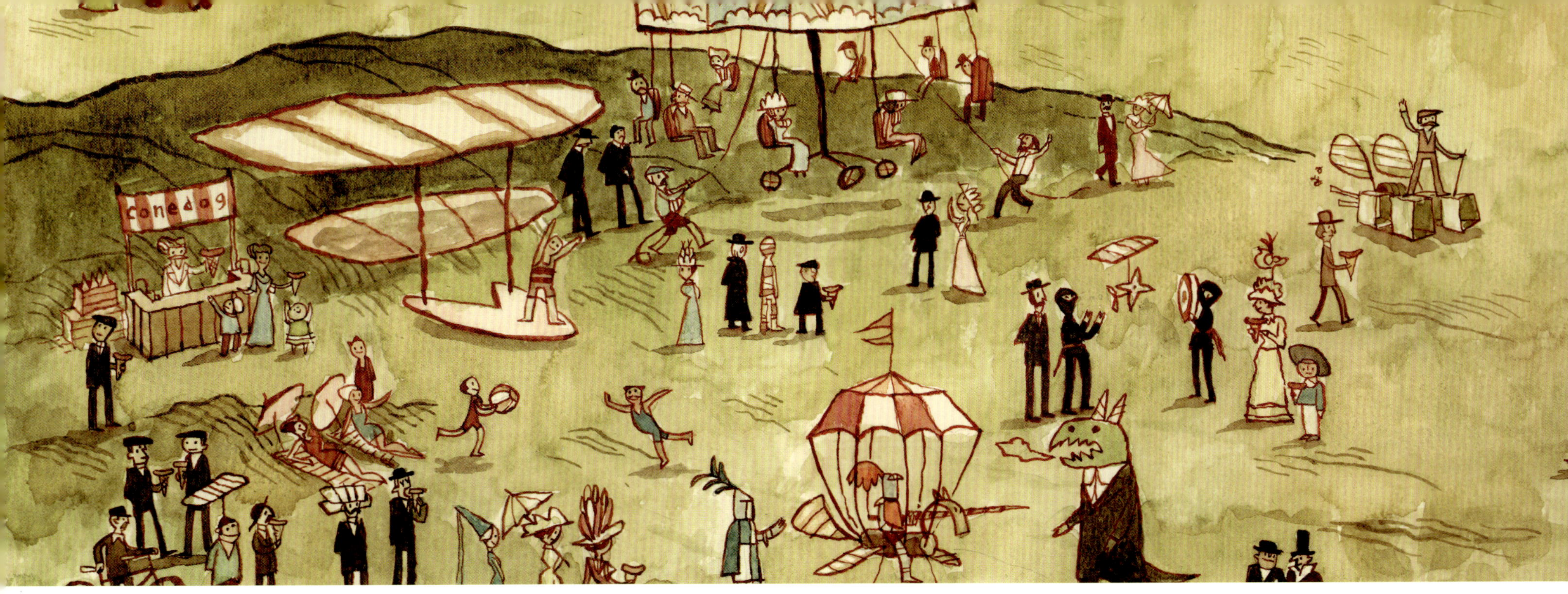

I was not a tormented soul that must paint to stay sane. I had a *Leave It to Beaver* upbringing with a pleasant family. I just liked to make jokes and be happy. I wanted to regain that feeling as a kid of getting so excited about finishing my cereal so that I might get back to that drawing I had been working on—that battle scene—because the drawings were more about having an adventure on paper and less about the end product. The end product was merely a chronicling of the good time I had had drawing it.

So I began to tell stories with my paintings. Another vow, everyone: to always have a bit of a narrative to my paintings and drawings. But not to spell it out—just to put the pieces there for people to discover and construct their own scenarios. Watching people enjoy my paintings in this fashion finally became satisfying. I like making people laugh and point and nudge one another.

SOME OF THE THINGS YOU WILL FIND IN THIS BOOK:

- There are monsters in this book, so do not freak out—but to balance that out, there is an equal amount of cute things as well.

- There are friends enjoying each other's company, but there are also awkward moments that must make us reflect on our own relationships.

- You might find some amazing hats in this book and some beautiful plant life. You may discover the secrets of ancient Egypt and the age of gallant knights.

- You may also come across those who enjoy the timber life.

- You may find zombies and ninjas, because they are quite popular right now and may forever be popular.

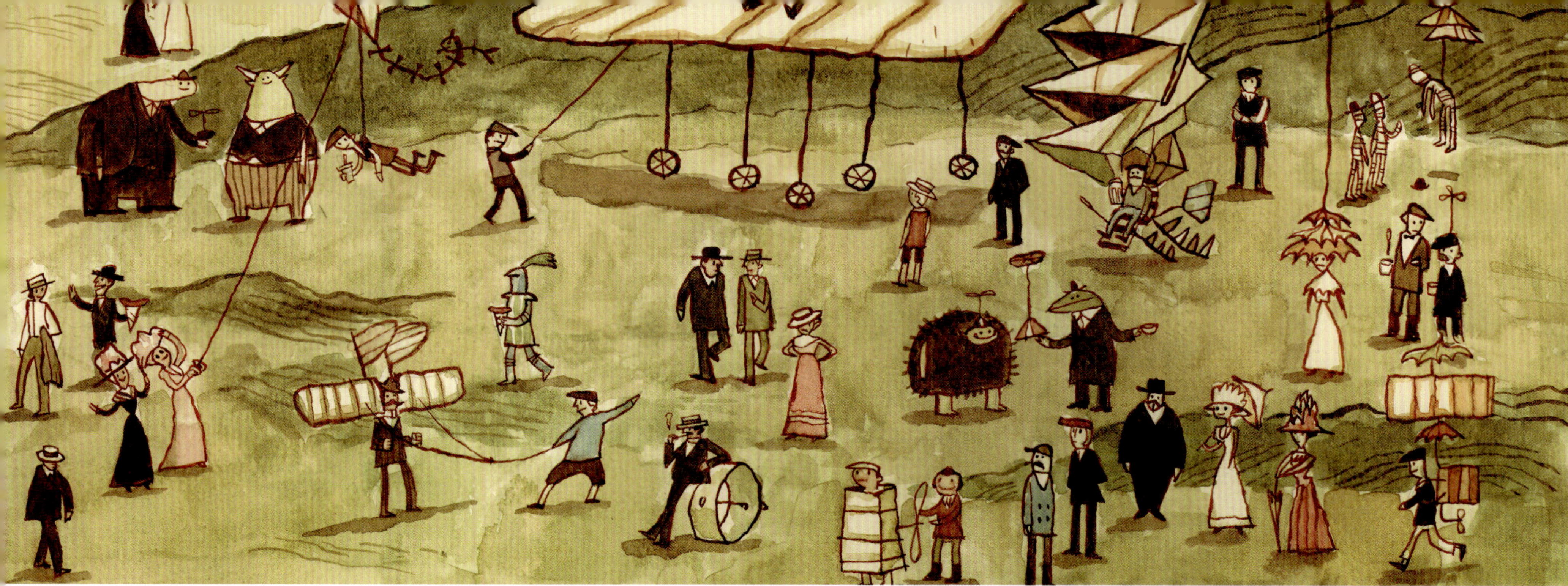

- There are cavemen in this book and dinosaurs that would like to be friends with these cavemen.

- My friends Igloo Head and Tree Head, you will be happy to know, make an appearance.

- There are some rainbows in this book.

- There are great houses in this book. You will see the glory of the residents that live in these houses and catch a glimpse of where they eat, sleep, and go hot-tubbing.

- There is fighting in this book. I will not lie. I wish there were not, but the world is full of fighting, and I must document it for you. So that we may learn from it. Learn fighting moves, mostly.

- There is pizza in this book. Quite a lot of pizza, actually.

- There are people hugging in this book. Beware. If you do not like hugging, you may want to shield your eyes in those parts.

- There are a couple of goats in this book.

- There is a map in this book that will teach you about maps. So get ready to learn about maps.

- Video games make an appearance in this book. So, if you are familiar with those, you will really get a kick out of that stuff. If you are unfamiliar with them, perhaps you will find something in them that resonates with you. Like the outfits.

- There are famous people in this book that I have paid great homage to, because I love them and respect them. Perhaps we can all learn to love and embrace famous people.

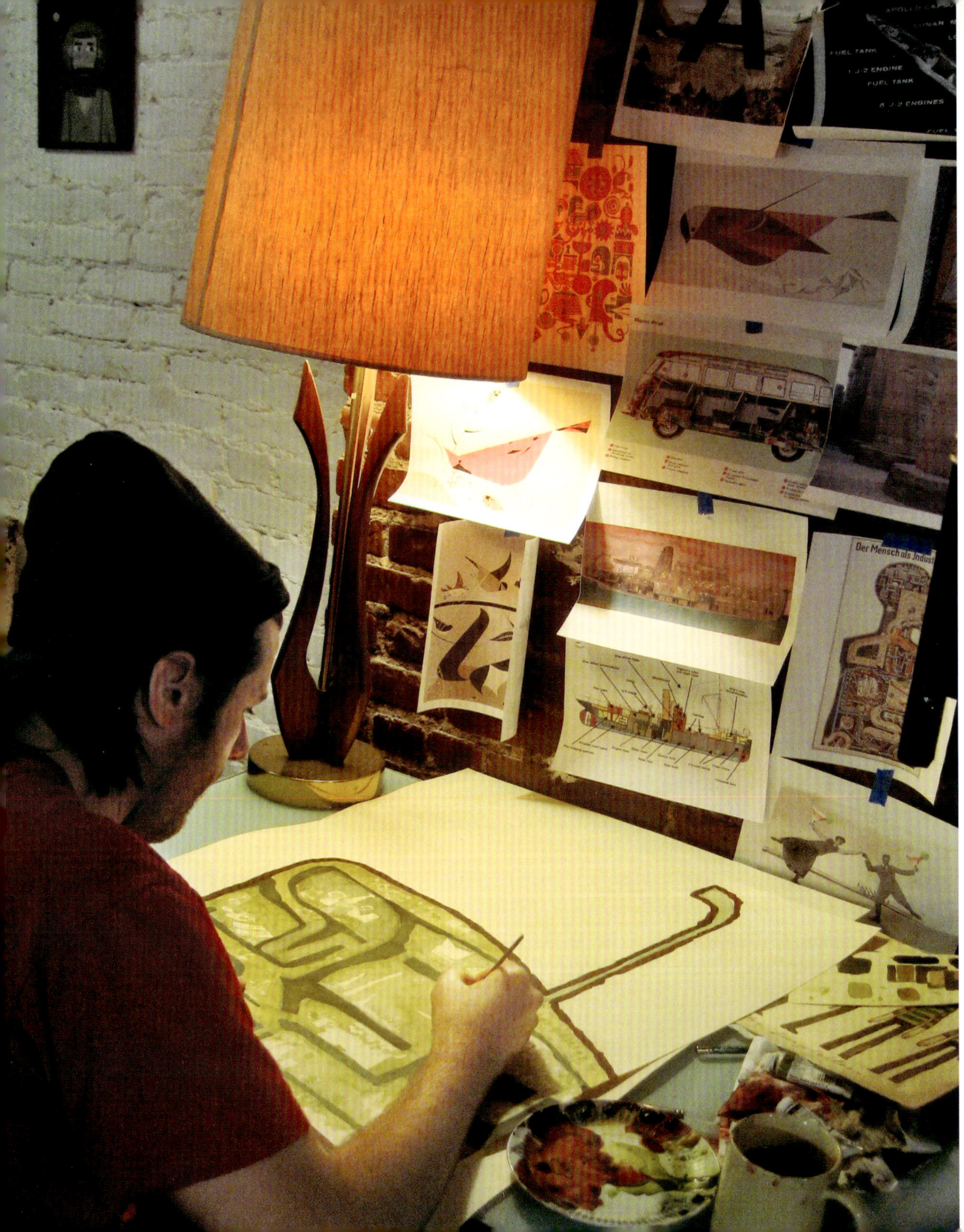

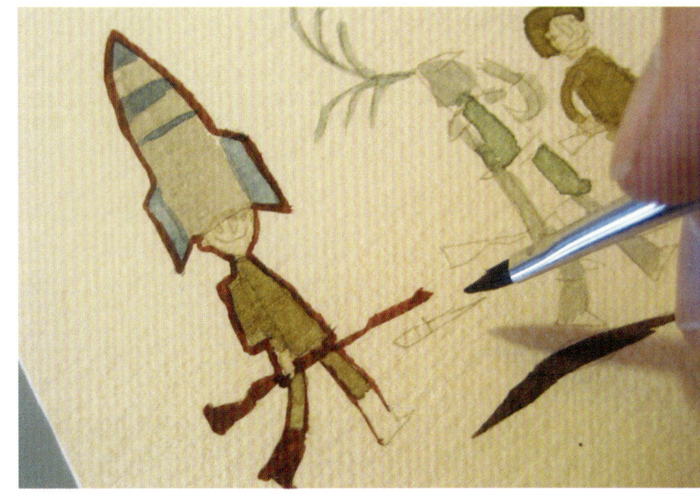

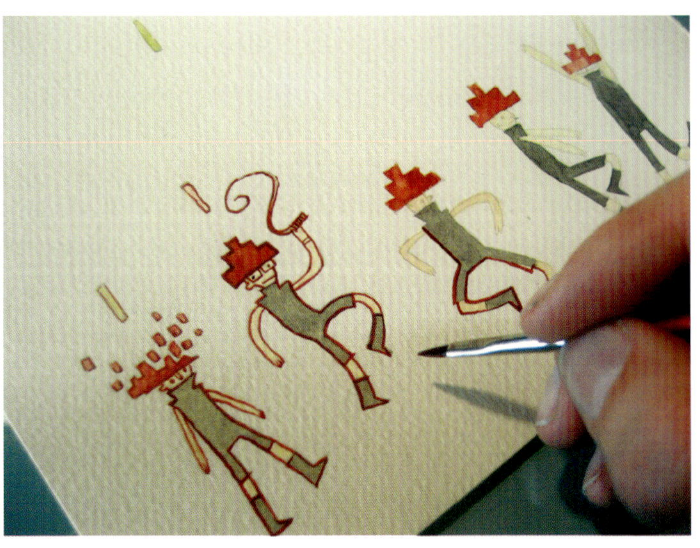

All these things are presented to you in adorable little watercolor paintings I have created with my hands. Why do I use watercolor? Because it enables me to have a muted and noncommittal palette with an airiness that relaxes me. My colors start out quite faint, but as I gain more confidence, the colors become more vibrant and contrasting. I start out by doodling on sheets of scratch paper and scanning them into the computer to compose in Photoshop. I have grown accustomed to the Undo button. I print the compositions out and trace them onto my watercolor paper like magic. My drawing table rests up against a brick wall in my apartment. I also print out inspiring art and images from the Internet and tape them to the brick wall so I may get pumped by them. I have three puppet friends: Knight, Mummy, and Caveman. Mummy is the smartest and likes to discuss things. Interesting topics, mostly. They were born for the *Home Slice* show at Gallery Nucleus. They are always hanging about doing puppet things.

I believe that you are about to embark on an amazing journey, my friends. I am happy that you are here and holding this book in your hands and reading these words. I am looking forward to the adventure you shall take here. And by the end of the book, if you have learned some things about the world around you, then splendid. All I can ask for is that you be open-minded to things with cute faces.

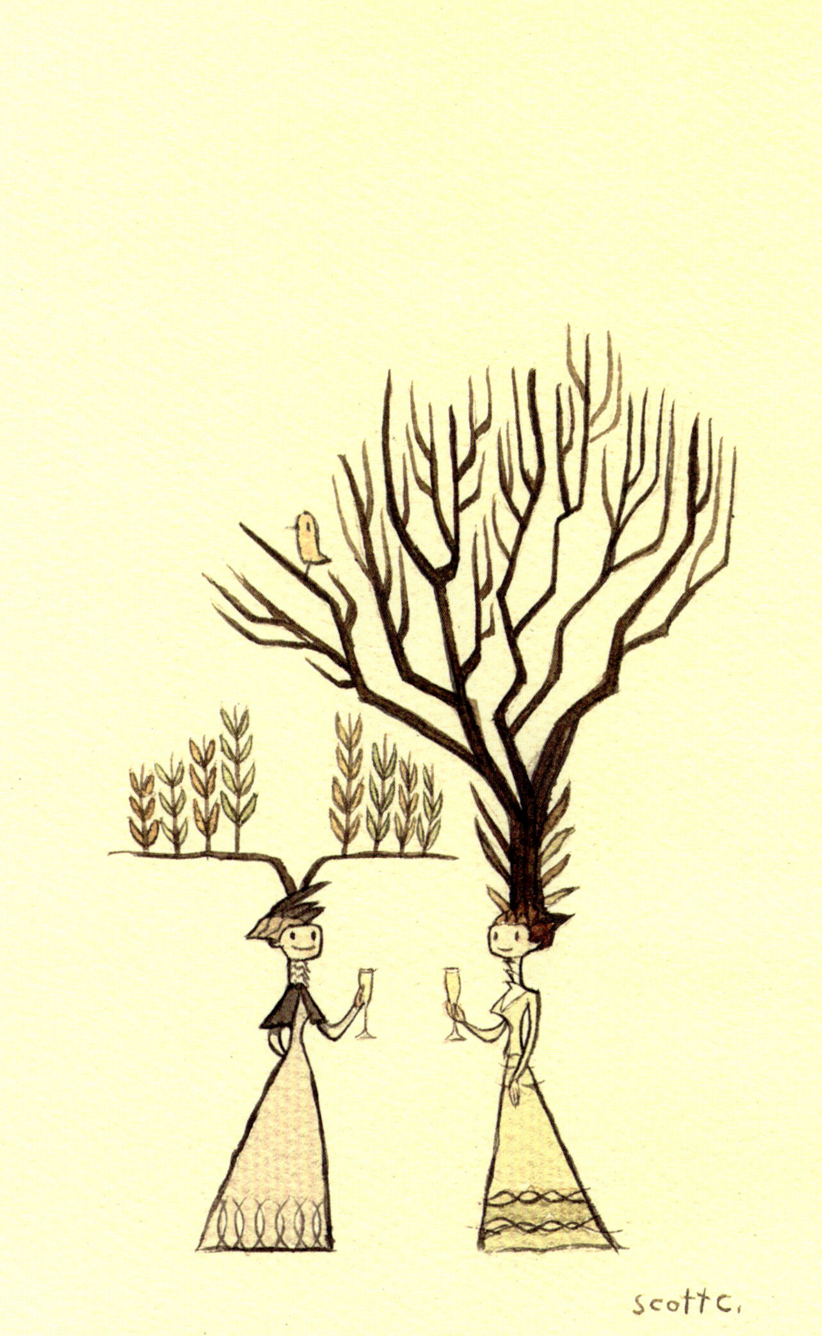

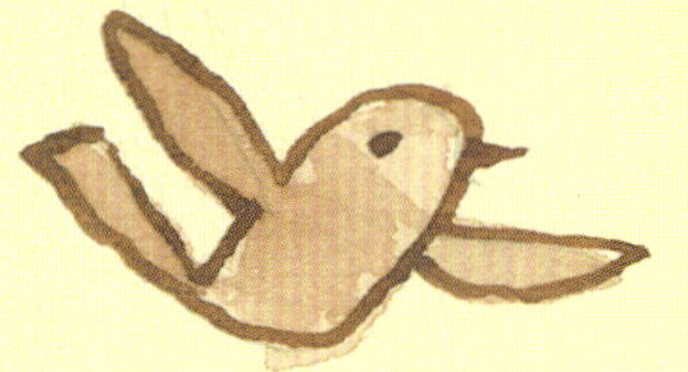

pop cultures

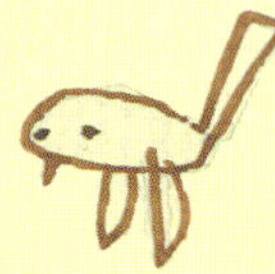

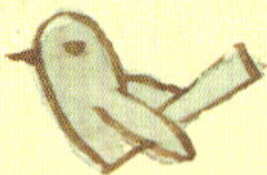

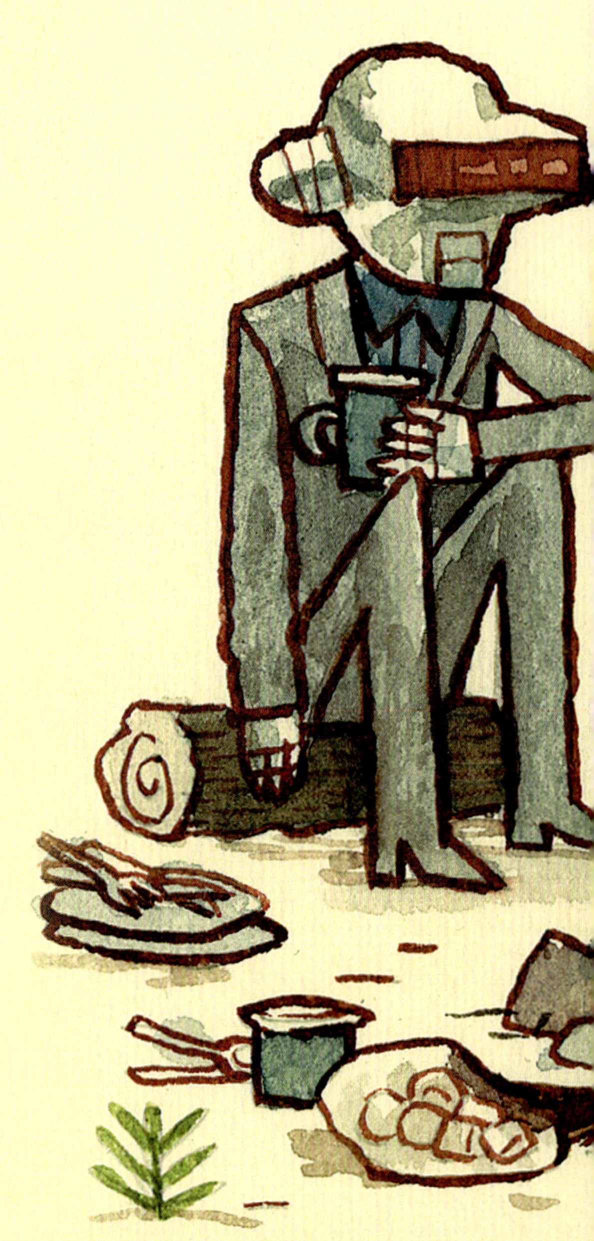

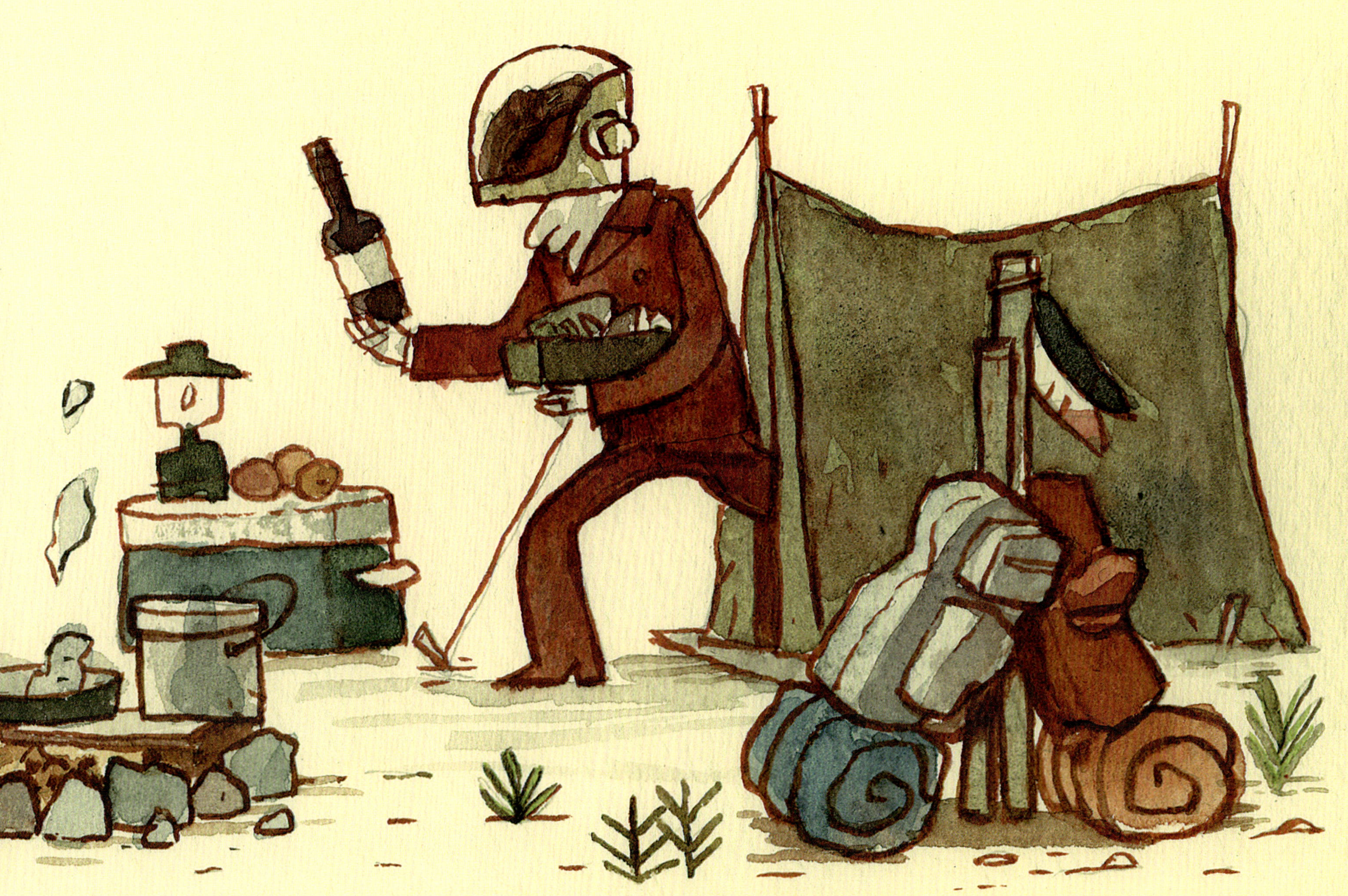

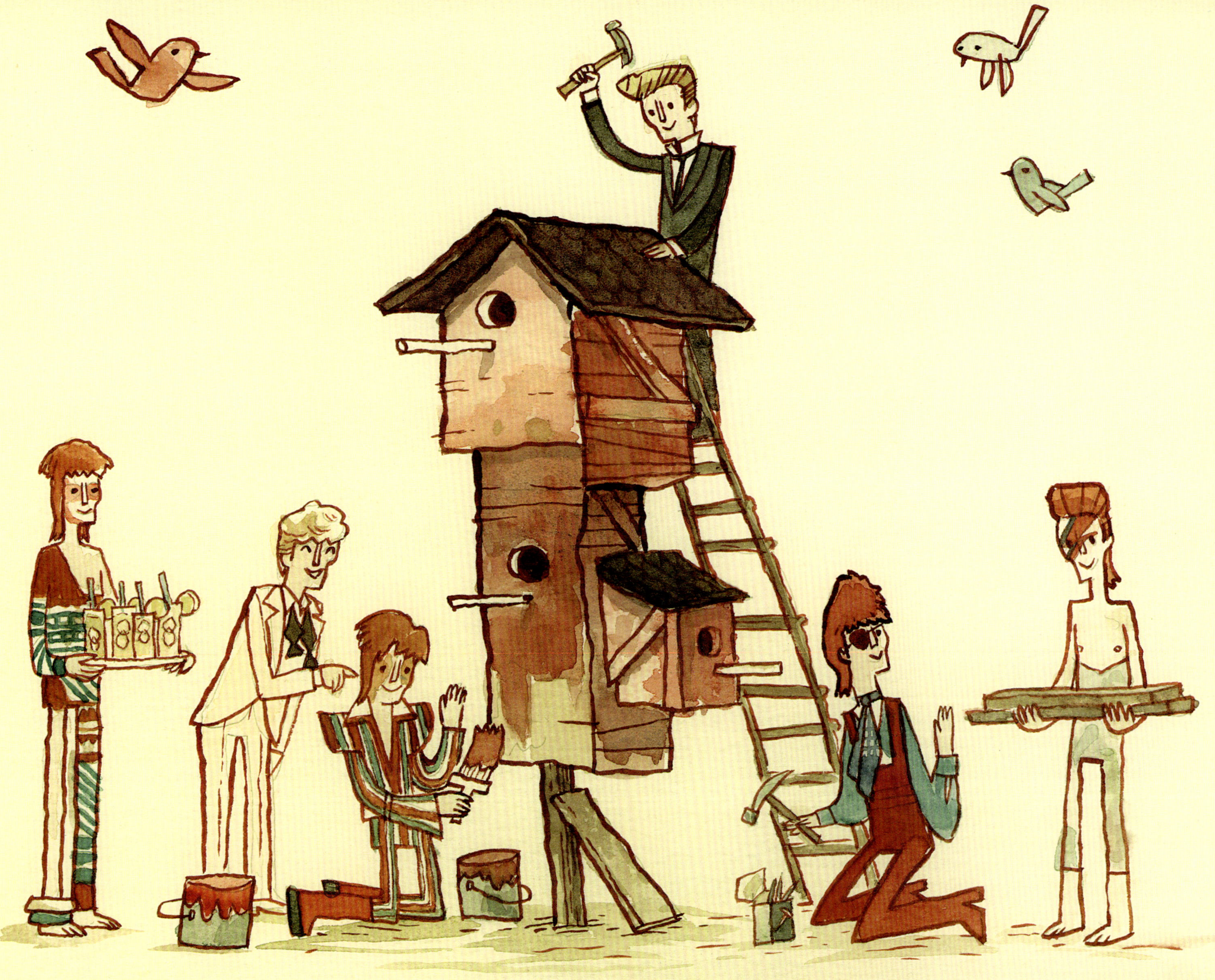

<< [section opener] | SOME WINE PERHAPS? | watercolor | 7" x 5" | 2009

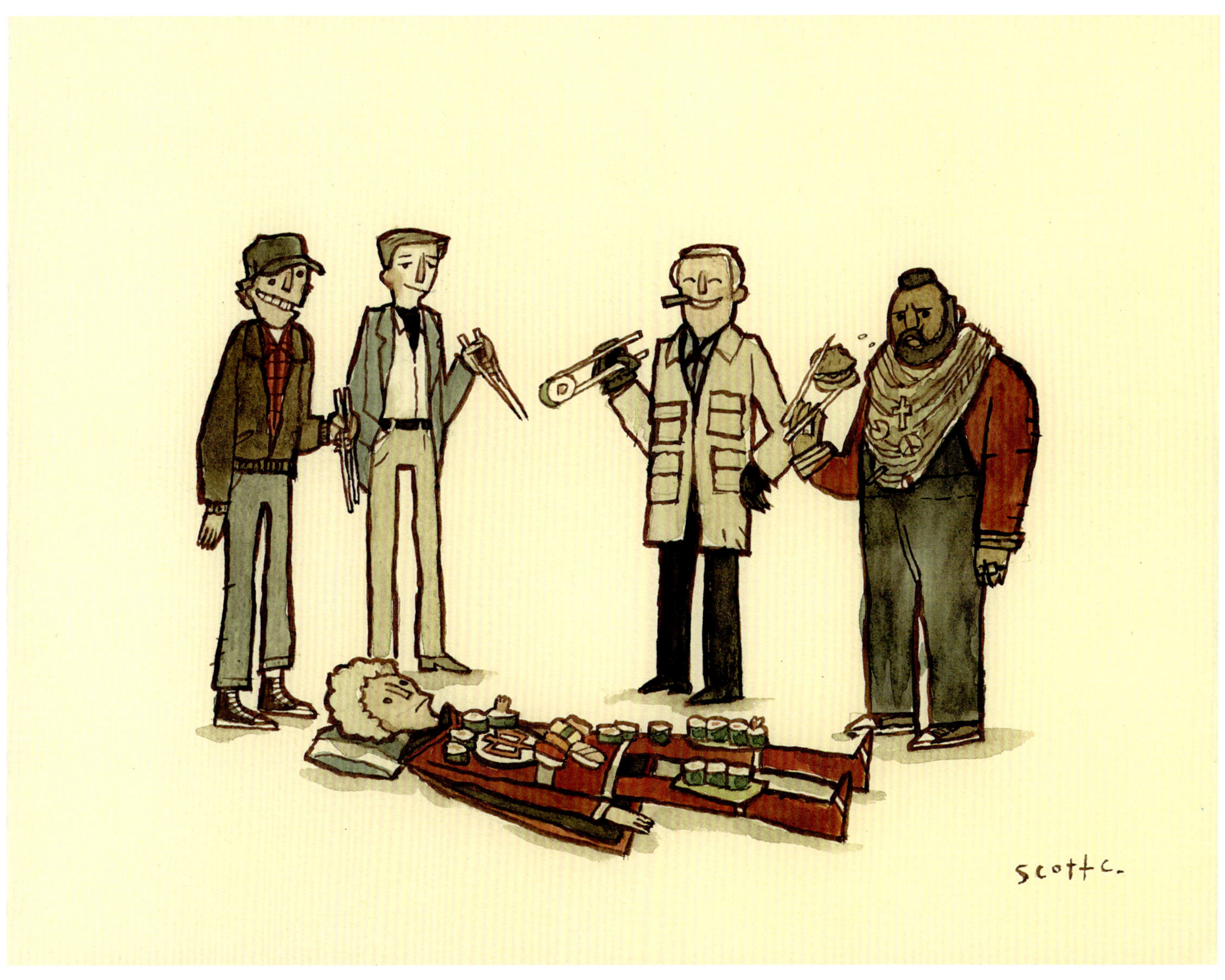

SUSHI OFF A FRIEND
watercolor
10" x 8"
2009

<< BUILDING WITH THE BOWIES | watercolor | 10" x 8" | 2009

22

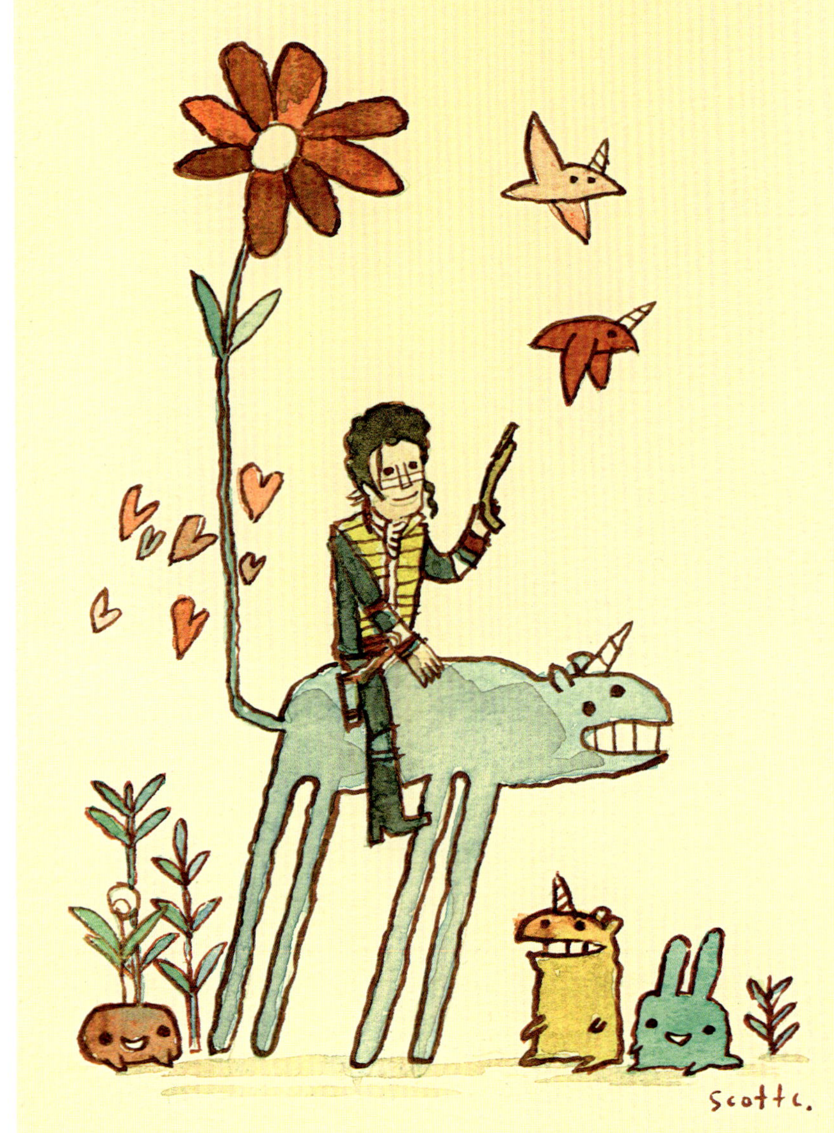

STANDING AND DELIVERING (SOME LOVE)
watercolor
8" x 10"
2009

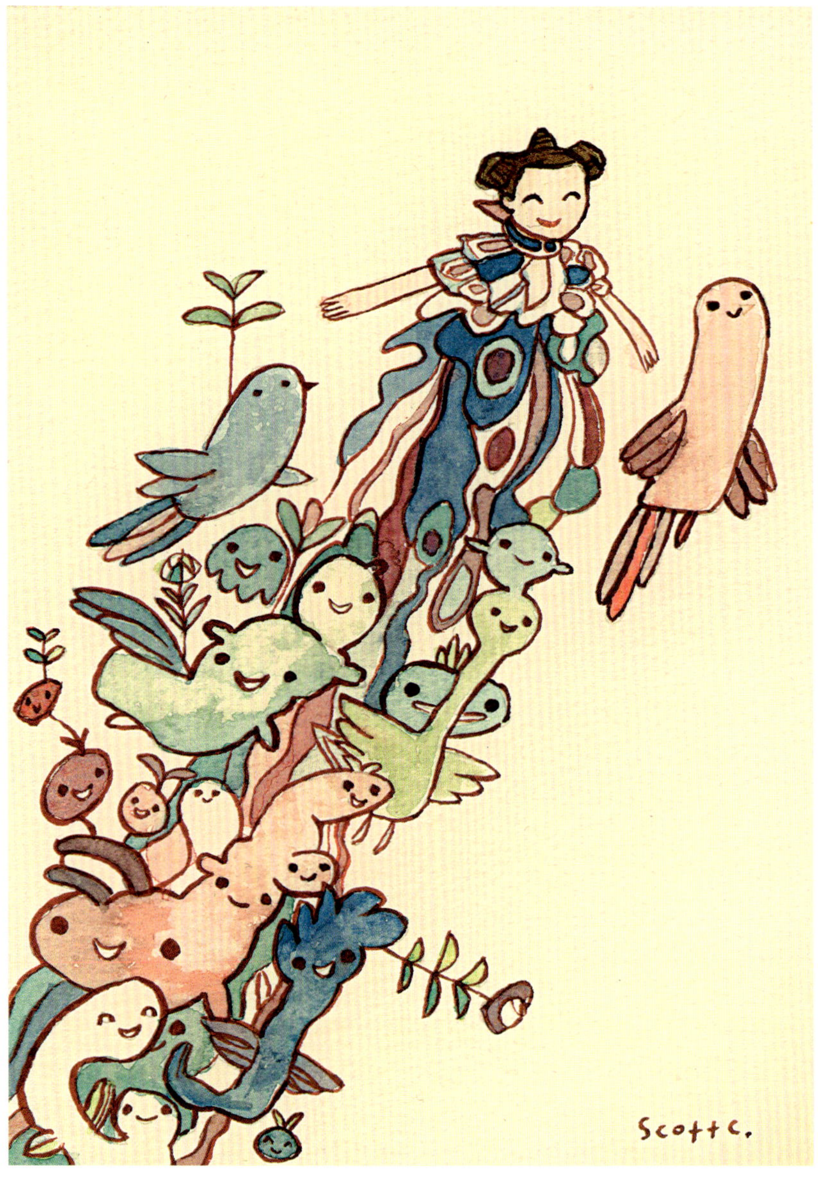

SEARCH FOR THE PERFECT SPOT
watercolor
8" x 10"
2009

THE TEA SPILLING | watercolor | 10" x 8" | 2009 >>

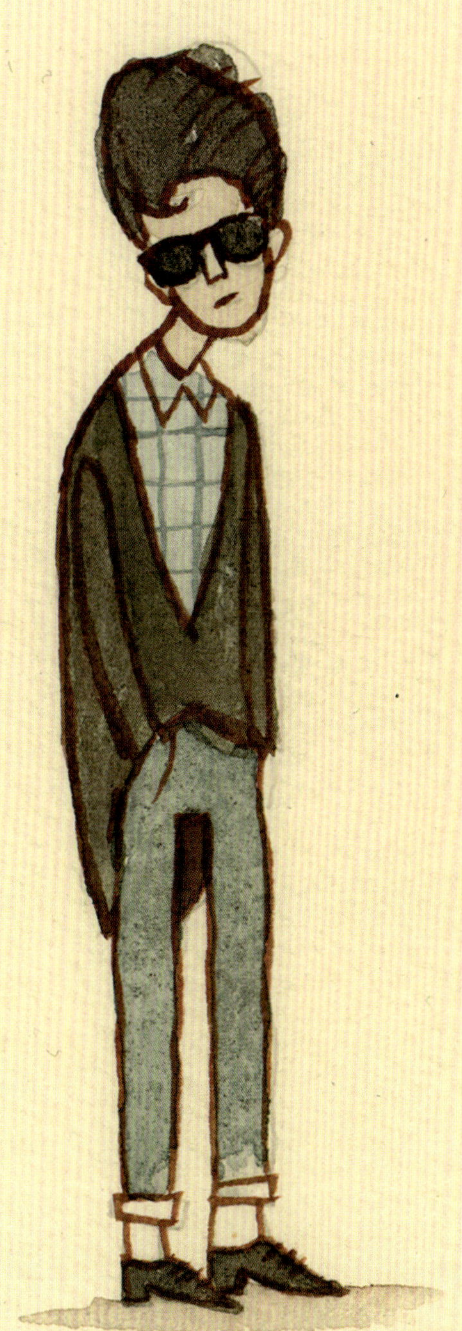

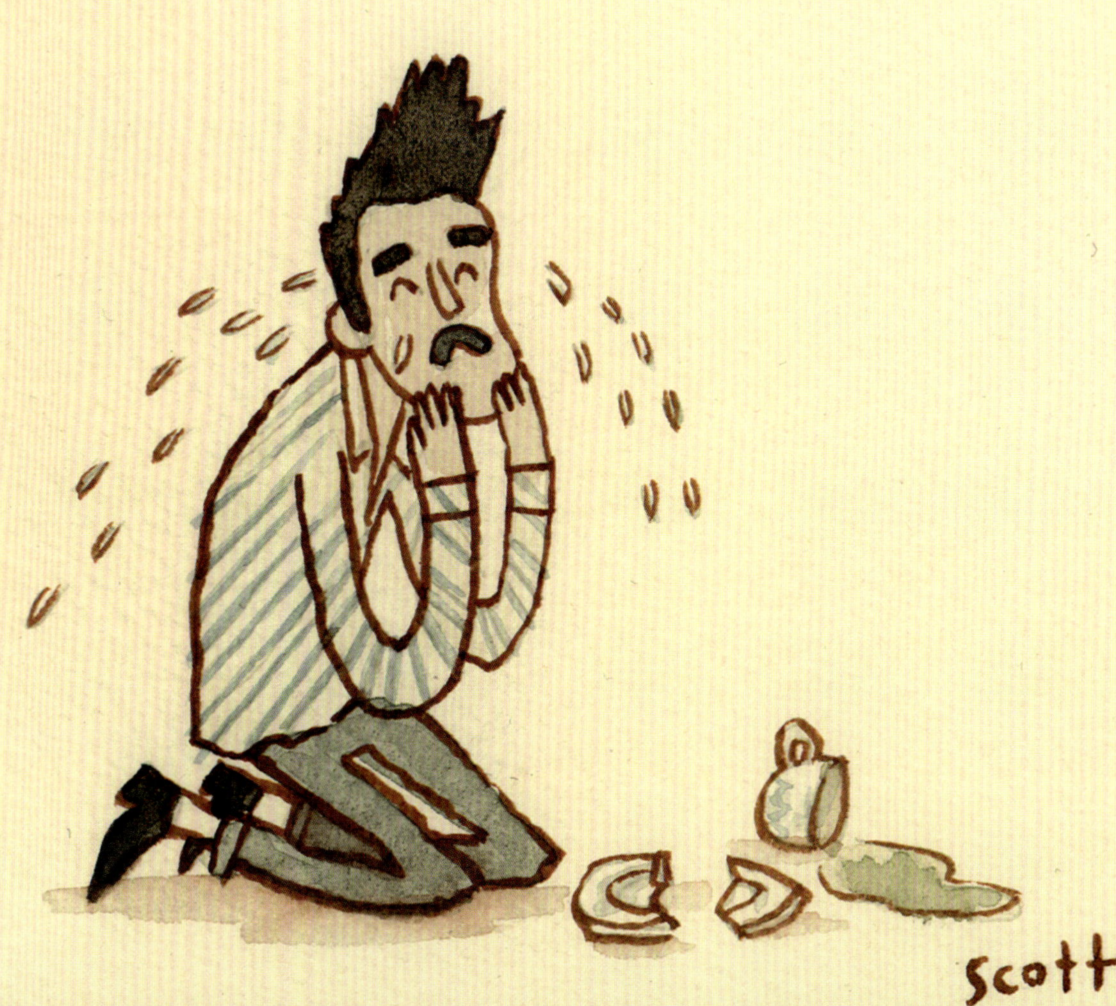
scott c.

I used to go to Bullwinkle's pizza place quite a lot and spent much of my time in the arcade. My favorite game was *Paperboy*. In this game you play a little dude trying to deliver papers to good houses and break the windows of the evil houses while avoiding crazy nutballs like the dude doing backspins in his driveway. *Paperboy 1884* explores the game if it were made 100 years prior, in the days of the Old West. The dude doing backspins did not have a boom box in those days. Just a phonograph.

PAPERBOY 1884
watercolor
14" x 11"
2006

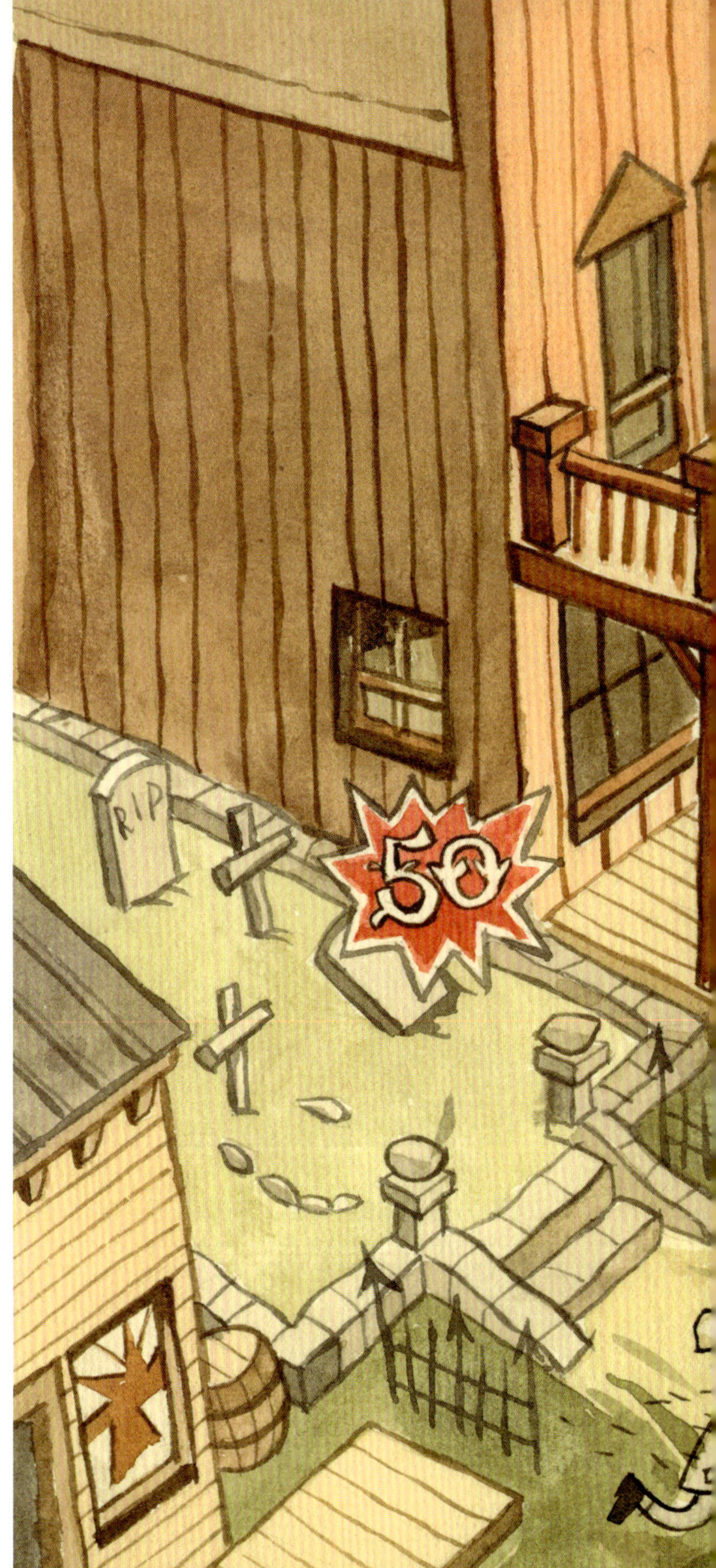

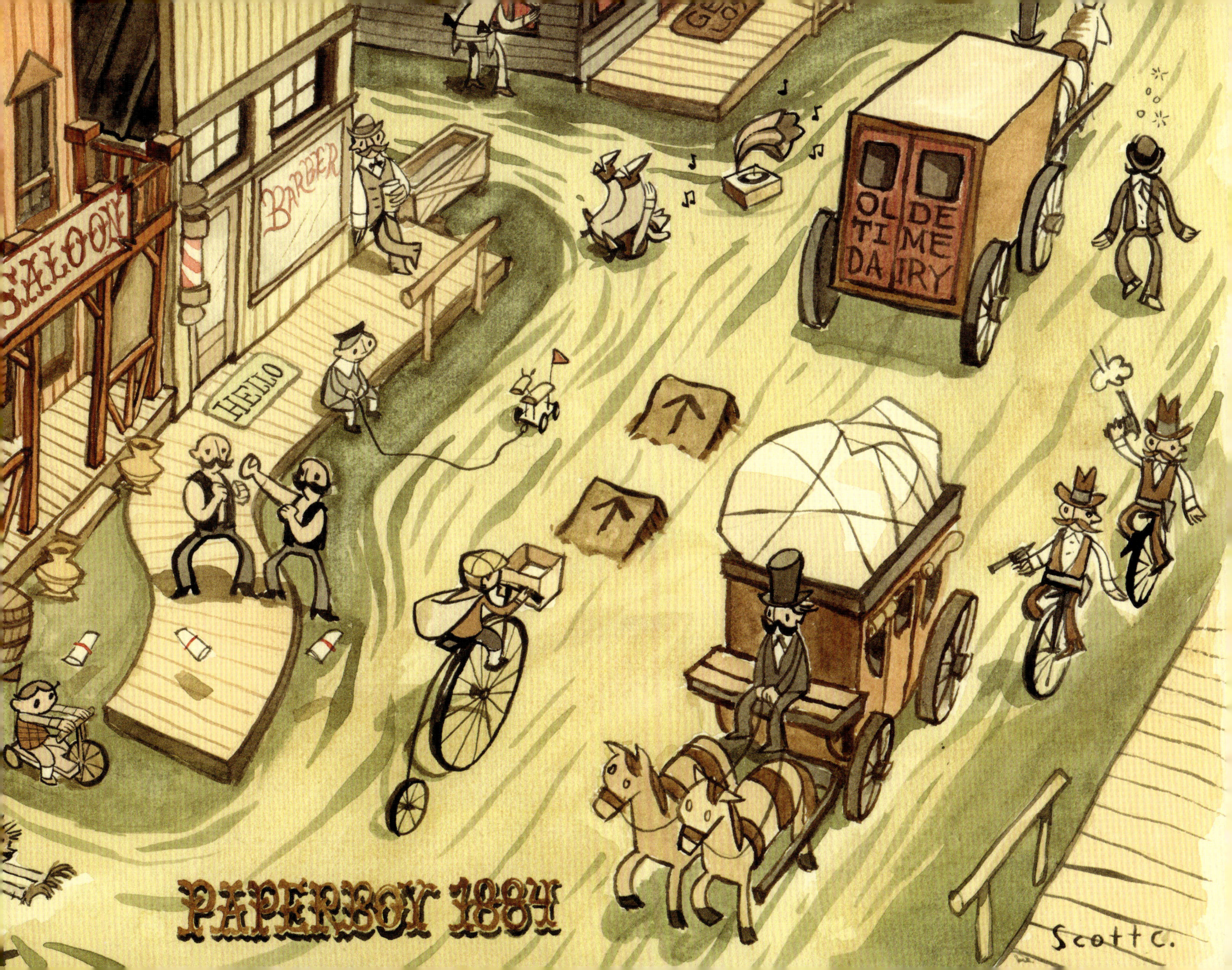
SALOON
BARBER
HELLO
OLDE TIME DAIRY
PAPERBOY 1884
Scott C.

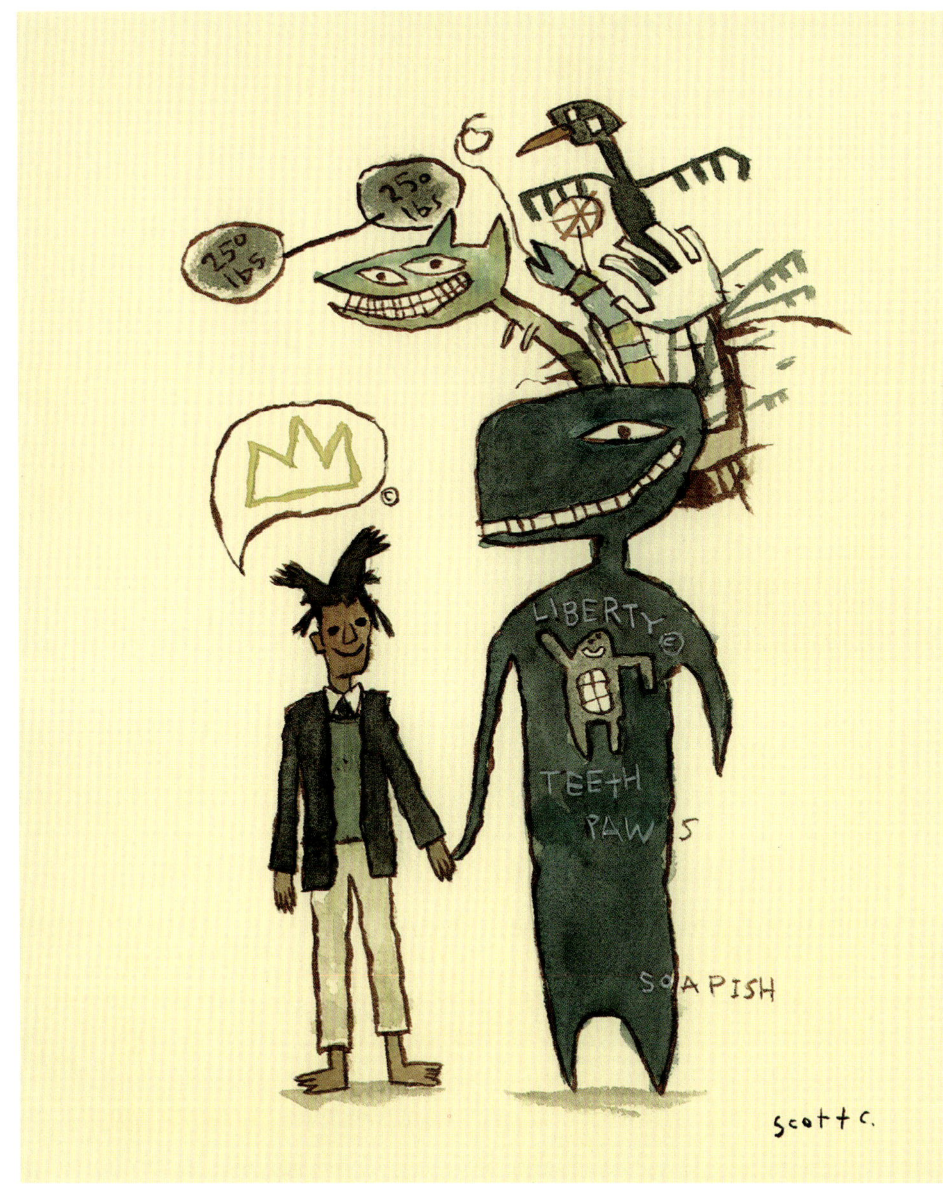

TAKING LIBERTY© FOR A STROLL
watercolor
8" x 10"
2009

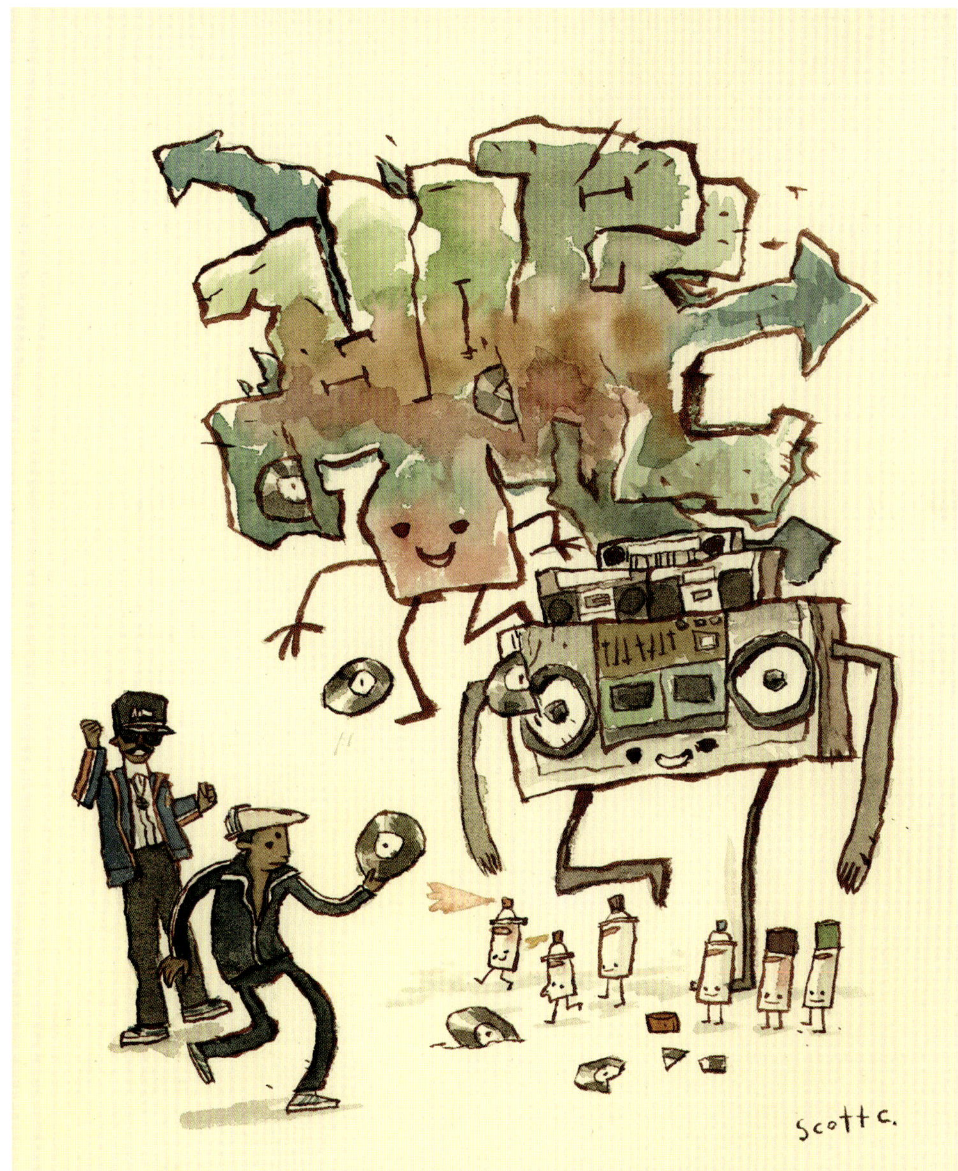

A DAY IN THE STREETS
watercolor
8" x 10"
2009

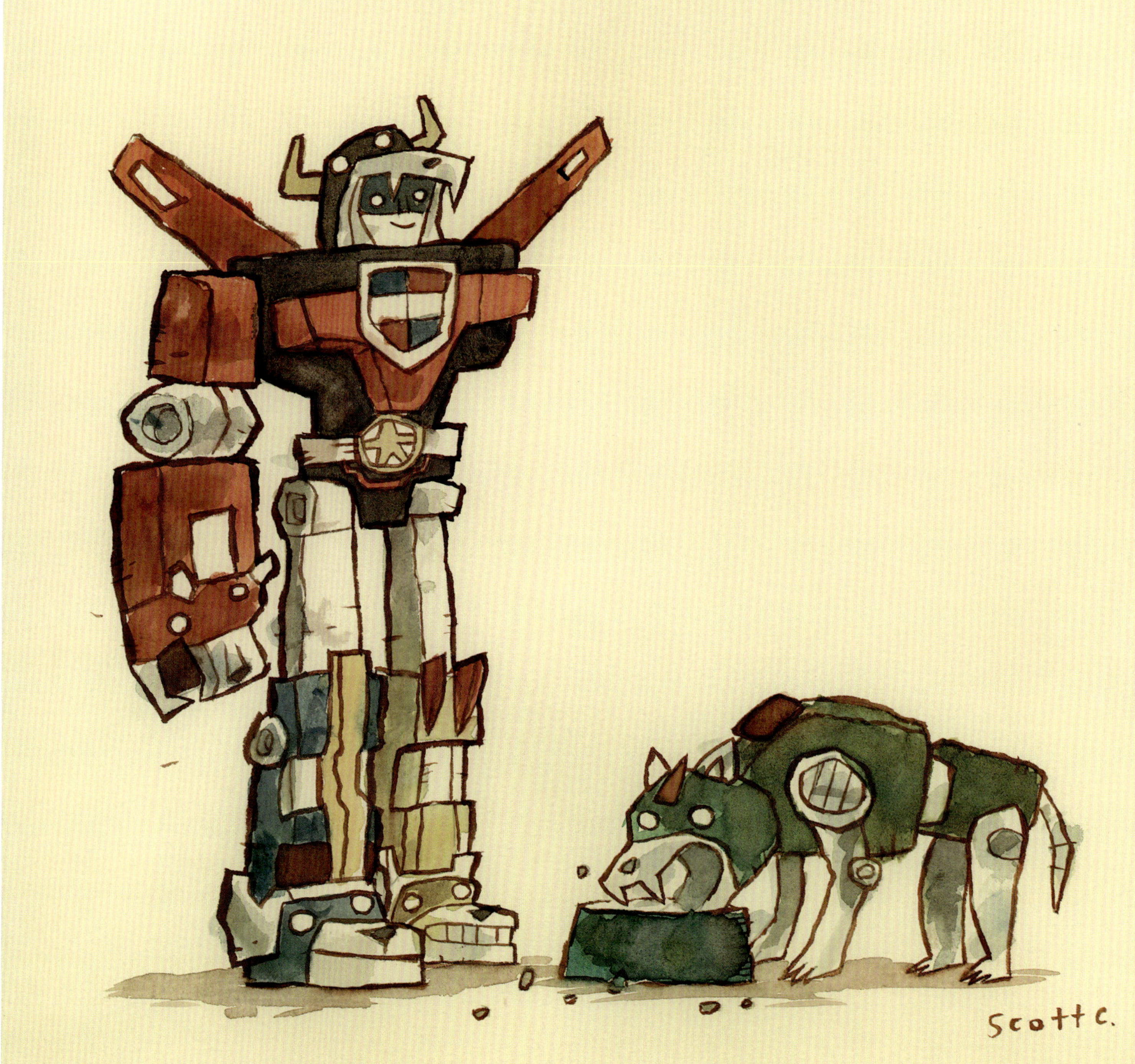

SUPER HUNGRY
watercolor
12" x 12"
2009

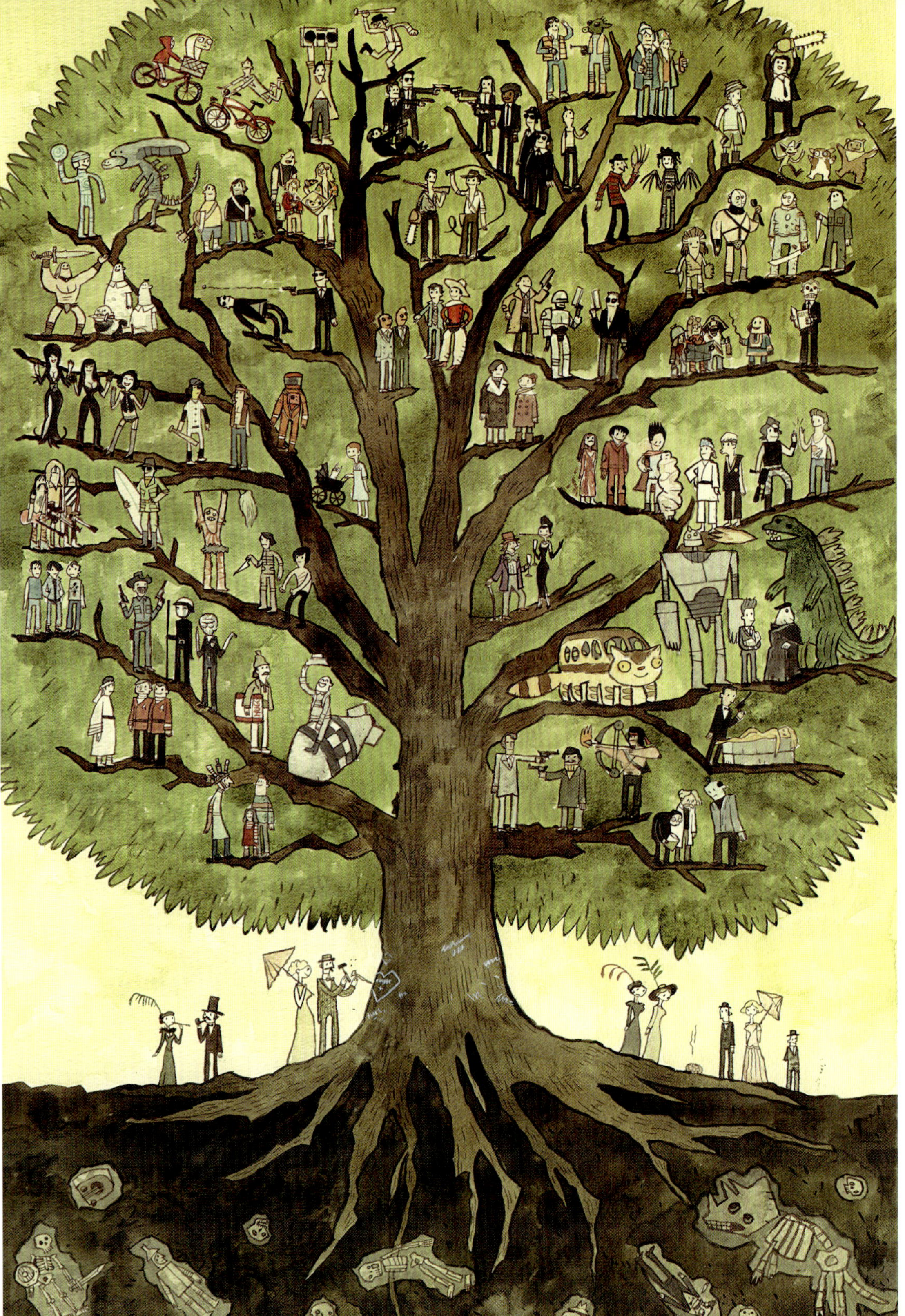

THE CULT TREE
watercolor
20" x 30"
2008

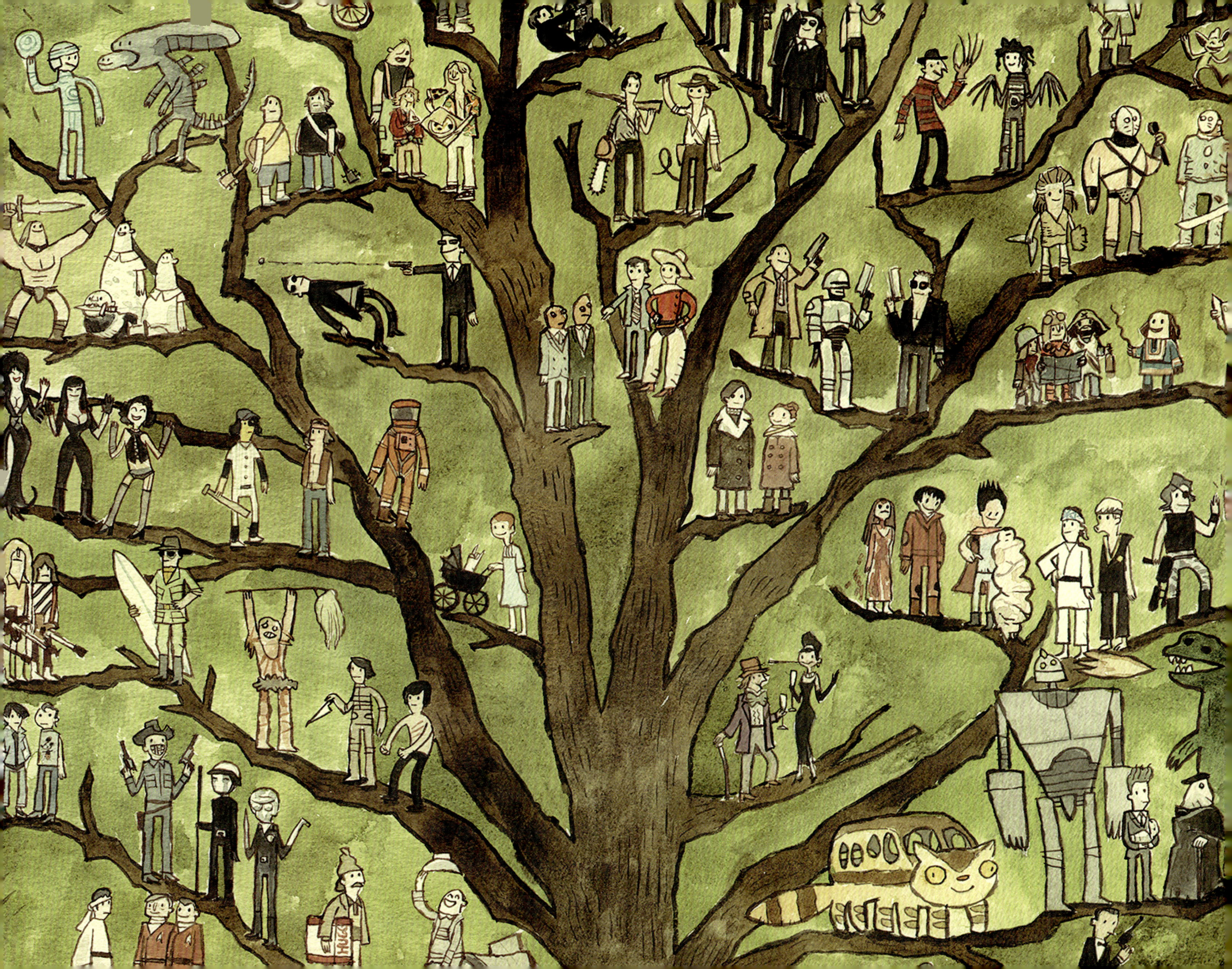

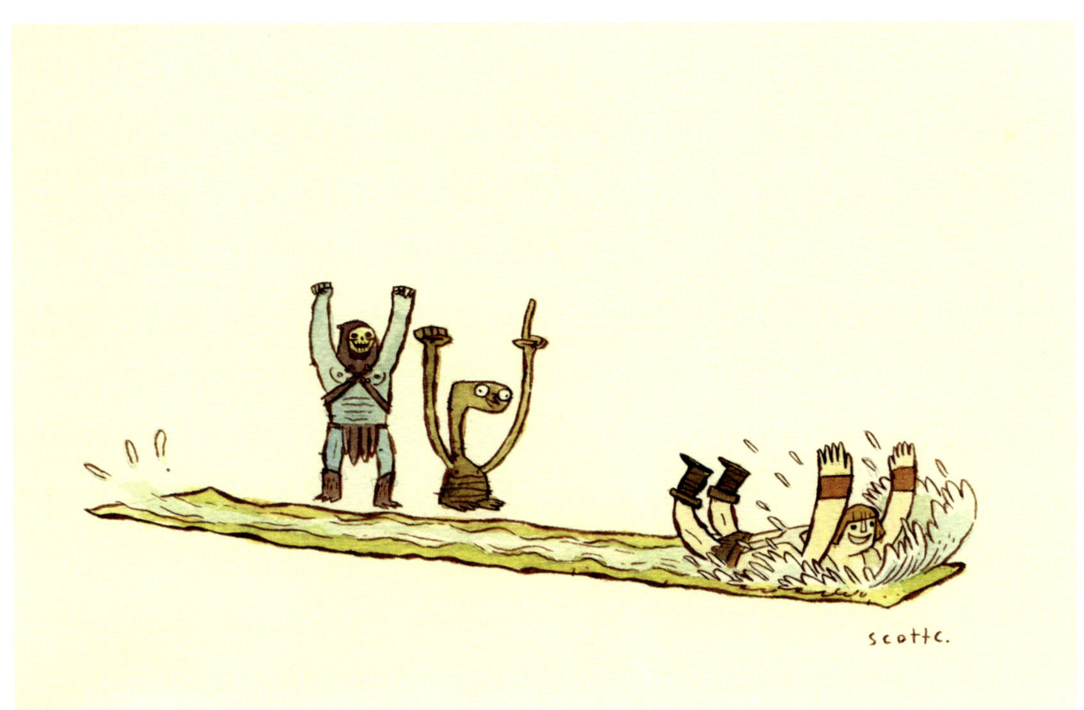

SLIDIN'
watercolor
10" x 8"
2008

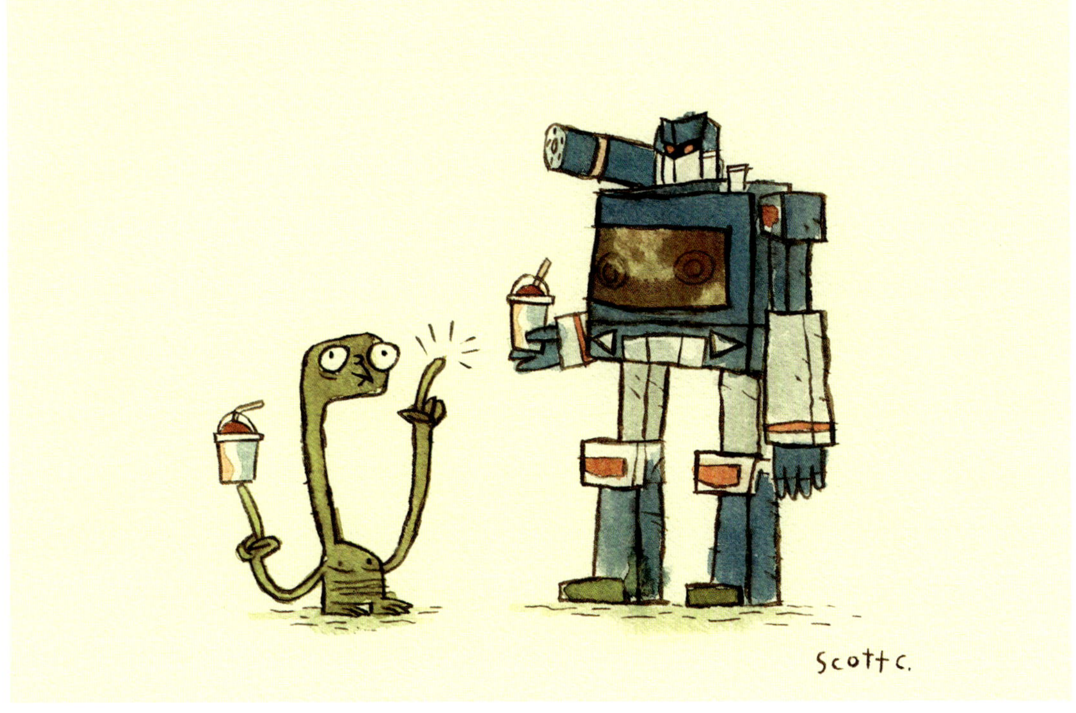

SOUNDWAVIN'
watercolor
10" x 8"
2008

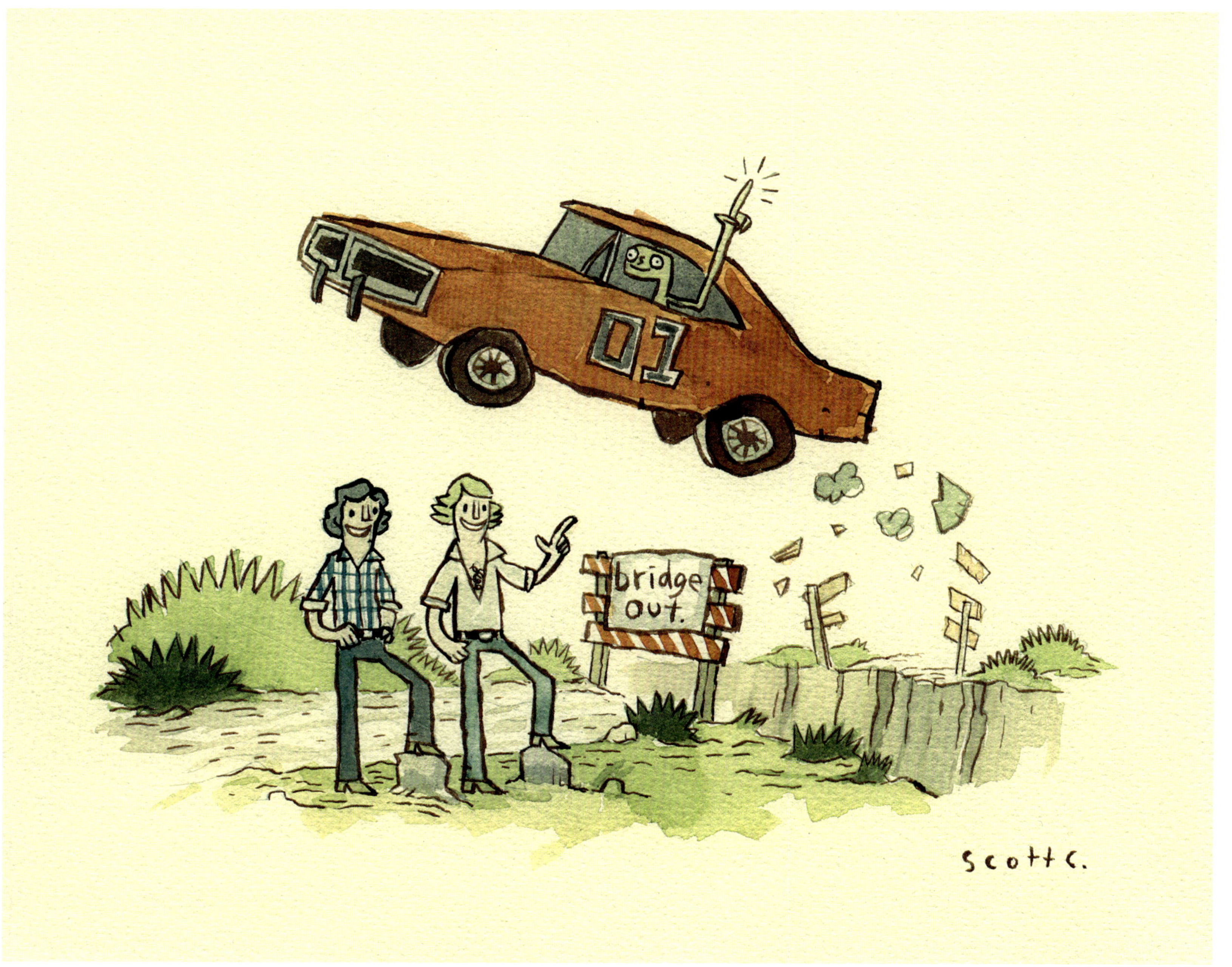

JUMPIN'
watercolor
10" x 8"
2008

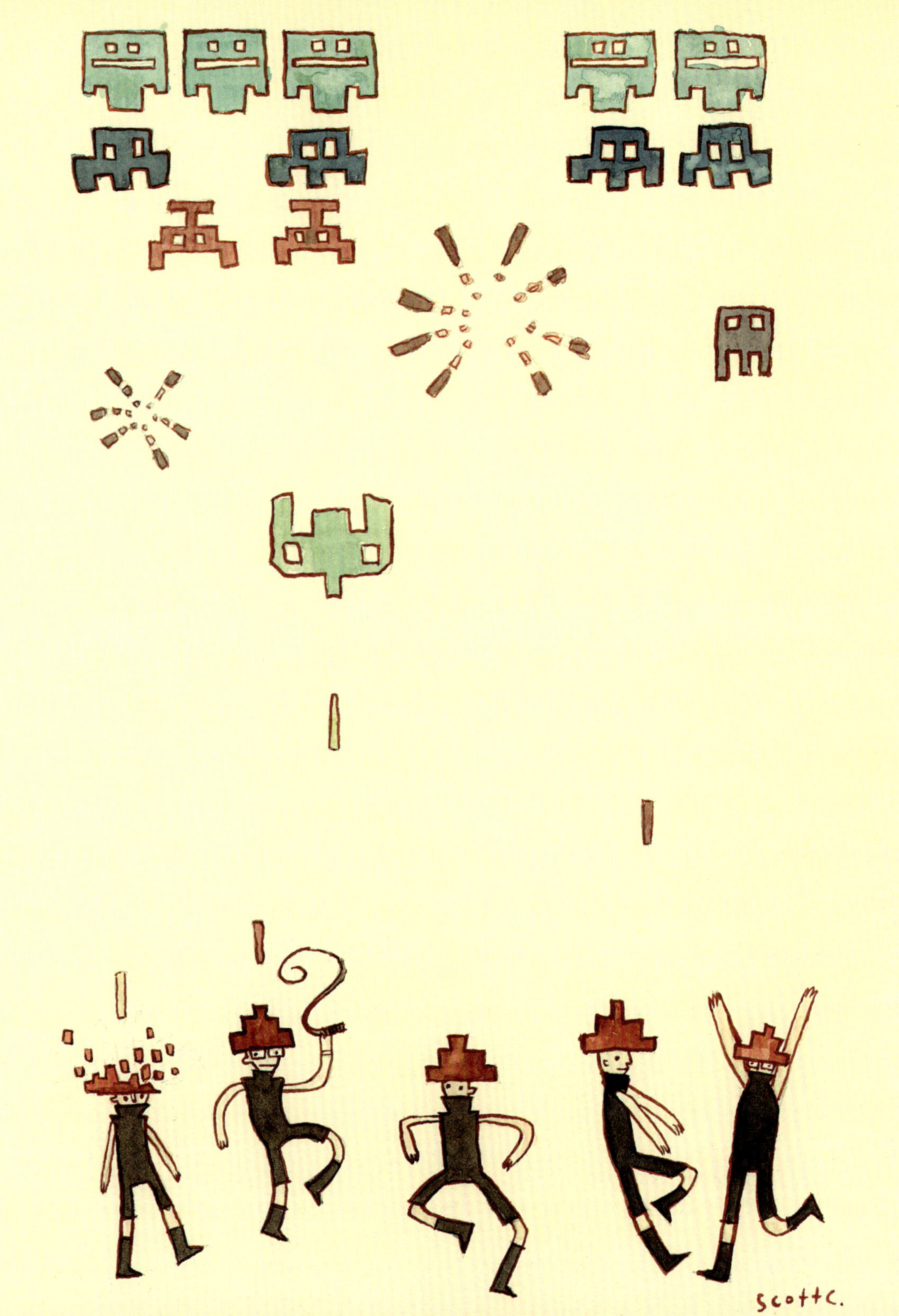

KEEPING THEM AT BAY
watercolor
8" x 10"
2009

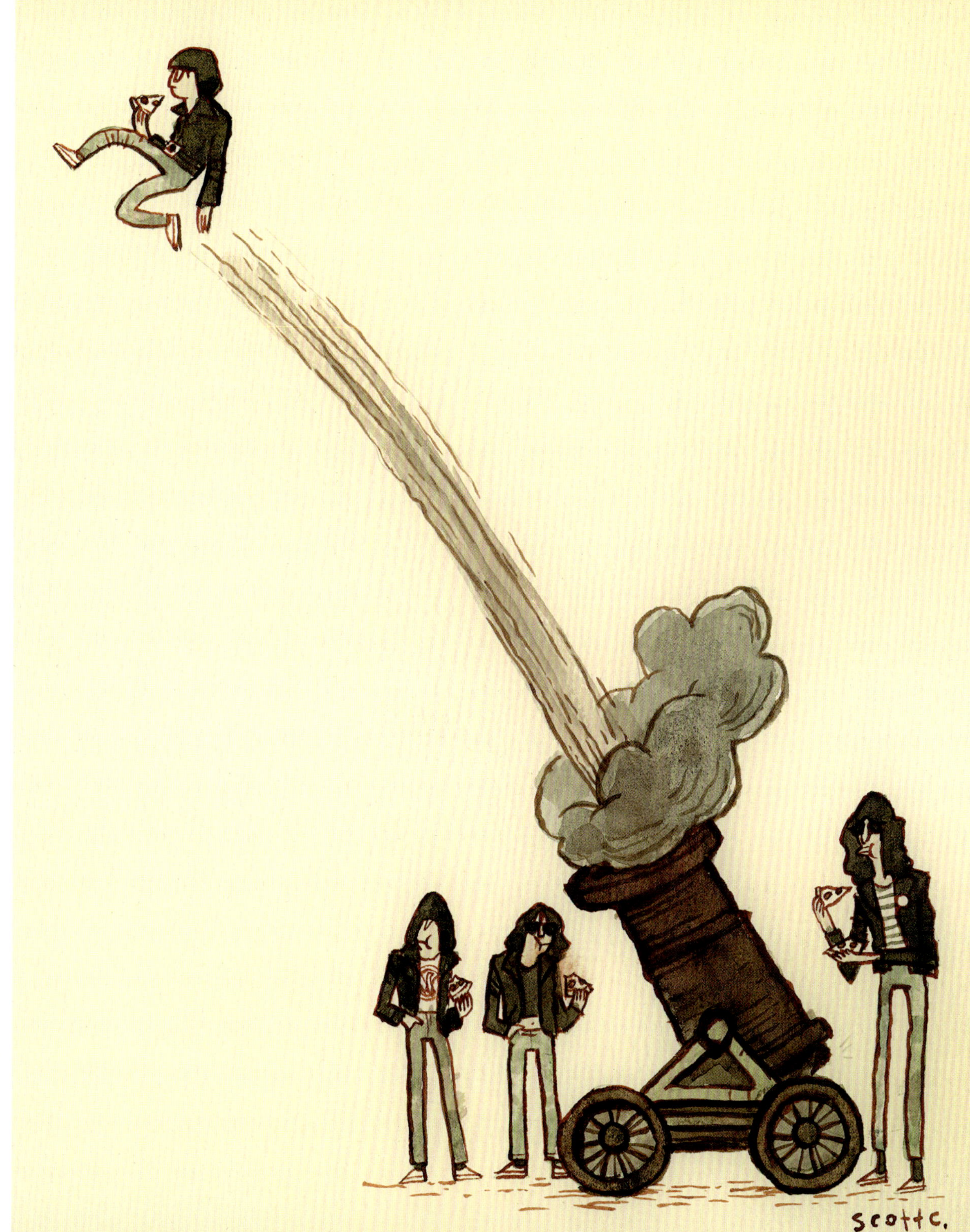

PIZZA (DIGGING IN)
watercolor
8"x 10"
2009

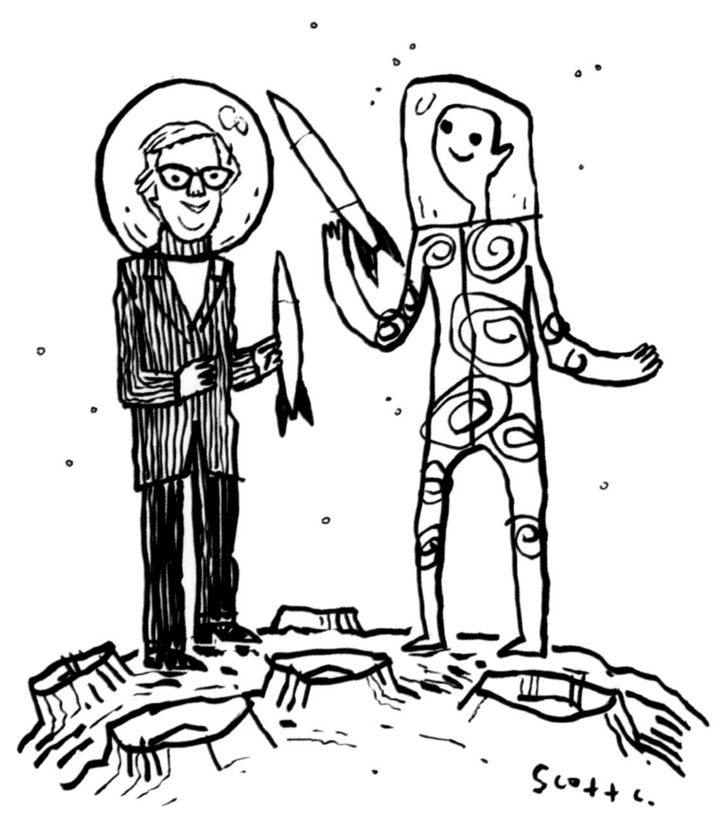

BRADBURY
pen on paper
8.5" x 11"
2009

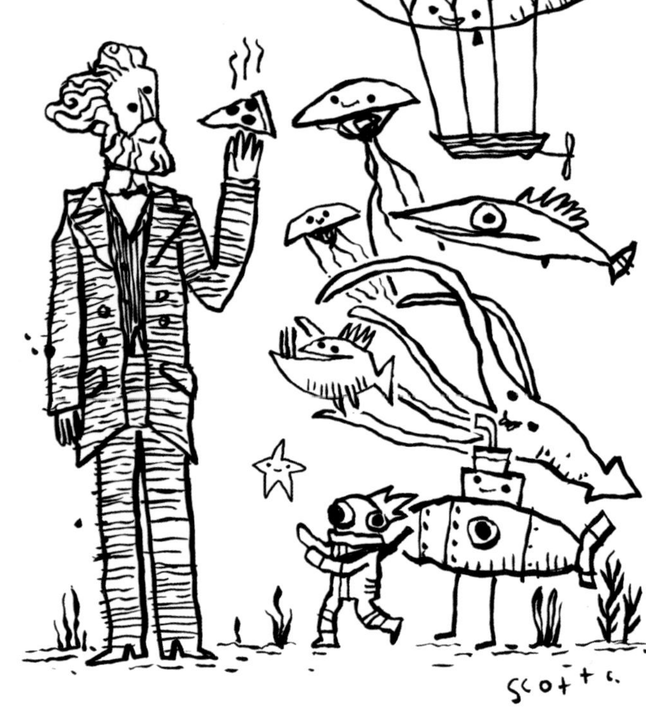

VERNE
pen on paper
8.5" x 11"
2009

These amazing drawings depict some of my favorite writers, hanging about with some of their favorite things. Ray Bradbury loves martians and rockets. Jules Verne loves balloons and underwater creatures. Rod Serling loves eyes with wings and clocks. Jules is enjoying a slice of pizza, that is true. Pizza is mostly something that I love, a gift that I gave to Jules in that drawing.

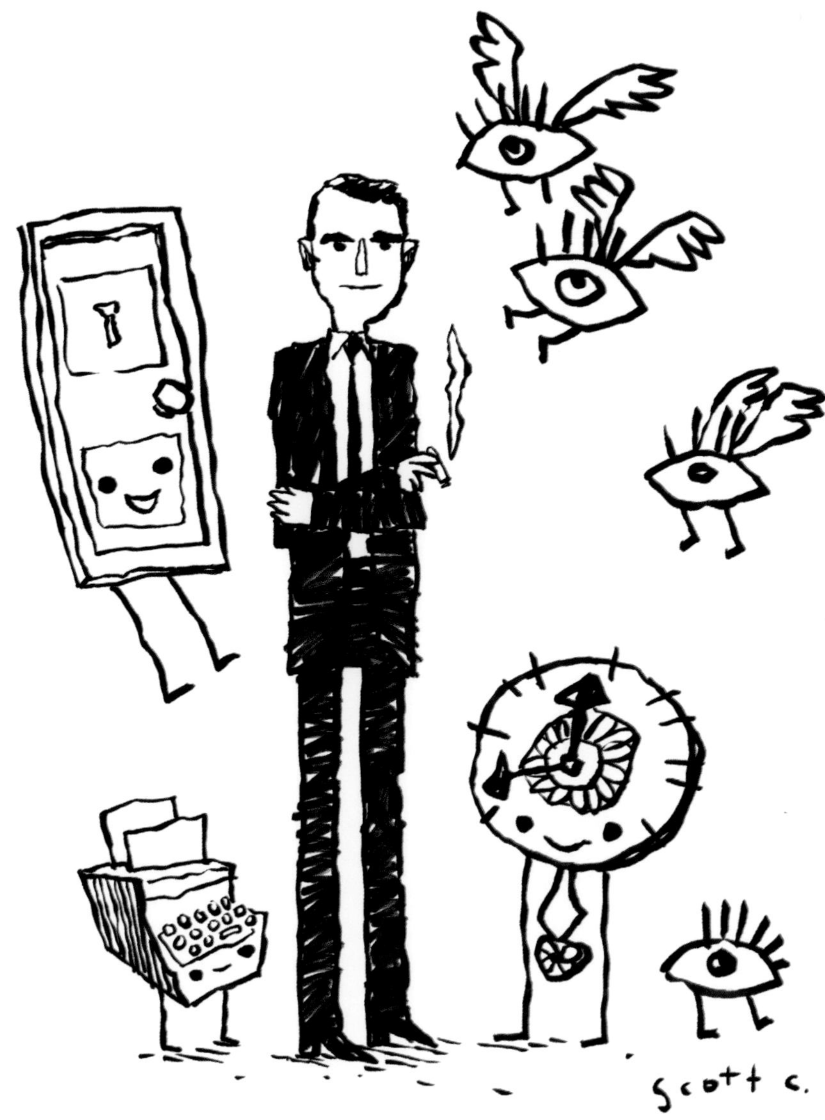

SERLING
pen on paper
8.5" x 11"
2009

everybody time

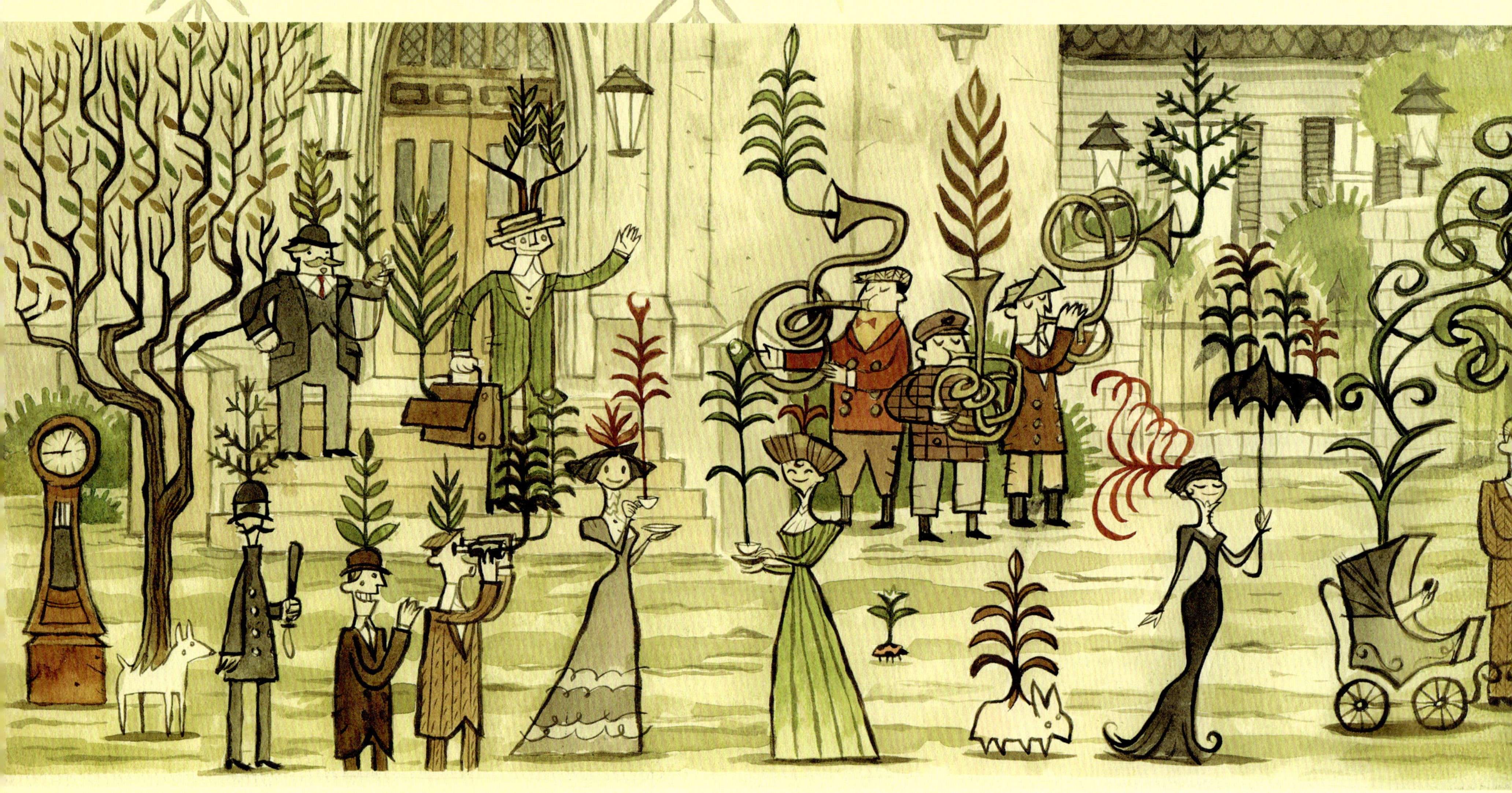

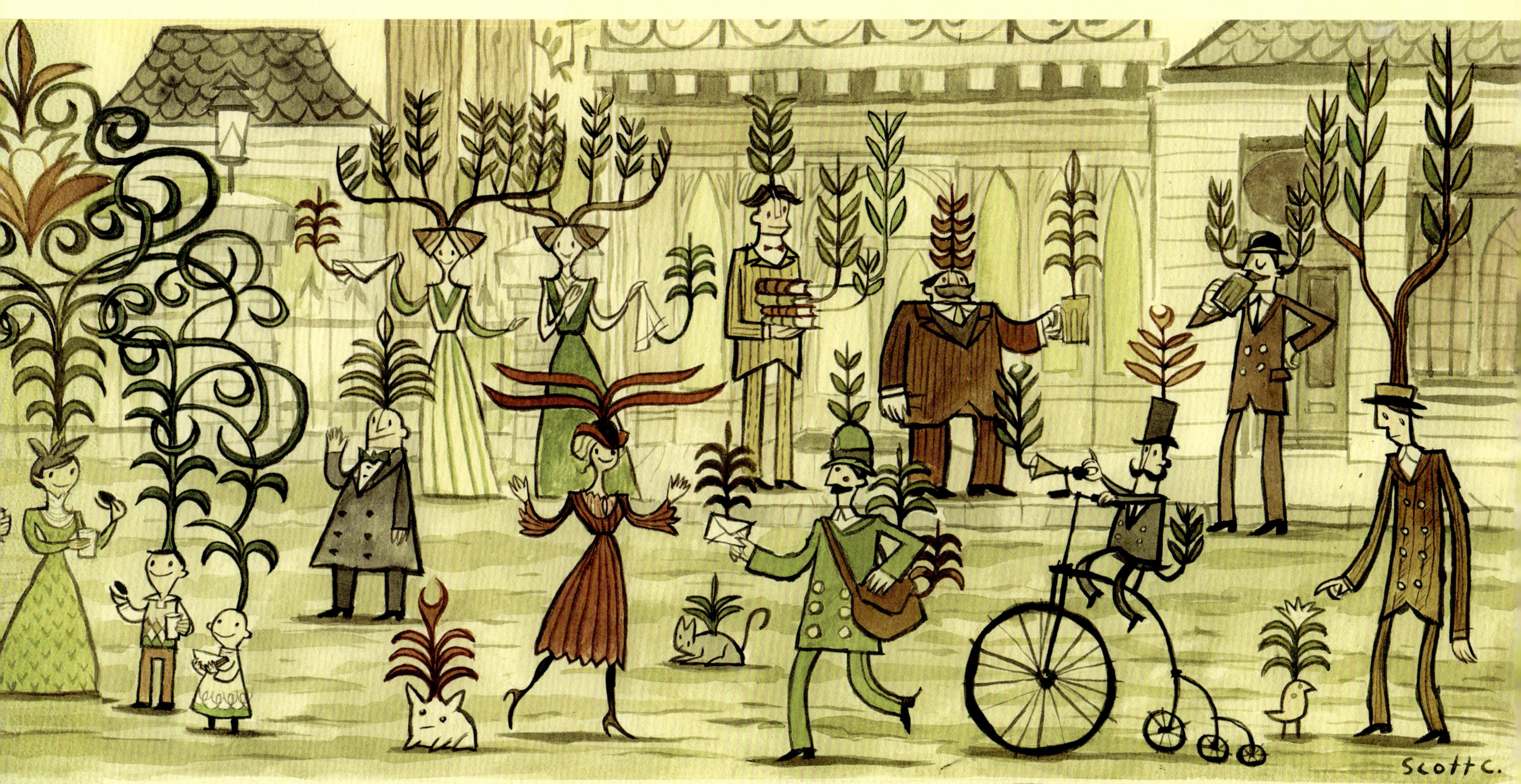
Scott C.

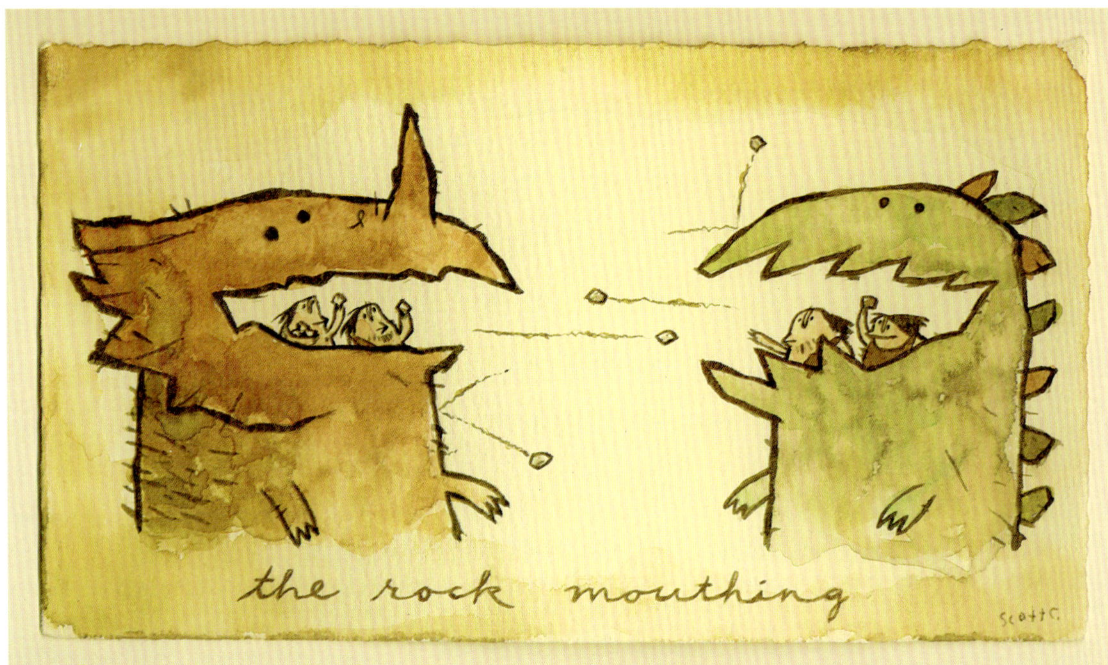

THE ROCK MOUTHING
watercolor
8" x 4"
2007

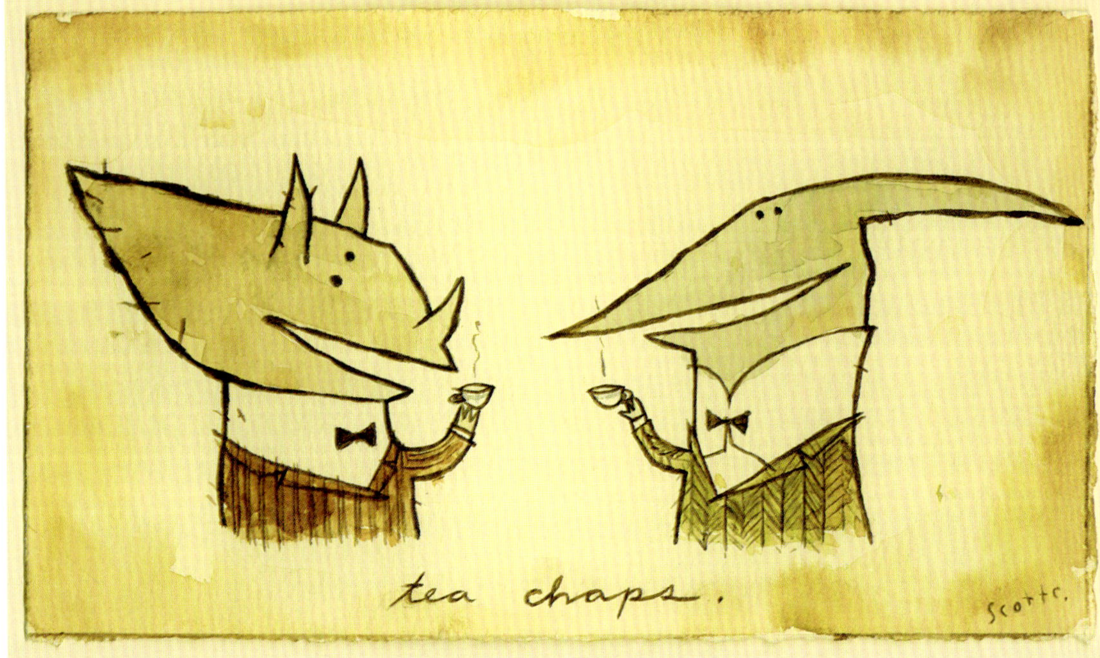

TEA CHAPS
watercolor
8" x 4"
2007

<< [section opener] A PLEASANT STROLL | watercolor | 35" x 9" | 2006

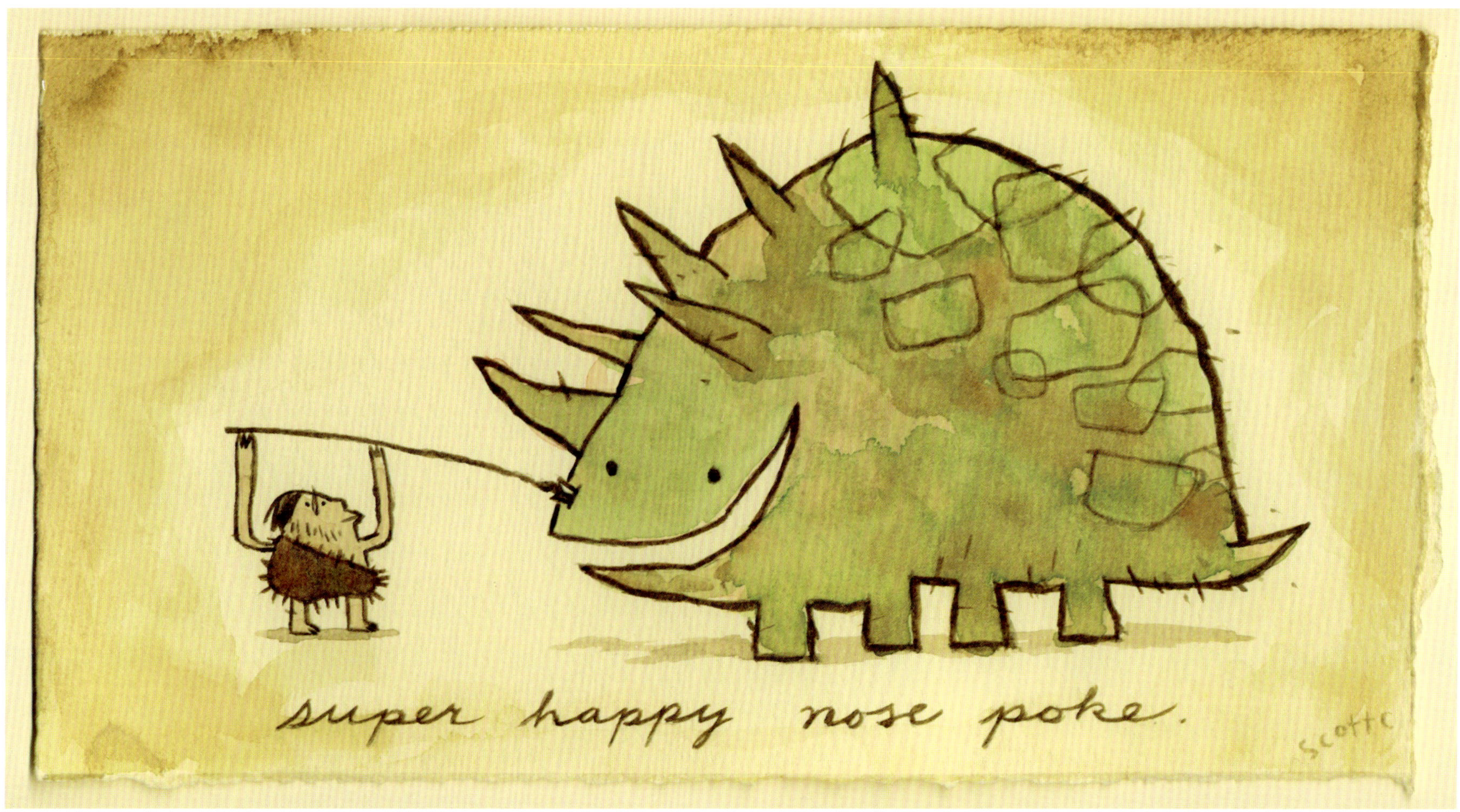

SUPER HAPPY NOSE POKE
watercolor
8.5" x 4.5"
2007

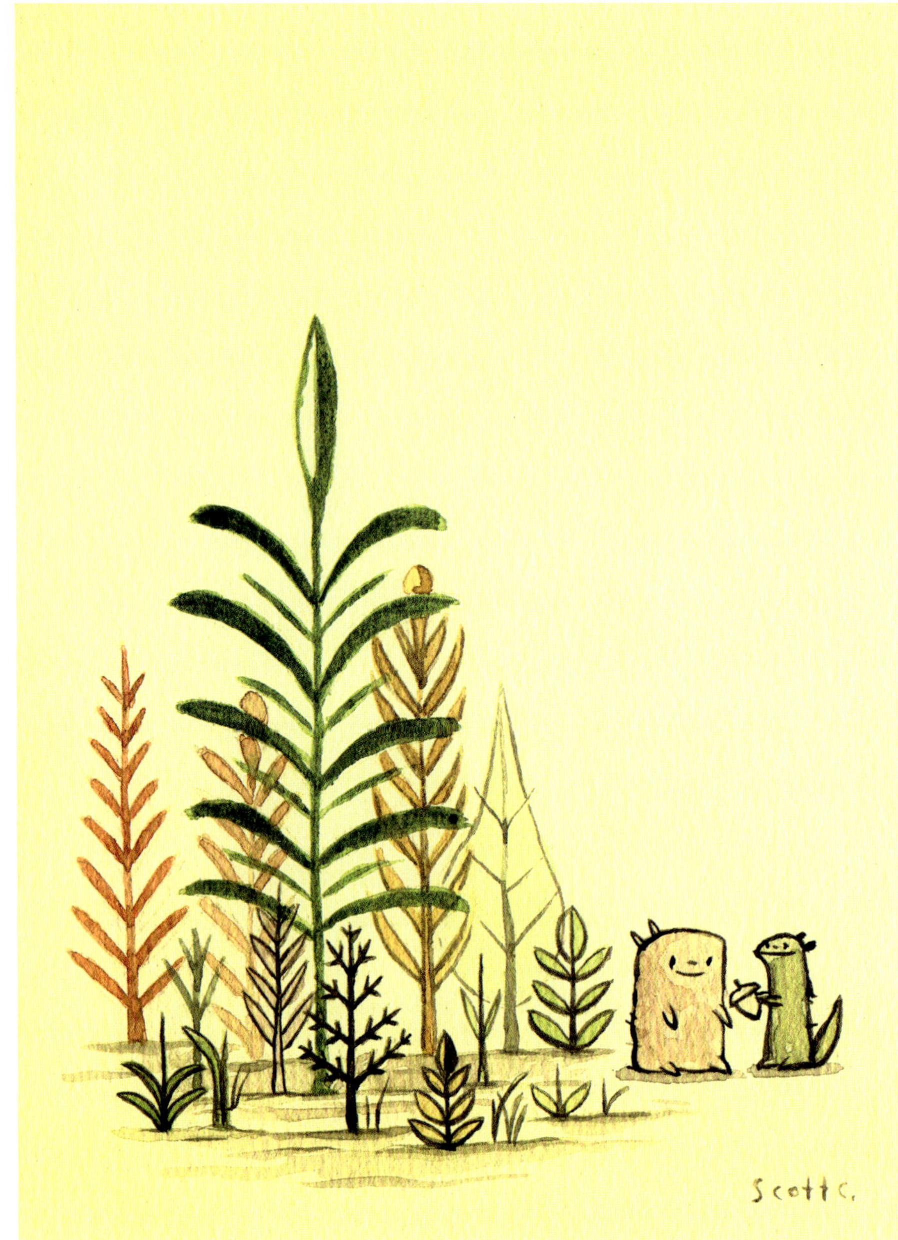

SHARING (NEXT TO PLANTS)
watercolor
8" x 10"
2007

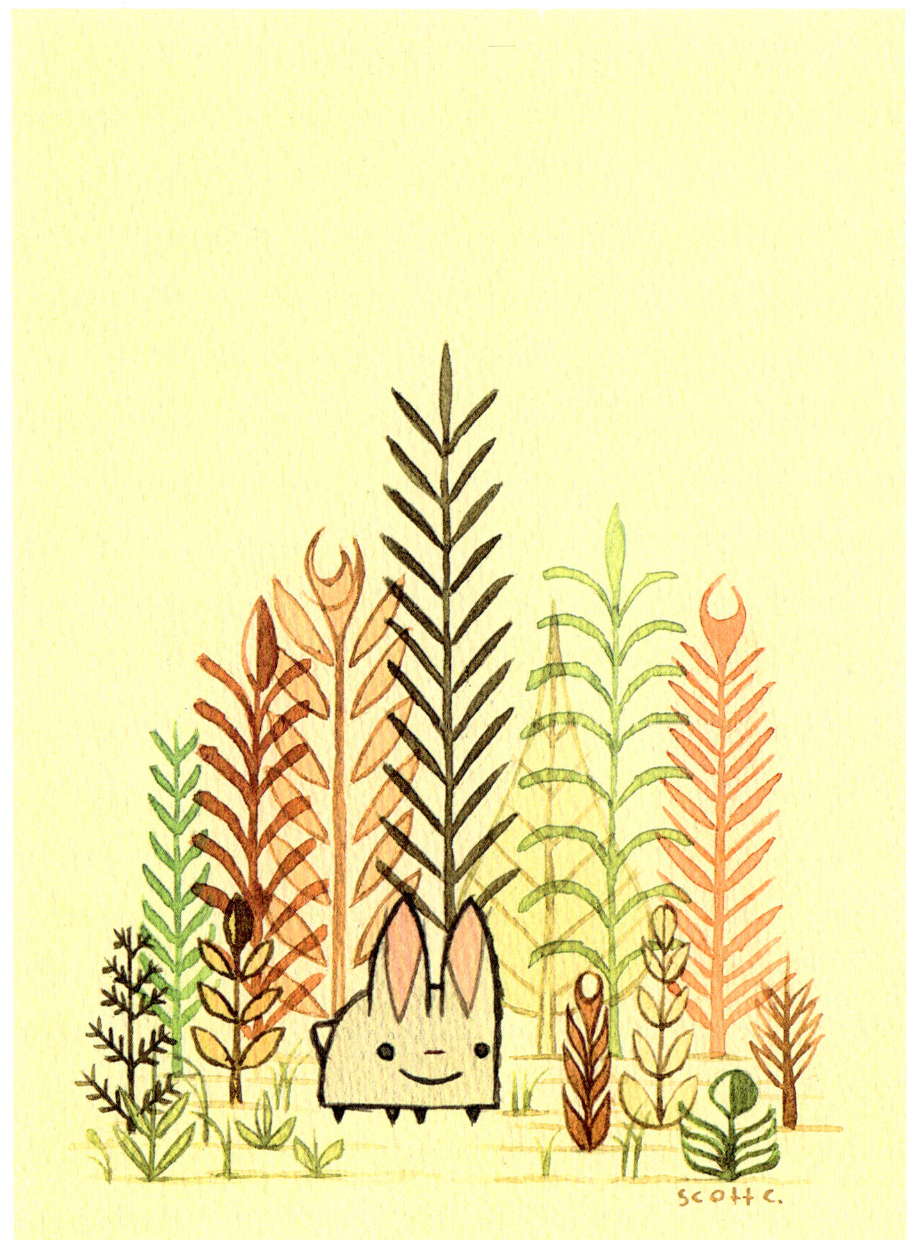

CUTEST THING EVER
watercolor
7" x 9"
2006

Friendship is a big deal in my paintings. These two old-timey ladies could perhaps be friends, but they are most likely competing for umbrella attention. There is give-and-take in any relationship. The little sharing creatures are reaping the benefits of friendship. The plants are acting as a chaperone to this exchange, making sure the creatures feel positive and comfortable. Cute creatures feel very pleasant next to pleasant plants. That is a rule of cute things. And umbrellas can really make the woman.

UMBRELLA PARTY
watercolor
8" x 10"
2006

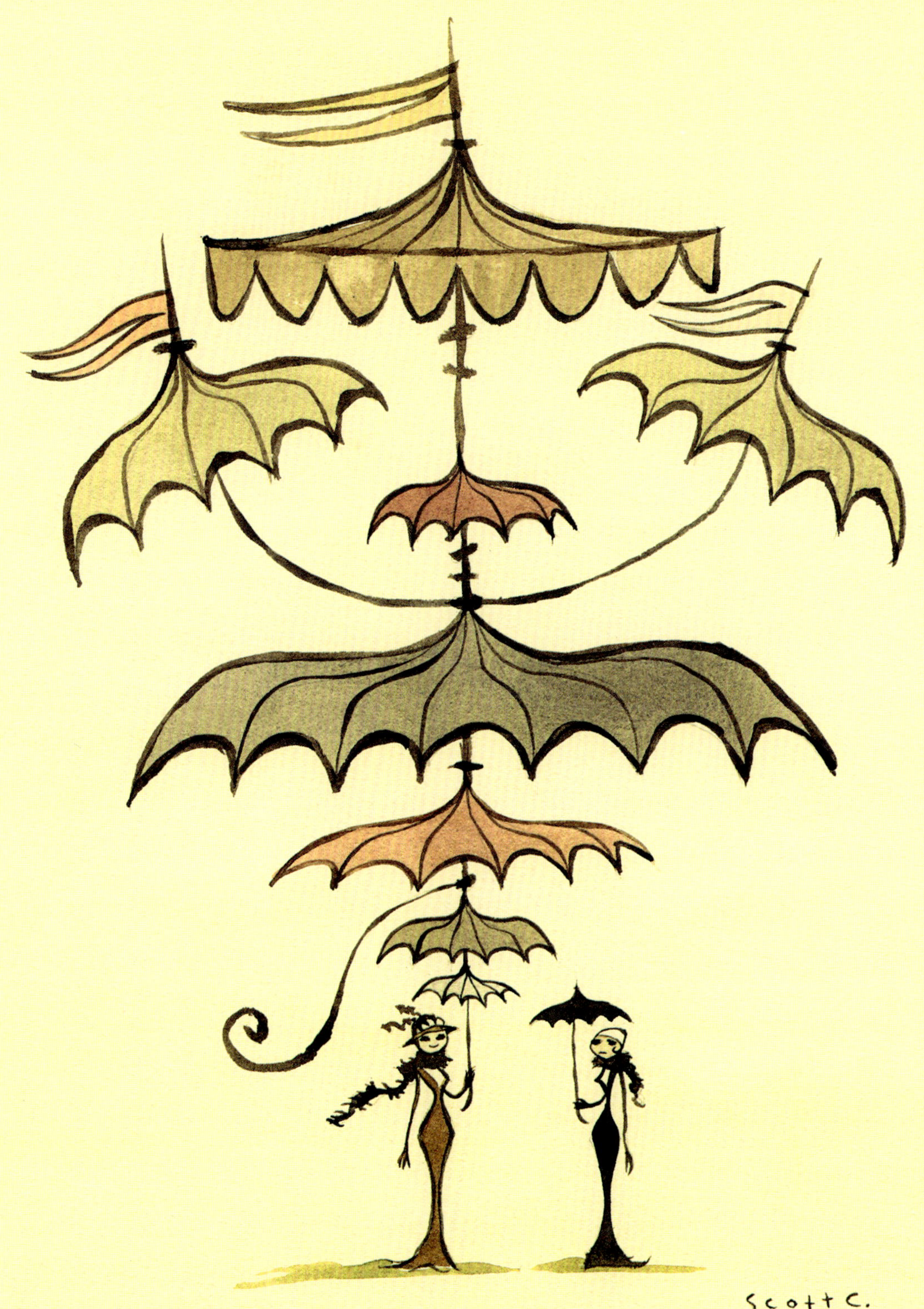

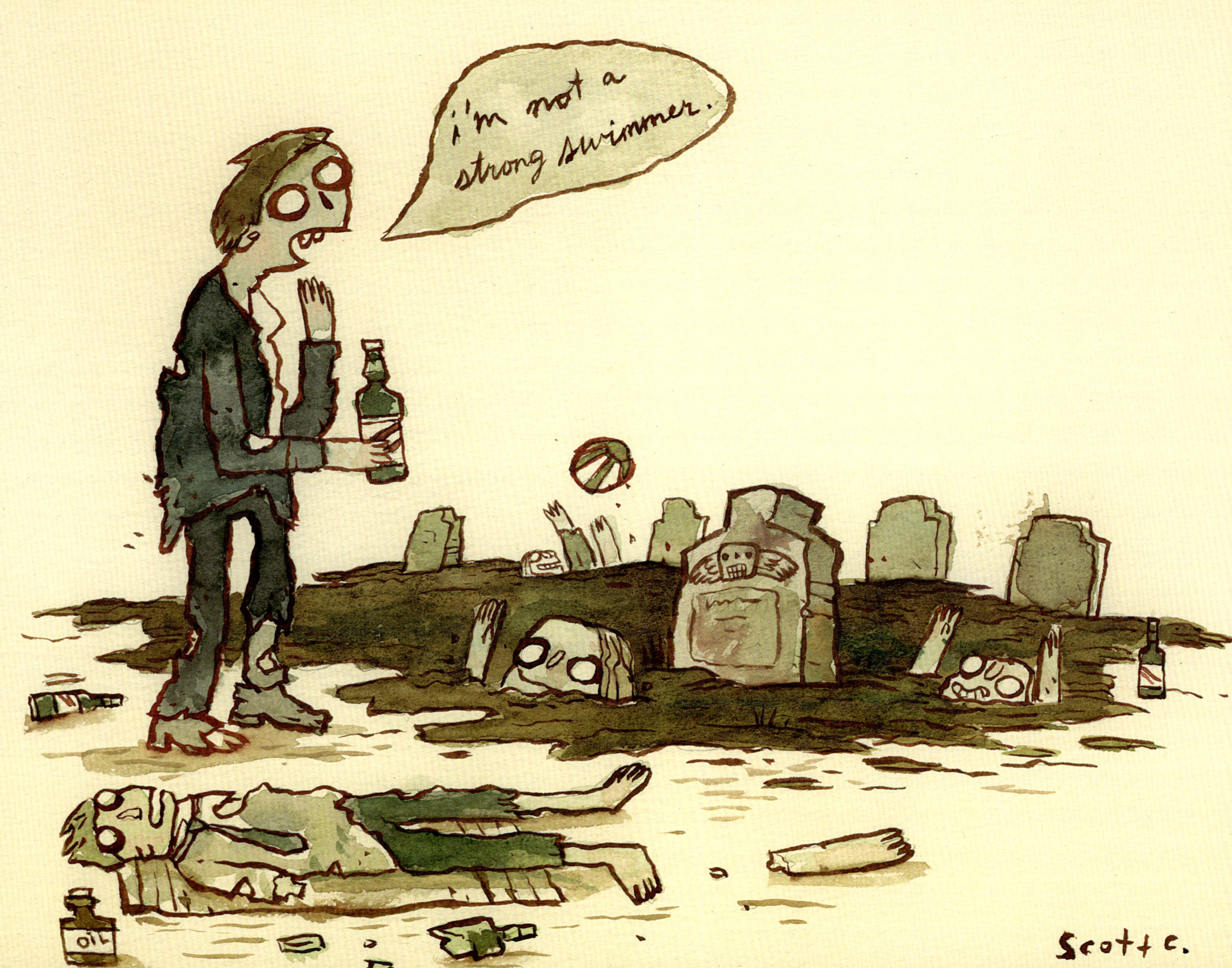
i'm not a strong swimmer.
OIL
Scott C.

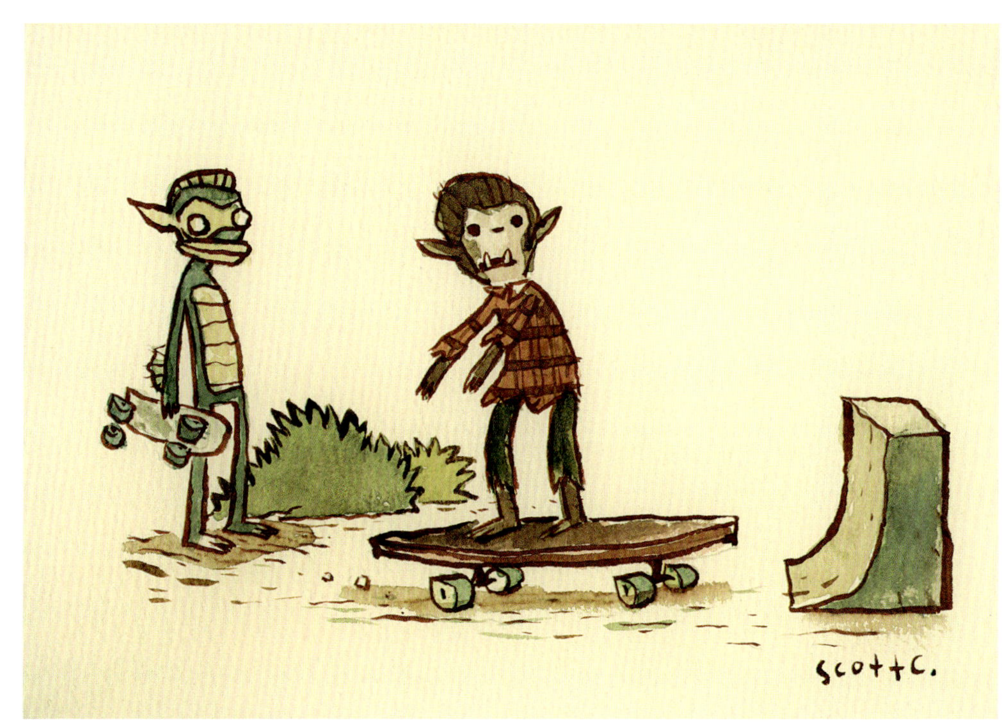

WOLFMAN RAMP
watercolor
7" x 5"
2009

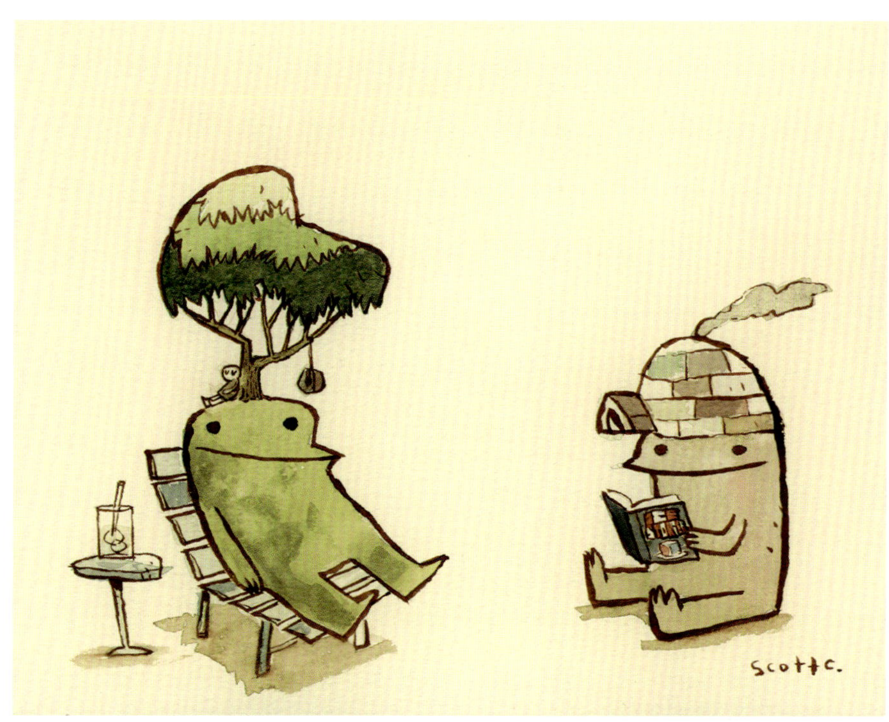

IGLOO HEAD AND TREE HEAD (DAY OFF)
watercolor
10" x 8"
2009

< < NOT A STRONG SWIMMER | watercolor | 10" x 8" | 2009

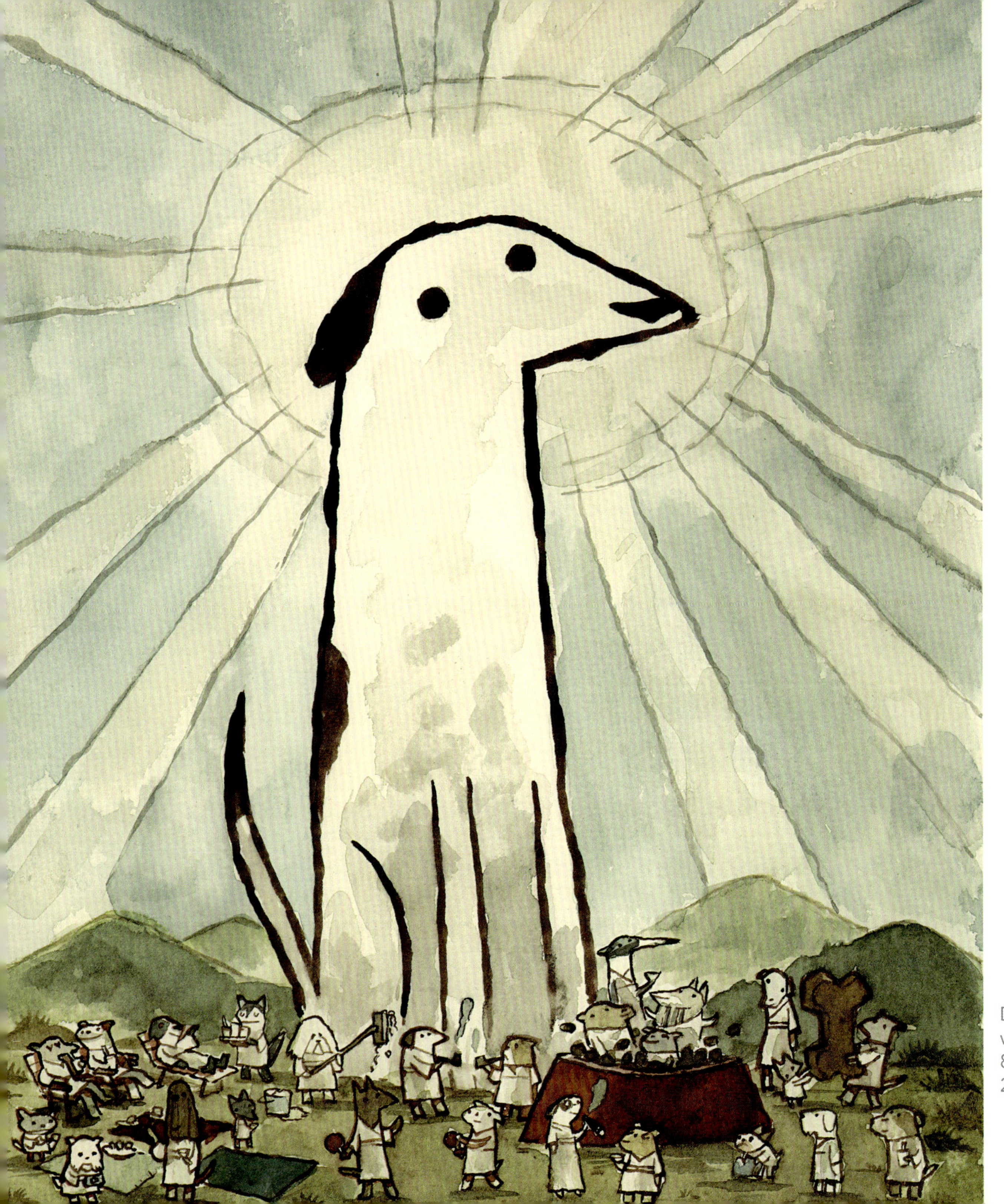

Ah. To relax in the warmth of the Great Dog. The little dogs feel at peace in its glow. They are the keepers of the Dog and must keep it fresh and clean for all to enjoy. They wear robes to encourage a relaxed togetherness. There is no judgement of one another at the foot of the Dog. Just winding down and forgetting their busy dog day.

DOG AMONGST DOGS
watercolor
8" x 10"
2009

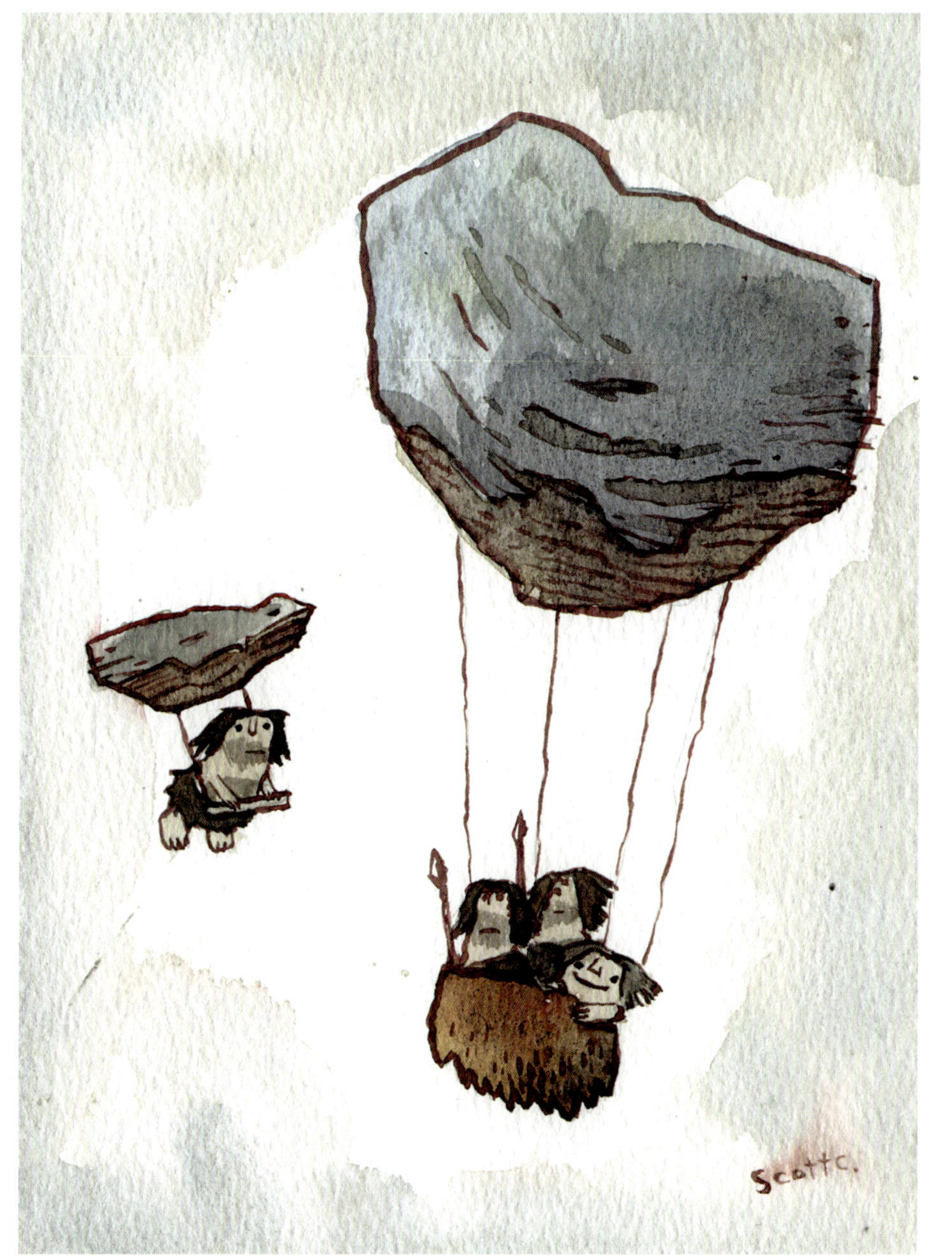

HUNTING FROM ABOVE
watercolor
5" x 7"
2009

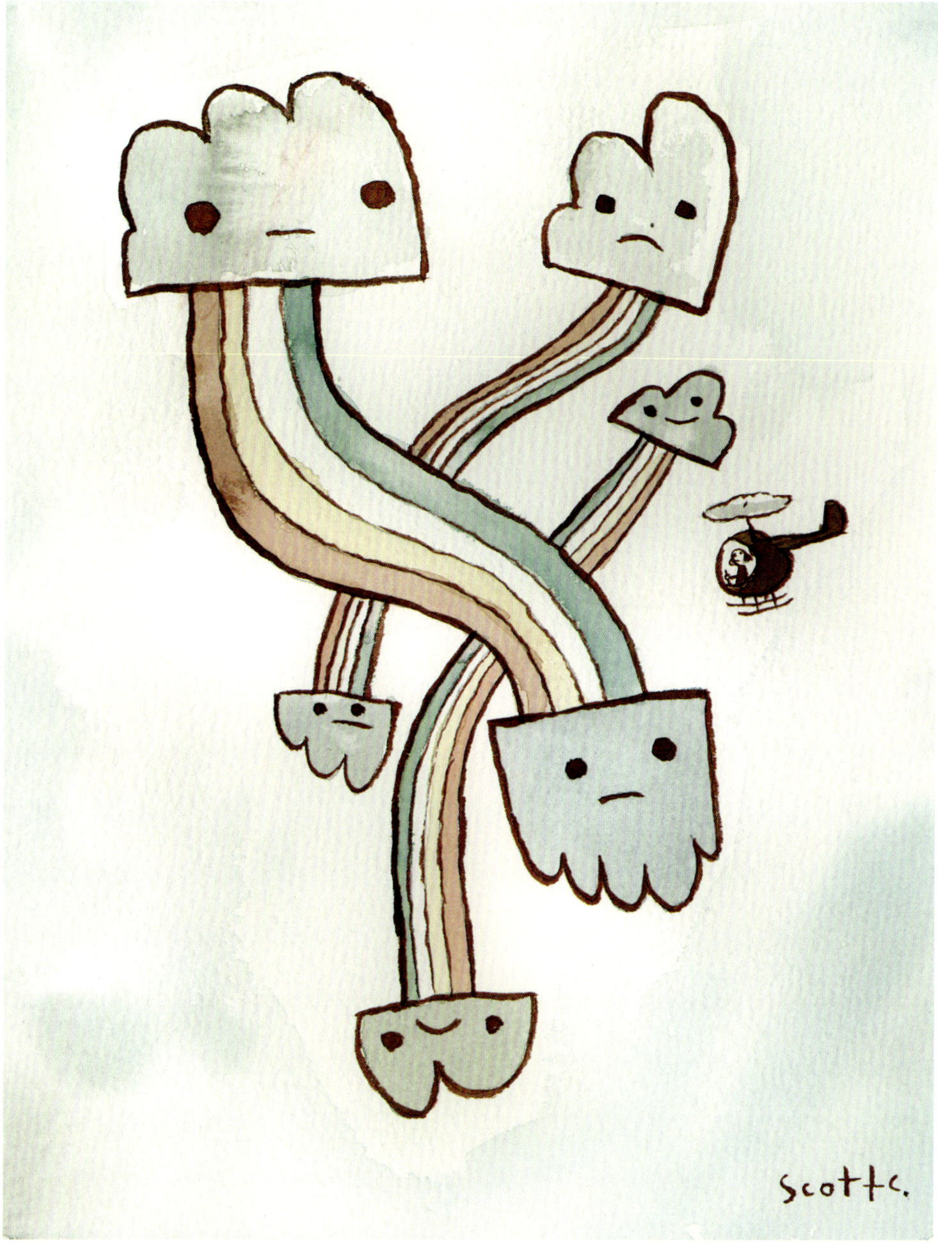

TWISTING THE BOWS
watercolor
8" x 10"
2009

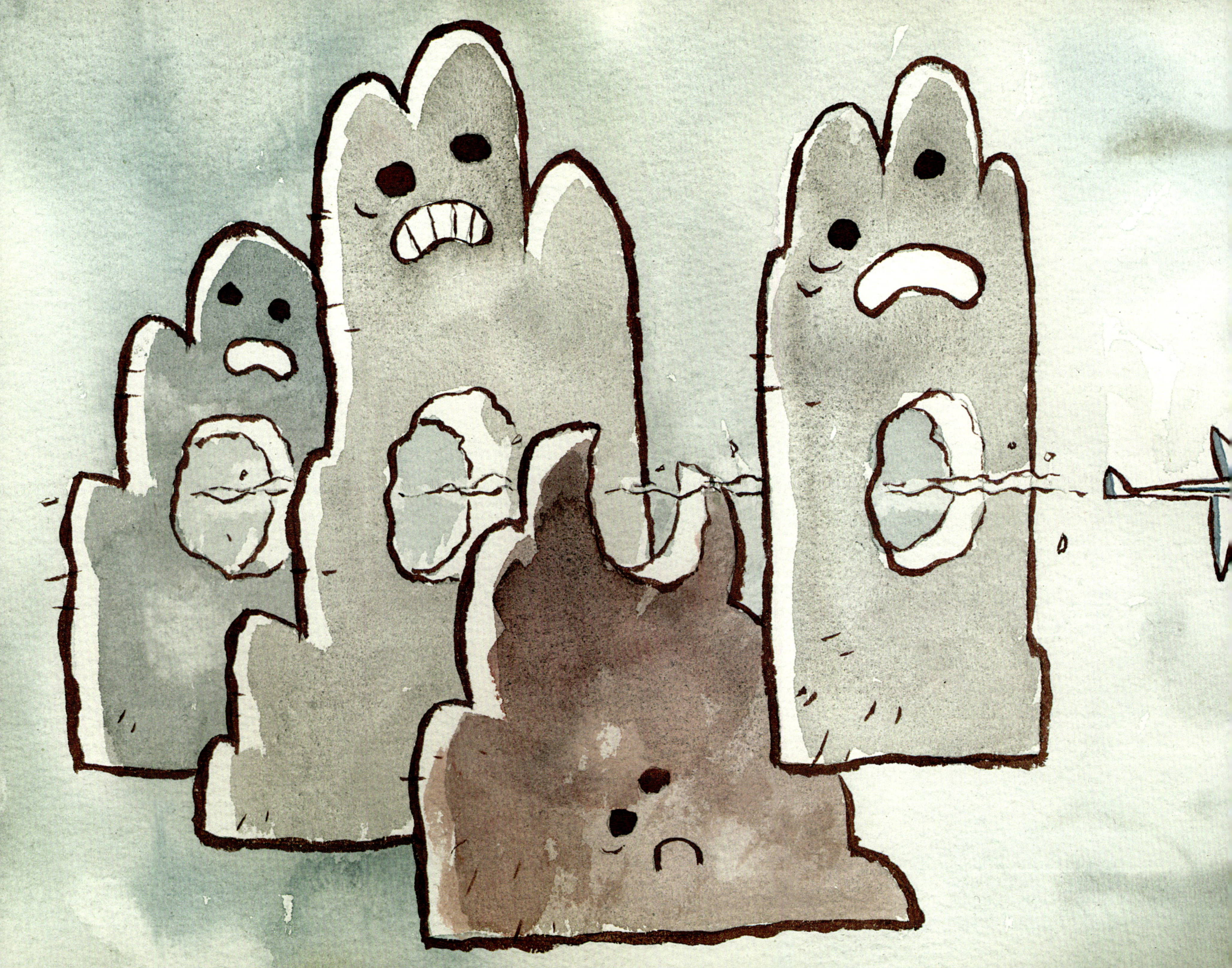

<< OOF, OH, MAN | watercolor | 10" x 8" | 2009

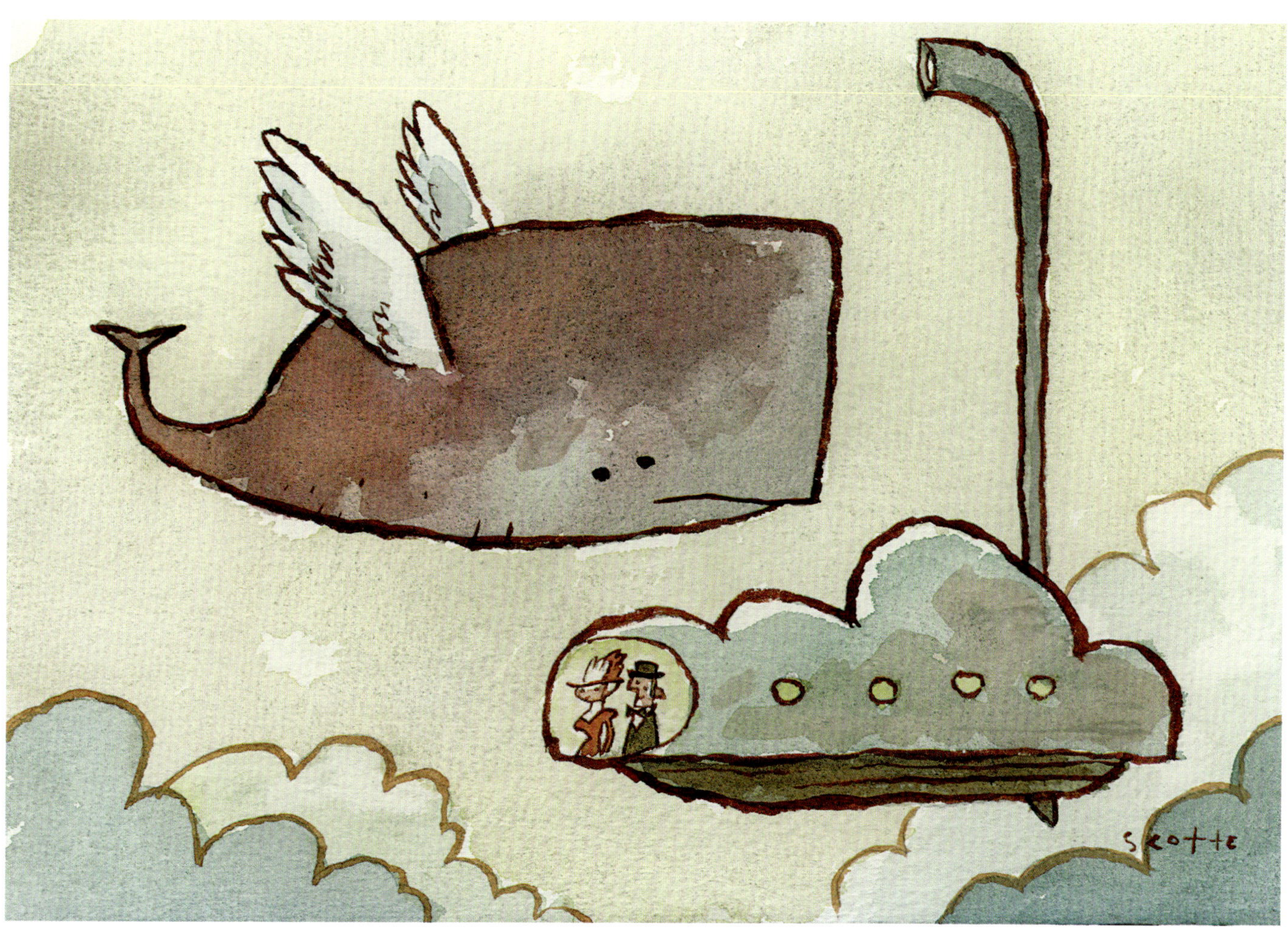

THE TOUR
watercolor
7" x 5"
2009

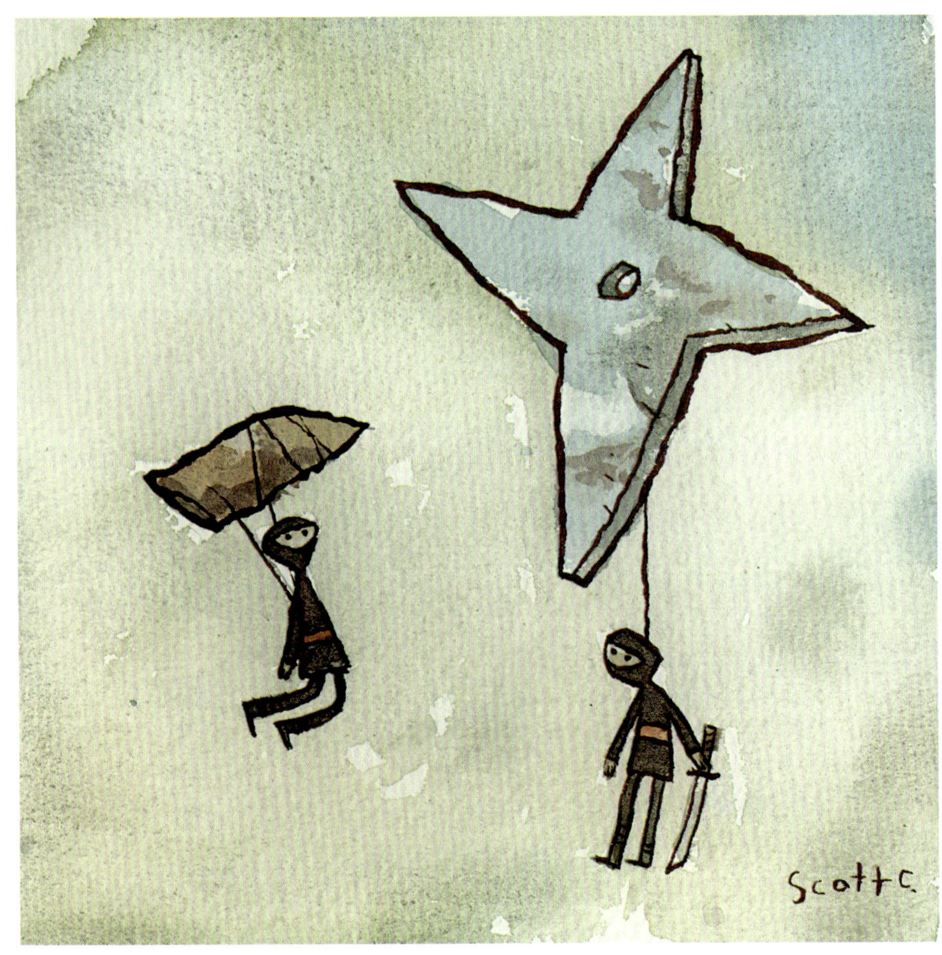

ASSASSINS IN FLIGHT
watercolor
5" x 5"
2009

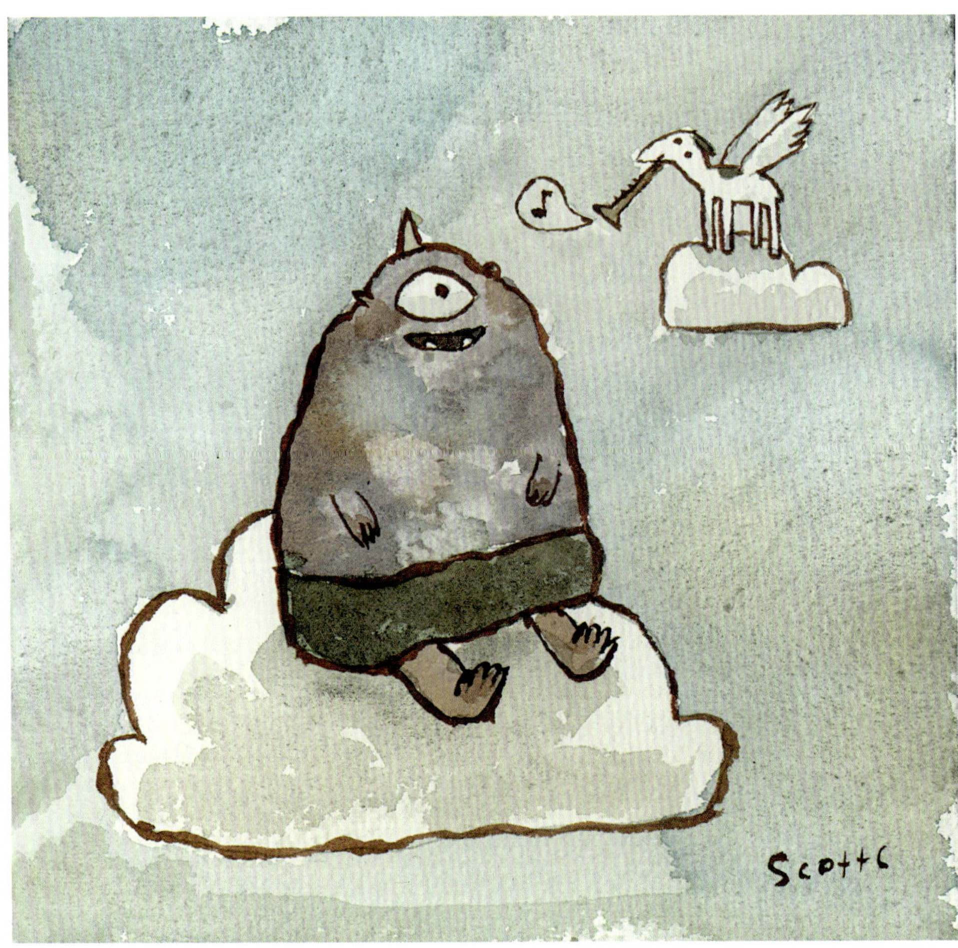

NOTE ENJOYED
watercolor
5" x 5"
2009

TEA DISTURBED | watercolor | 10" x 8" | 2009 >>

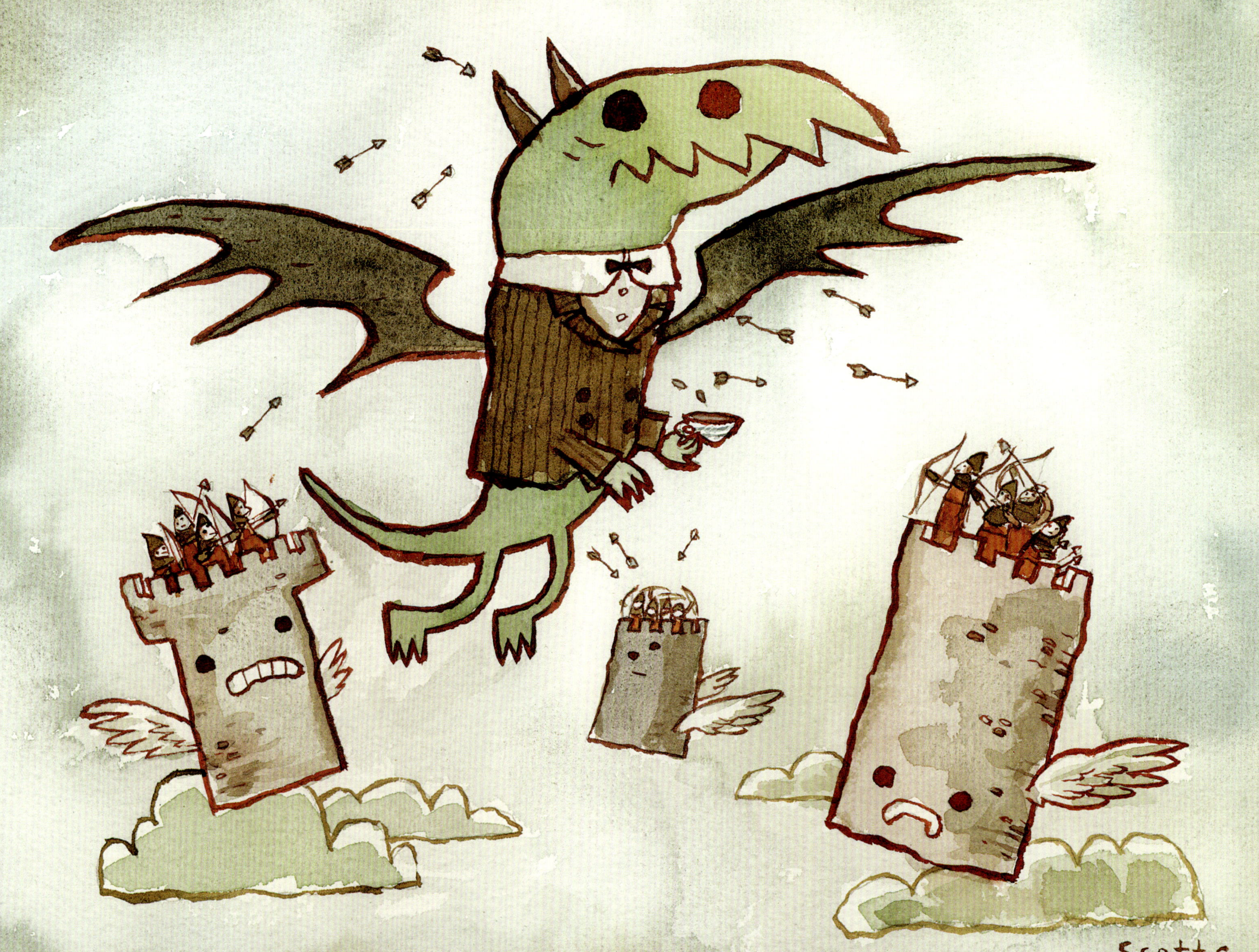
scott c.

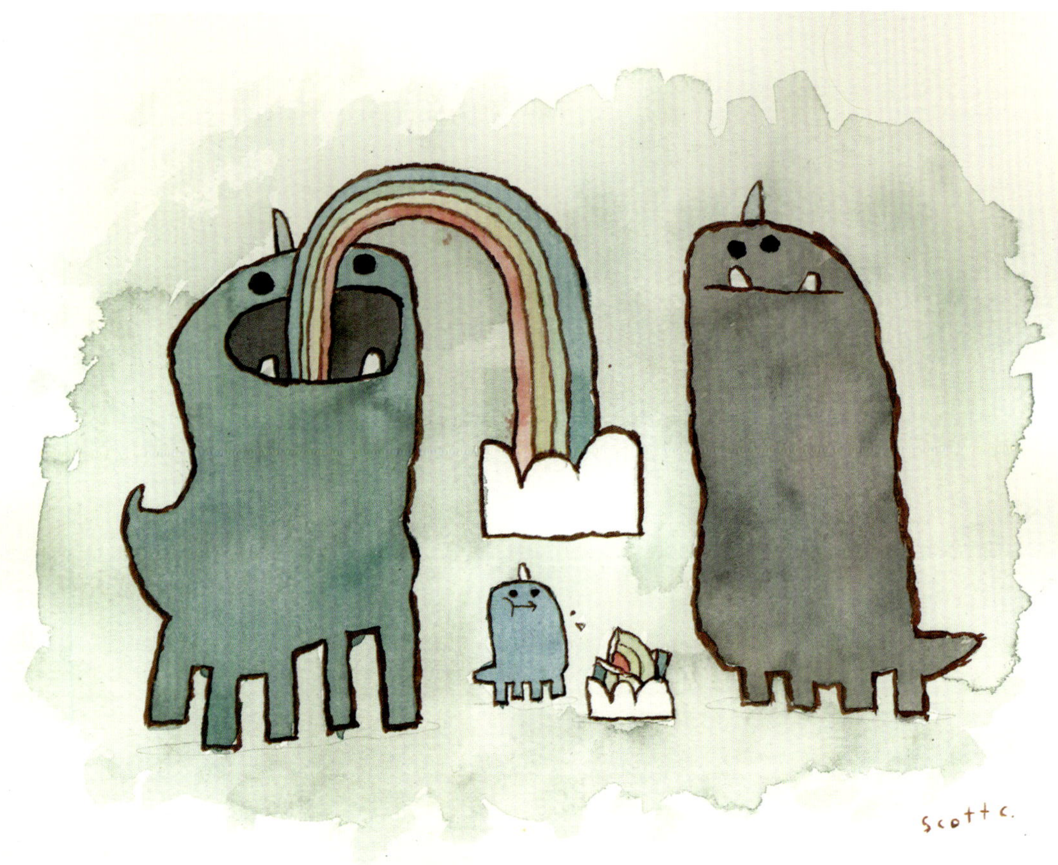

MAKING RAINBOWS
watercolor
10" x 8"
2010

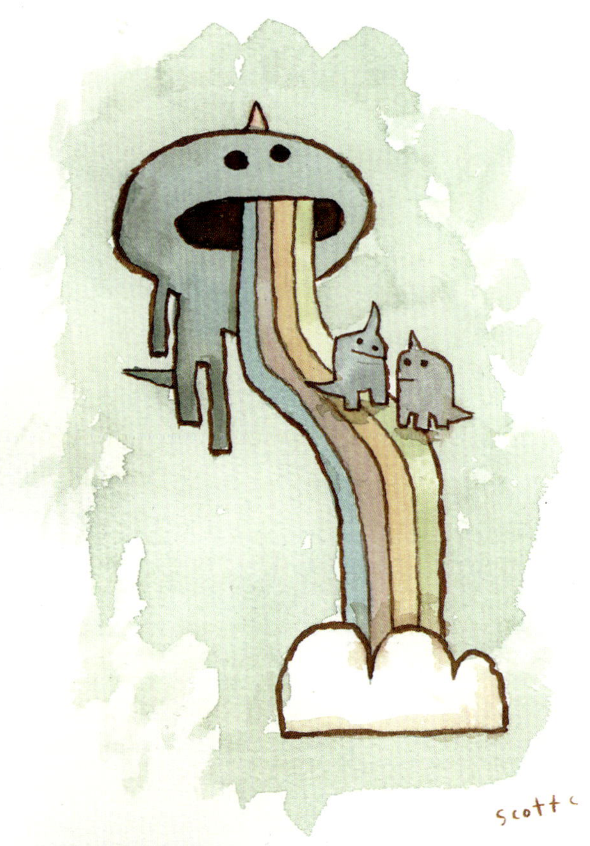

RIDE THE RAINBOW
watercolor
5" x 7"
2010

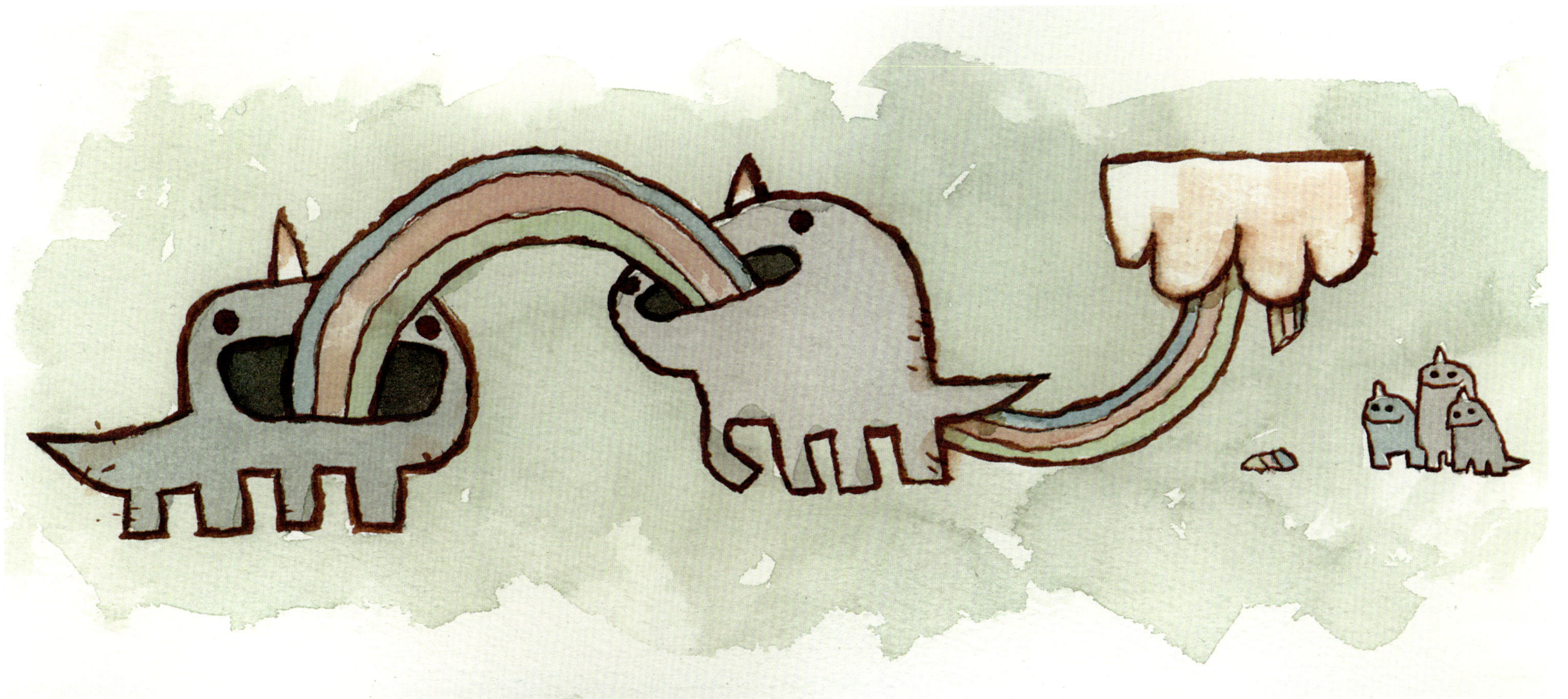

THE LIFE OF THE RAINBOW
watercolor
10" x 4"
2010

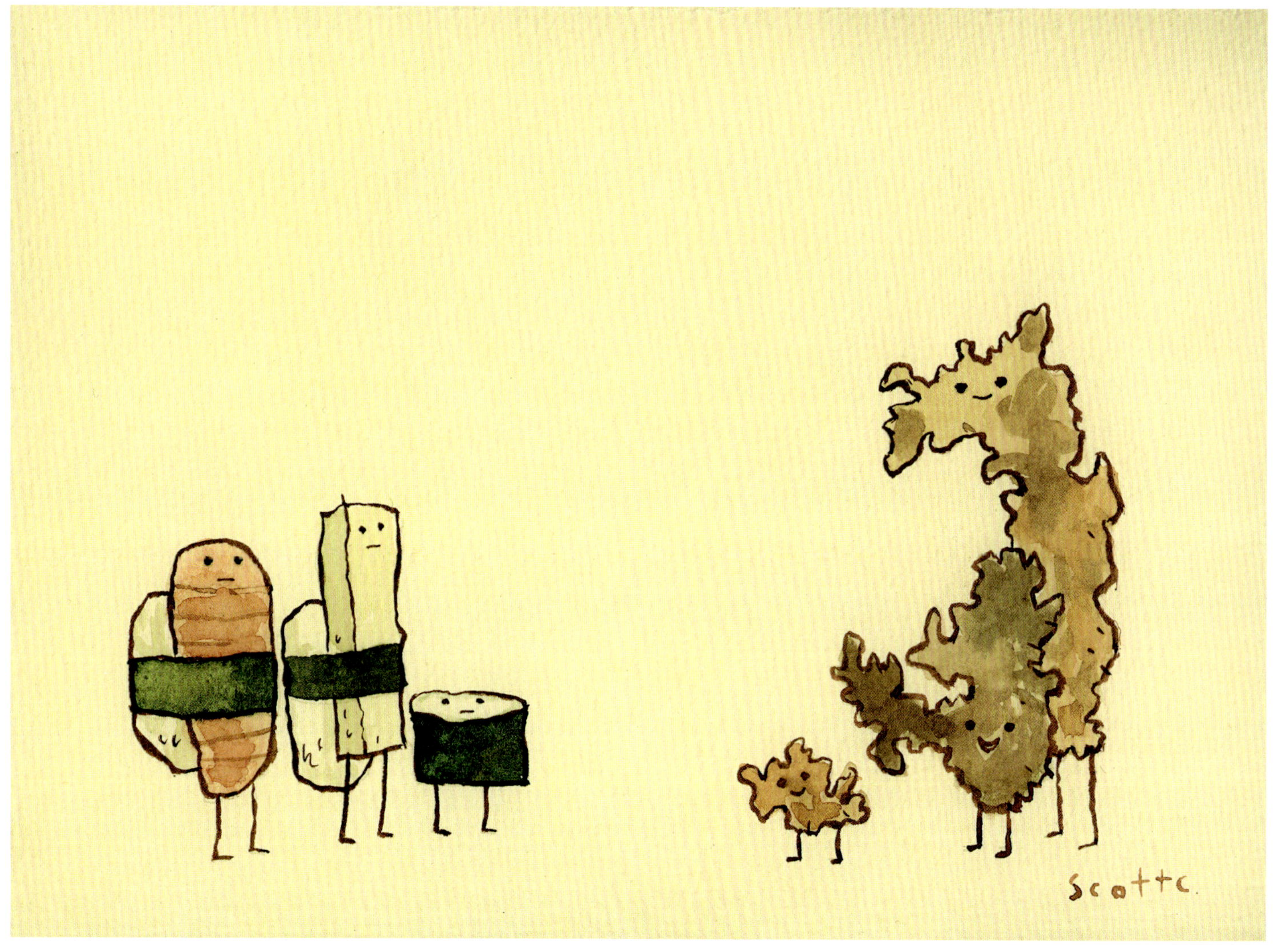

SUSHIS MEET THE TEMPURAS
watercolor
7" x 5"
2008

THE BLESSING | watercolor | 10" x 8" | 2009 >>

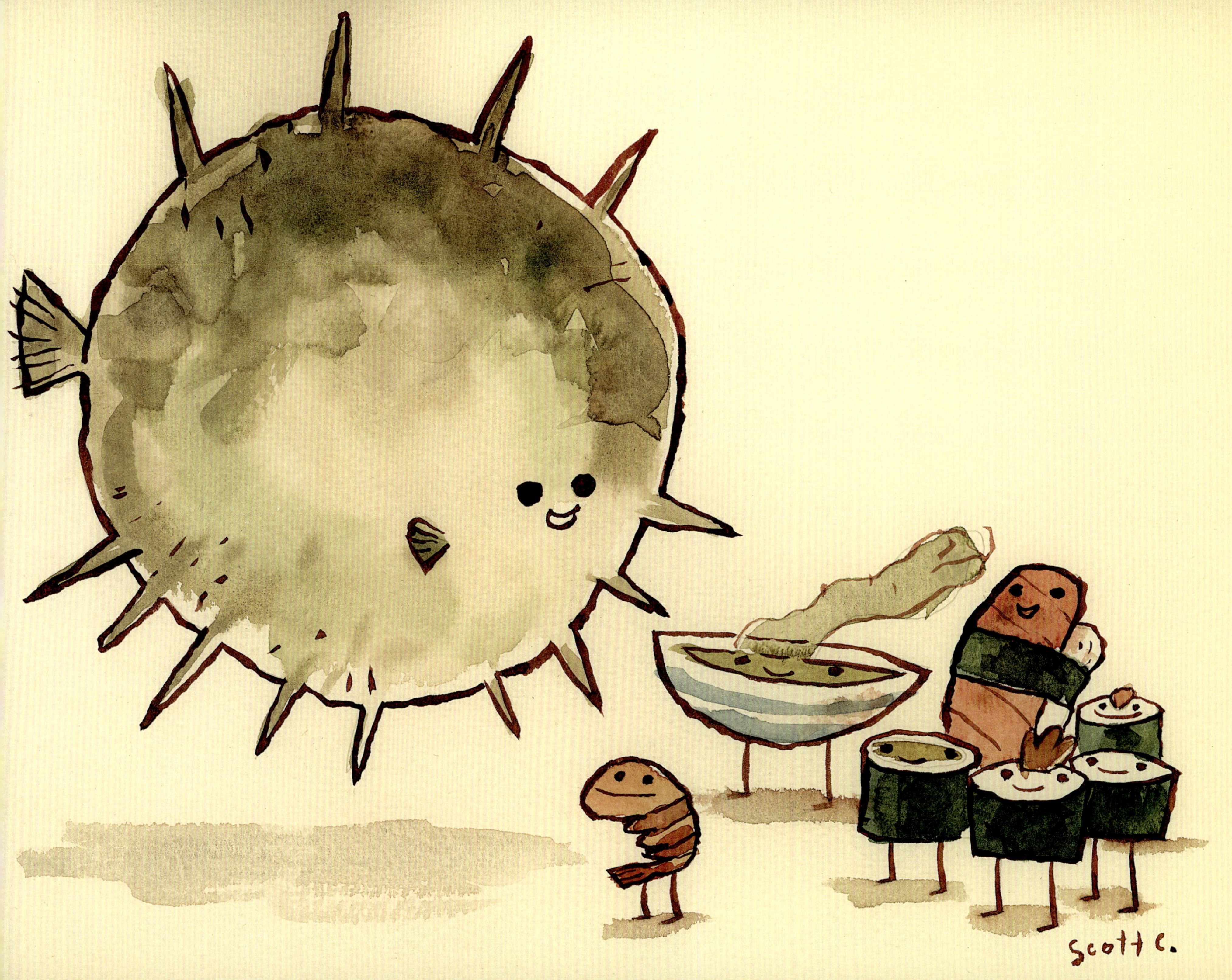
Scott C.

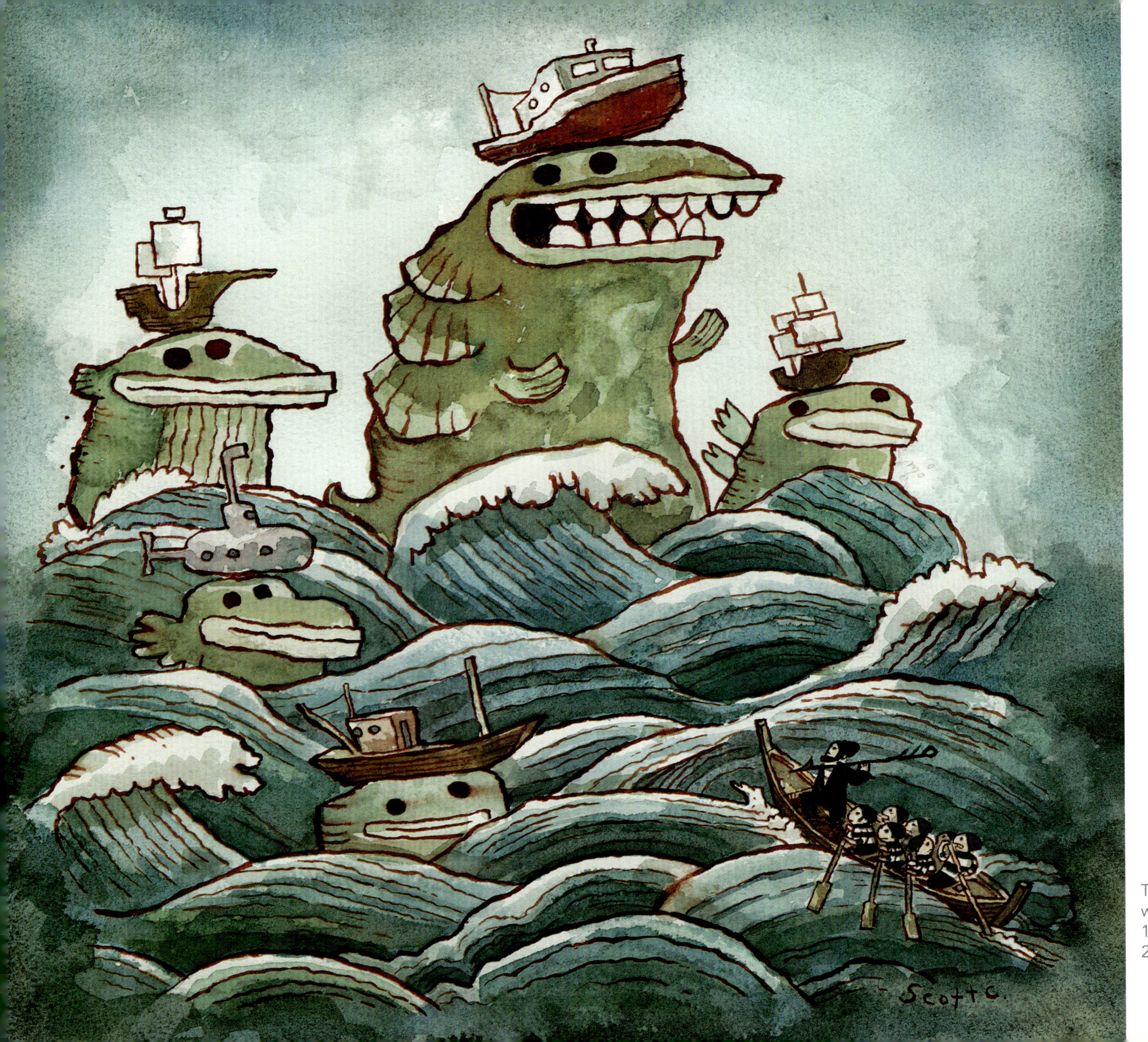

THE LOST SHIPS
watercolor
12" x 12"
2010

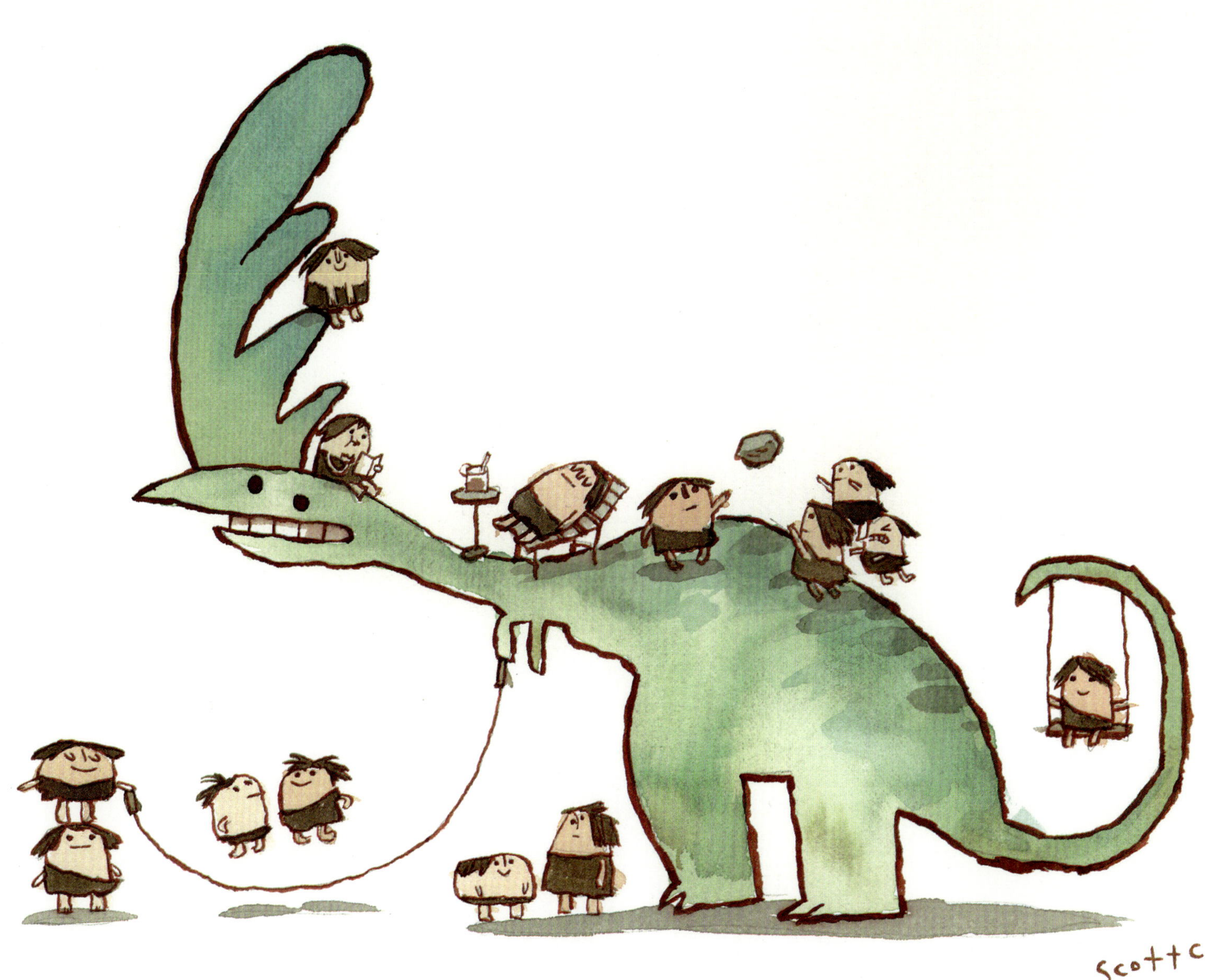

DINOSAUR PARK #1
watercolor
10" x 8"
2009

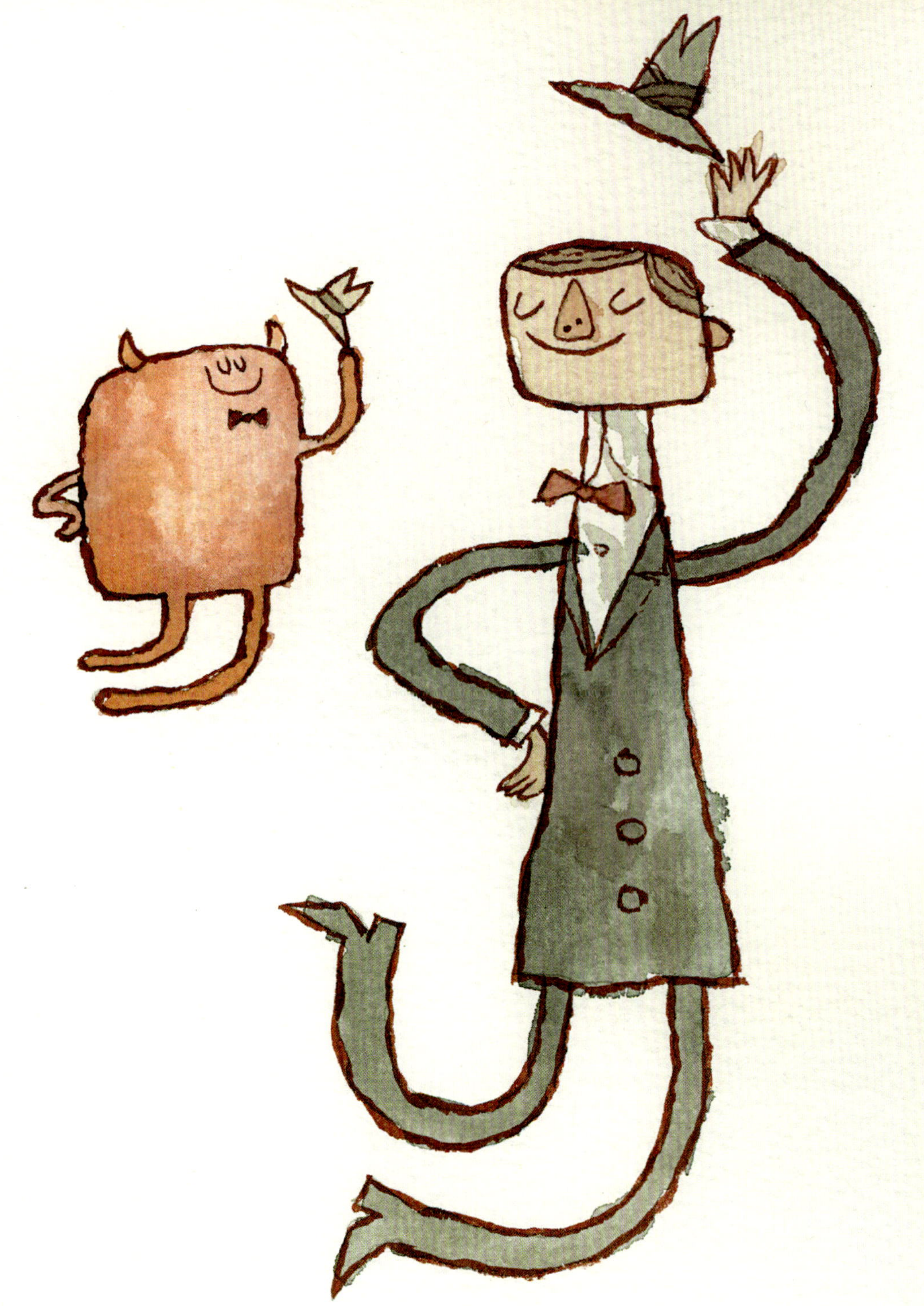

THE GREETINGS
watercolor
5" x 7"
2009

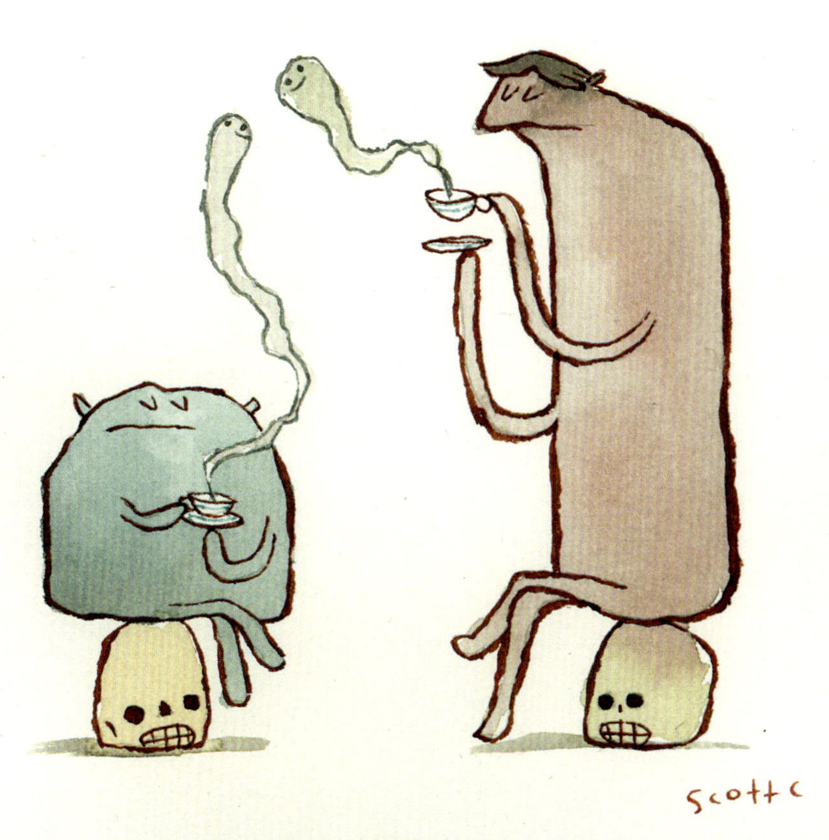

REUNITED
watercolor
5" x 5"
2010

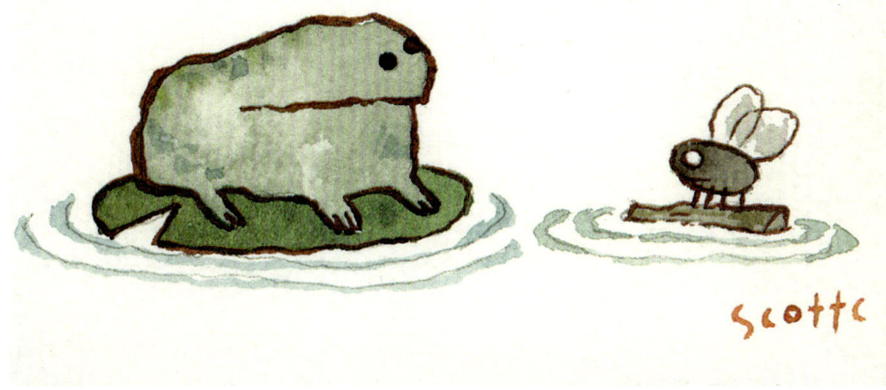

TENSION
watercolor
3.5" x 3.5"
2010

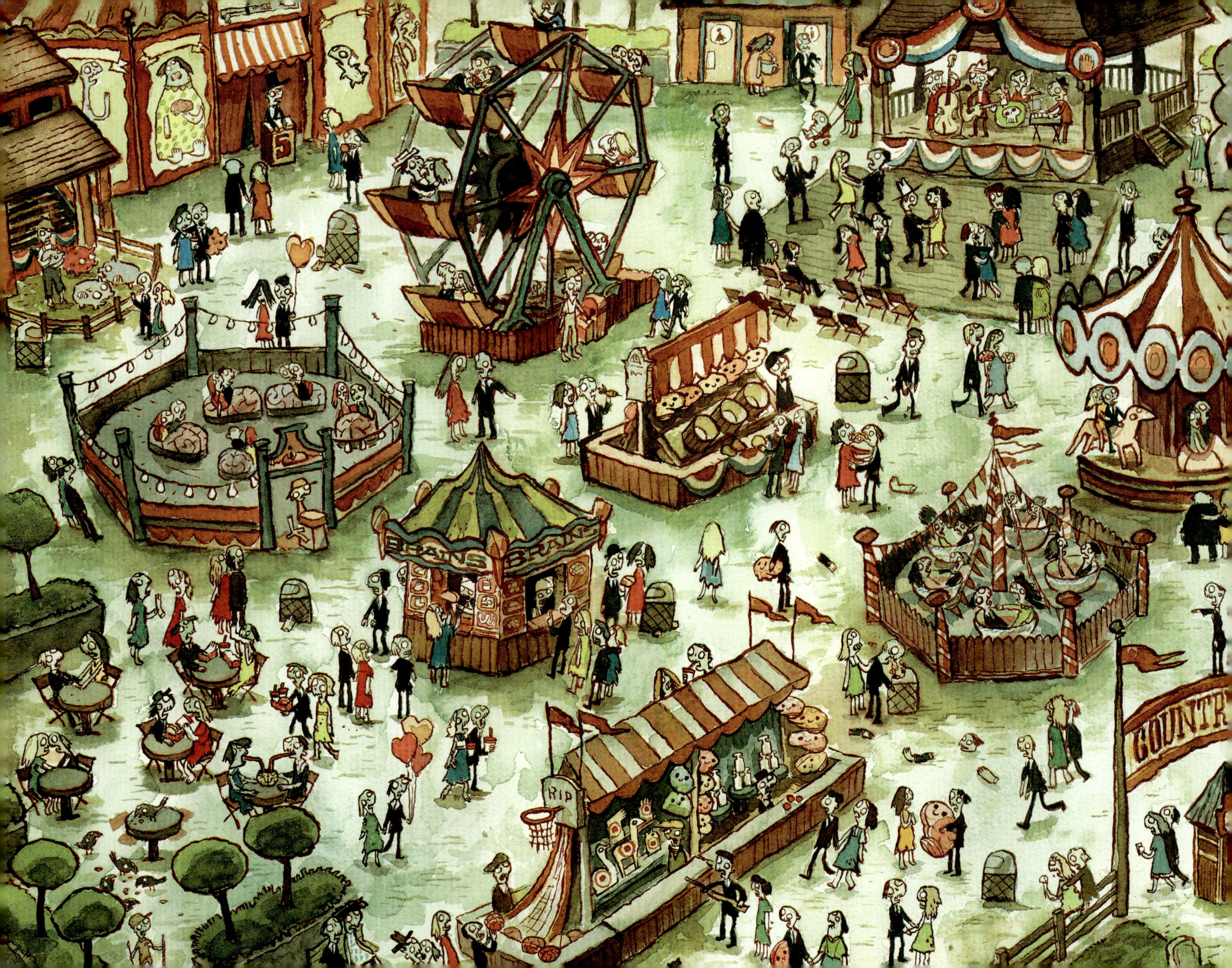
5
BRAINS
BRAINS
RIP
COUNTR

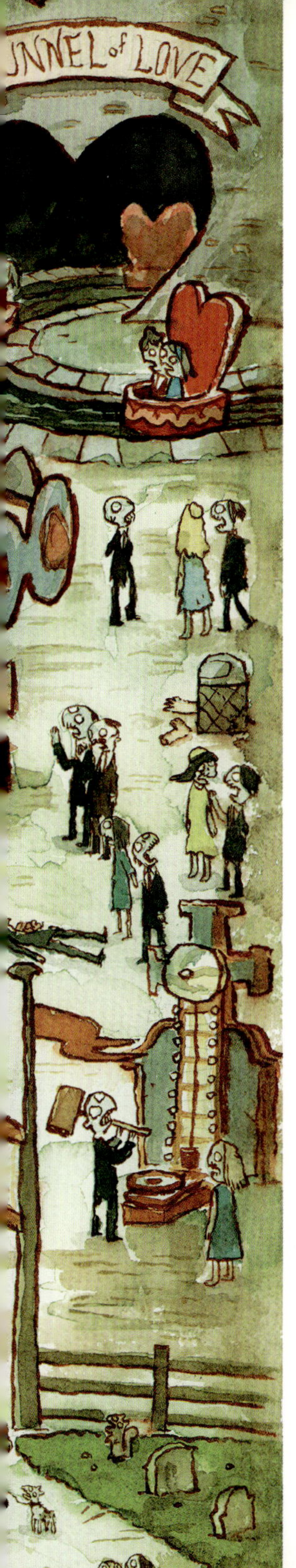

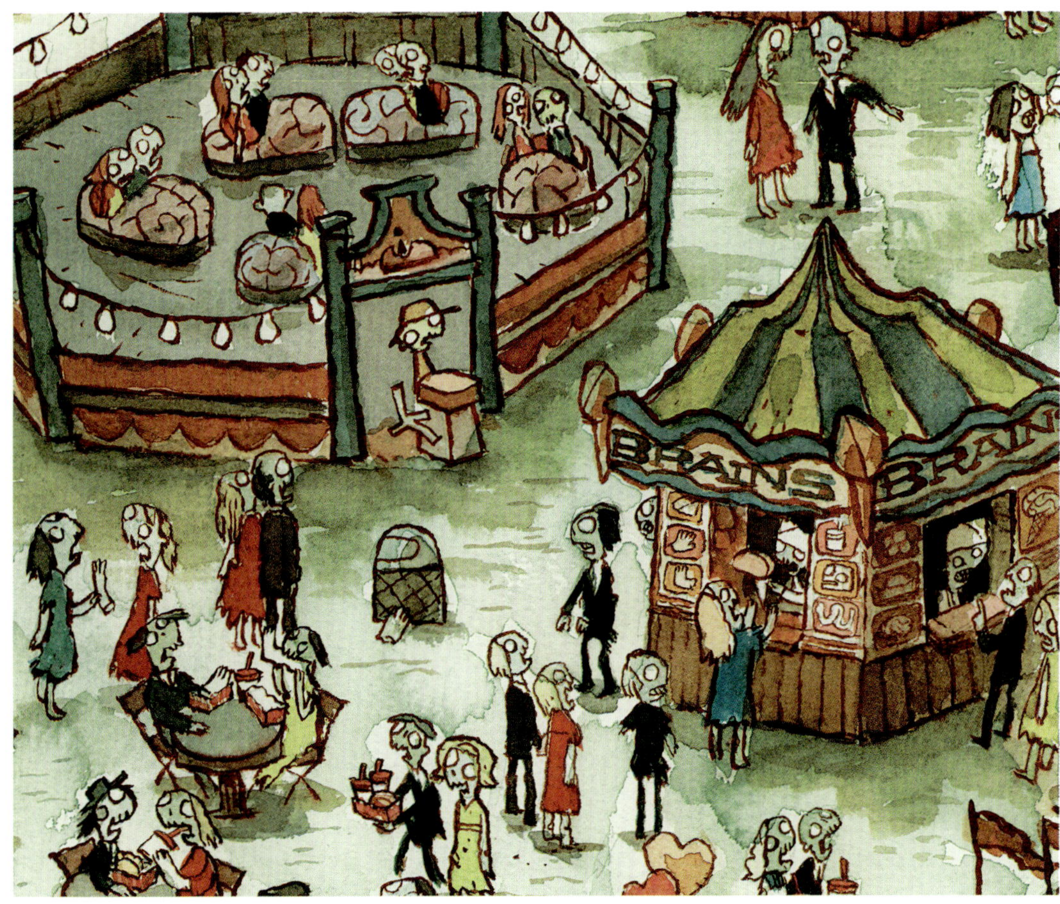

ZOMBIE FAIR
watercolor
22" x 16"
2010

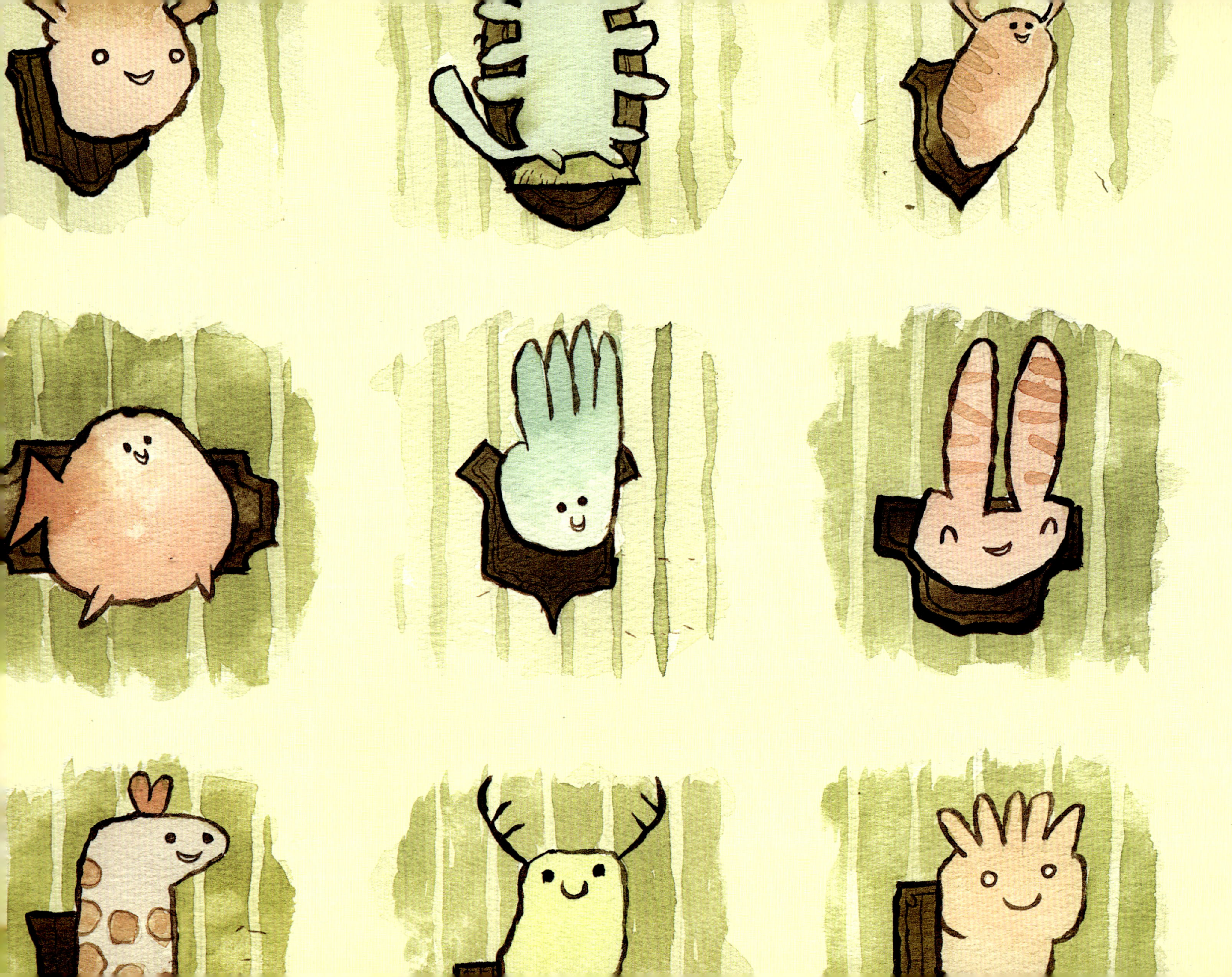

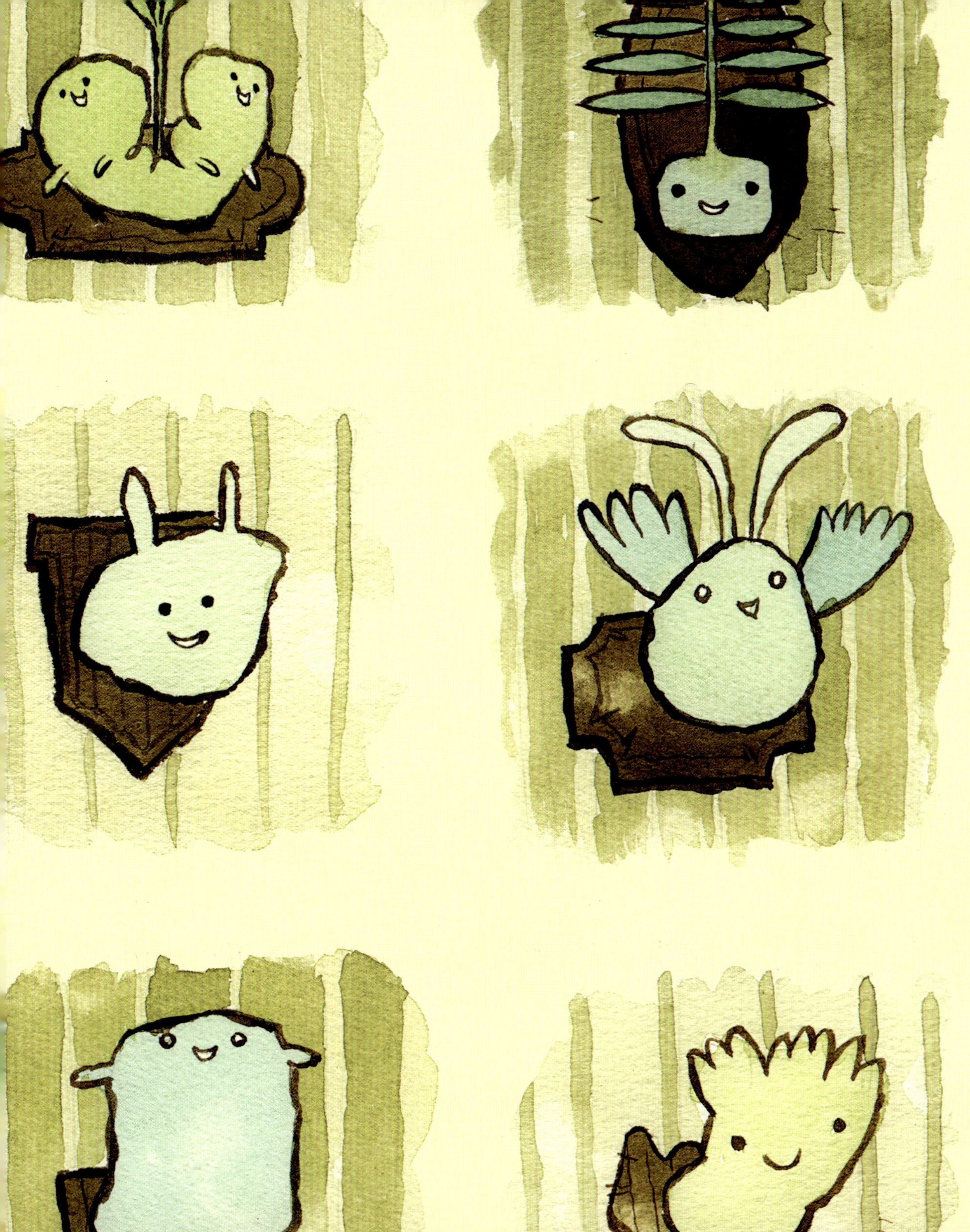

cute hunter

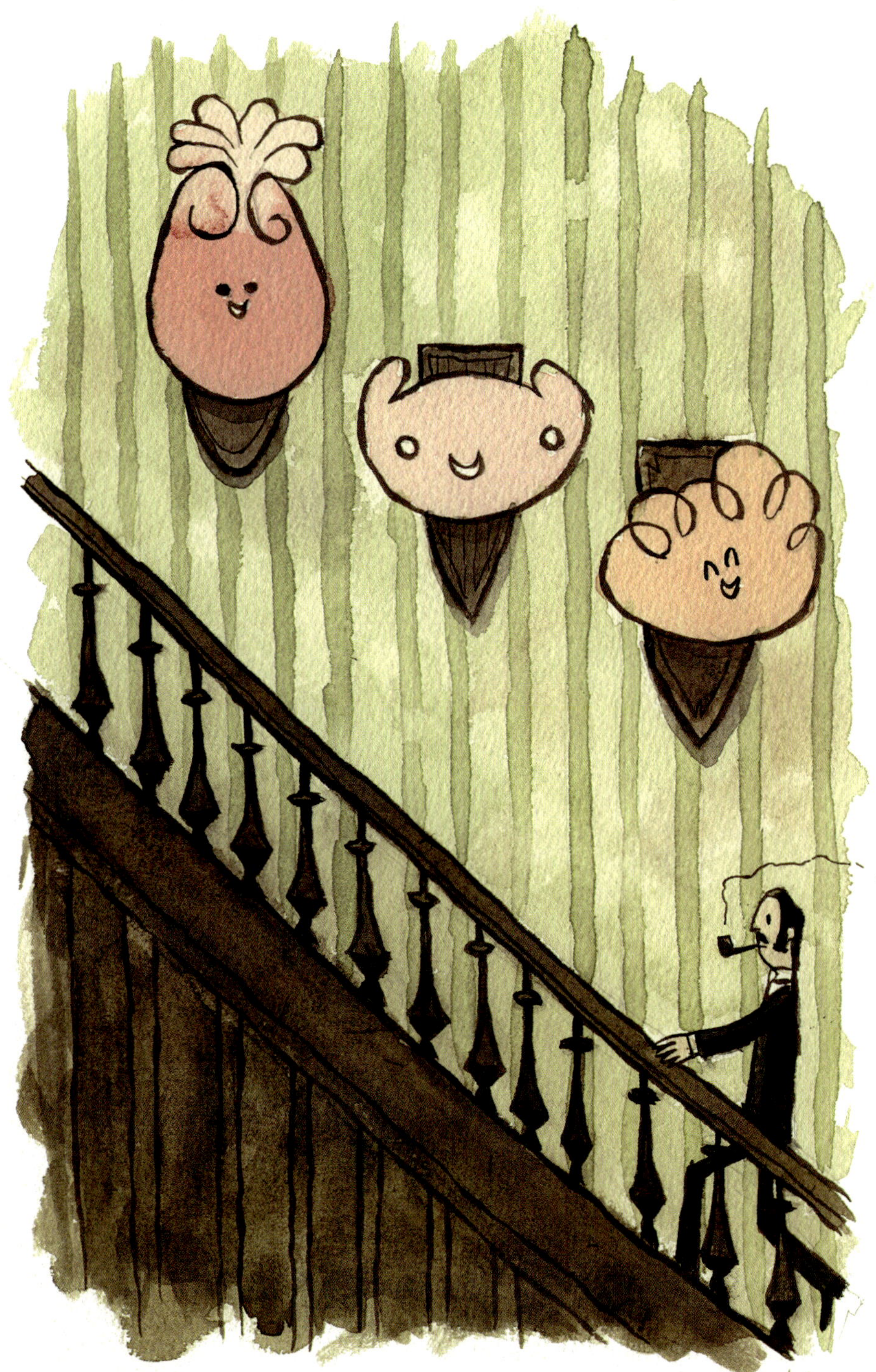

CUTE HUNTER ASCENDS
watercolor
8" x 10"
2008

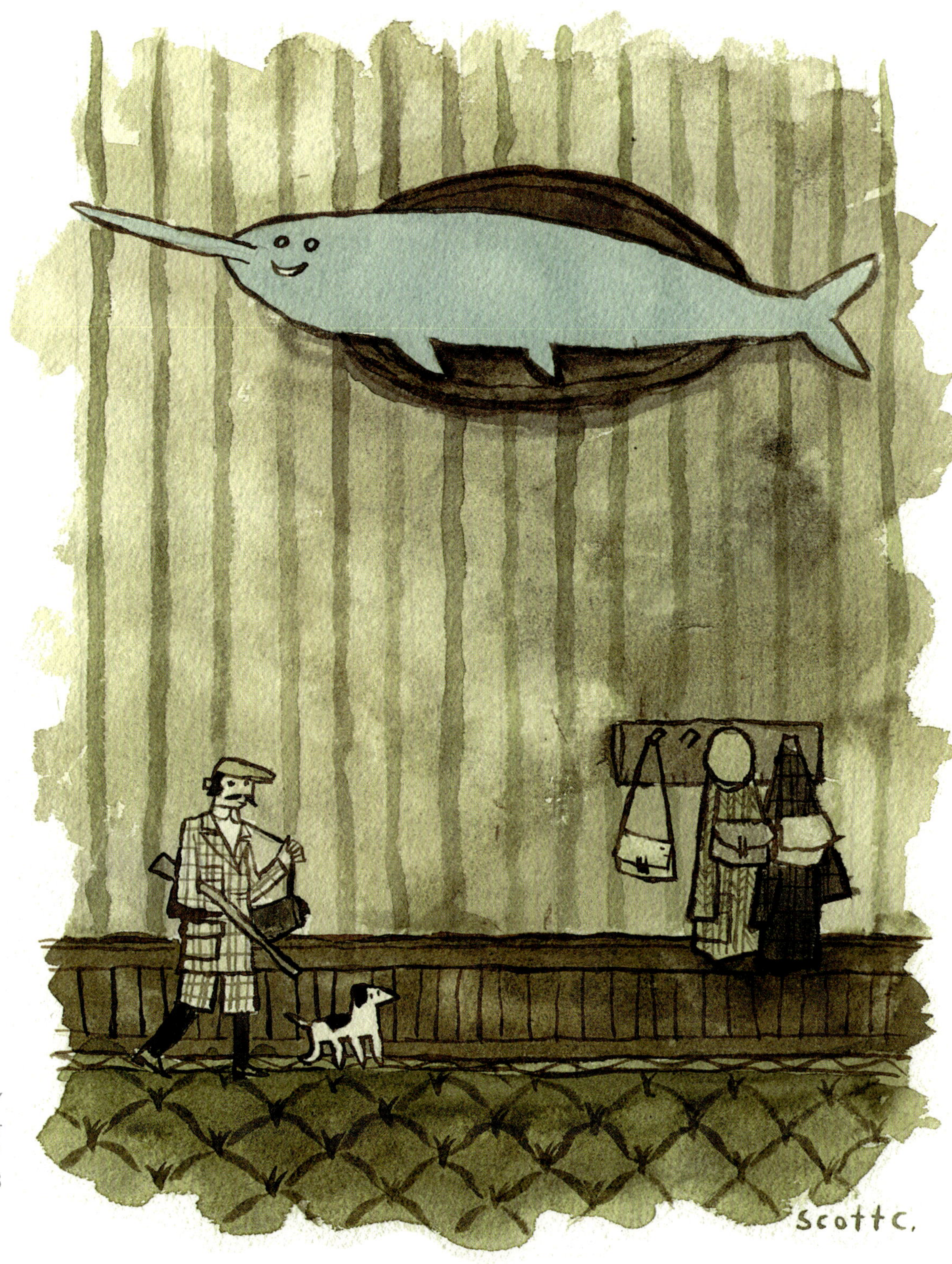

CUTE HUNTER LONG DAY
watercolor
8" x 10"
2008

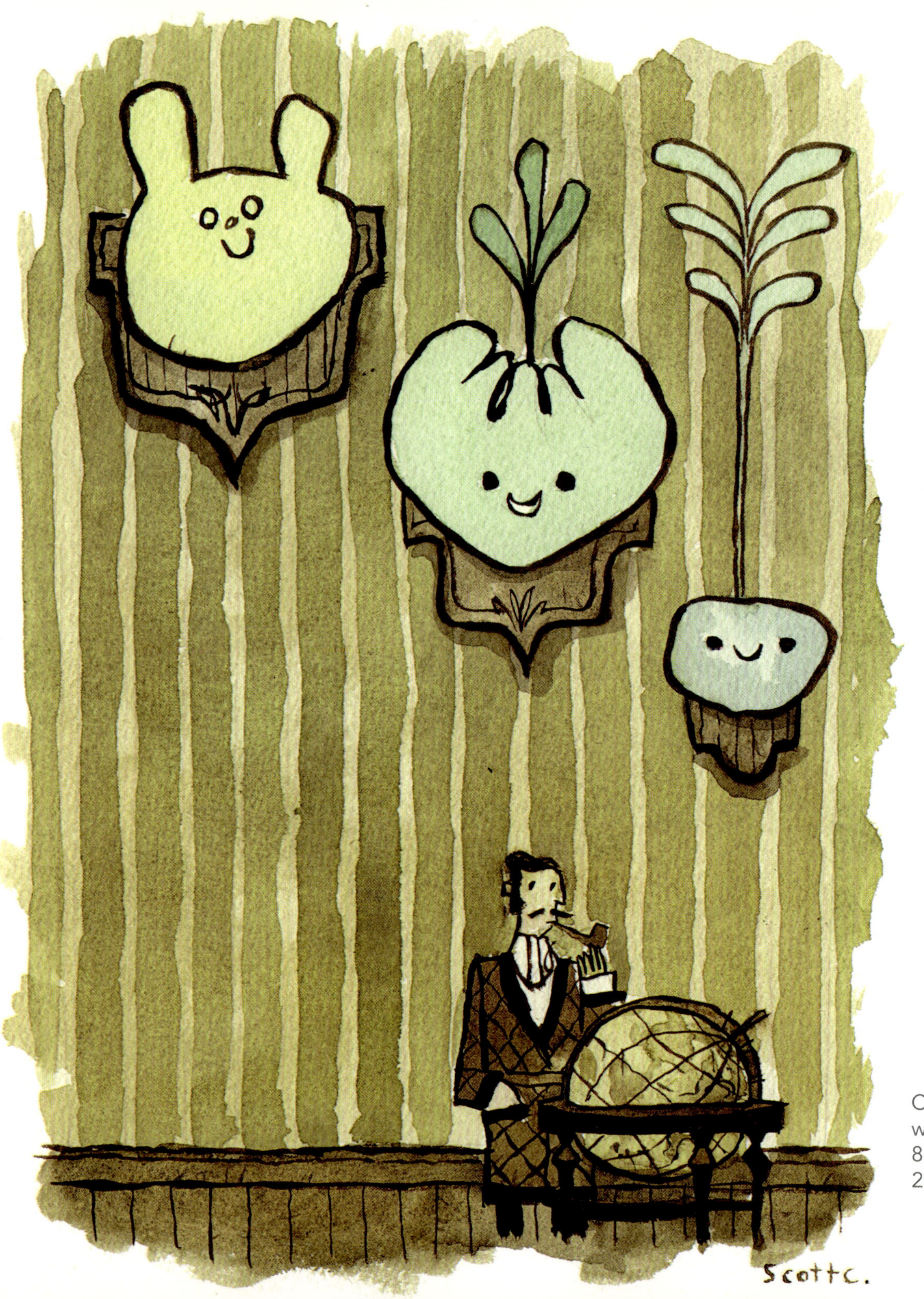

The Cute Hunter is a collector of all things cute. He is a skilled hunter and travels to exotic lands for the rarest of cute creatures. His collection is quite expansive and very famous. The cute creatures are overjoyed to be part of his collection and are oftentimes smiling, singing, and drooling.

CUTE HUNTER QUESTIONS GLOBE
watercolor
8" x 10"
2008

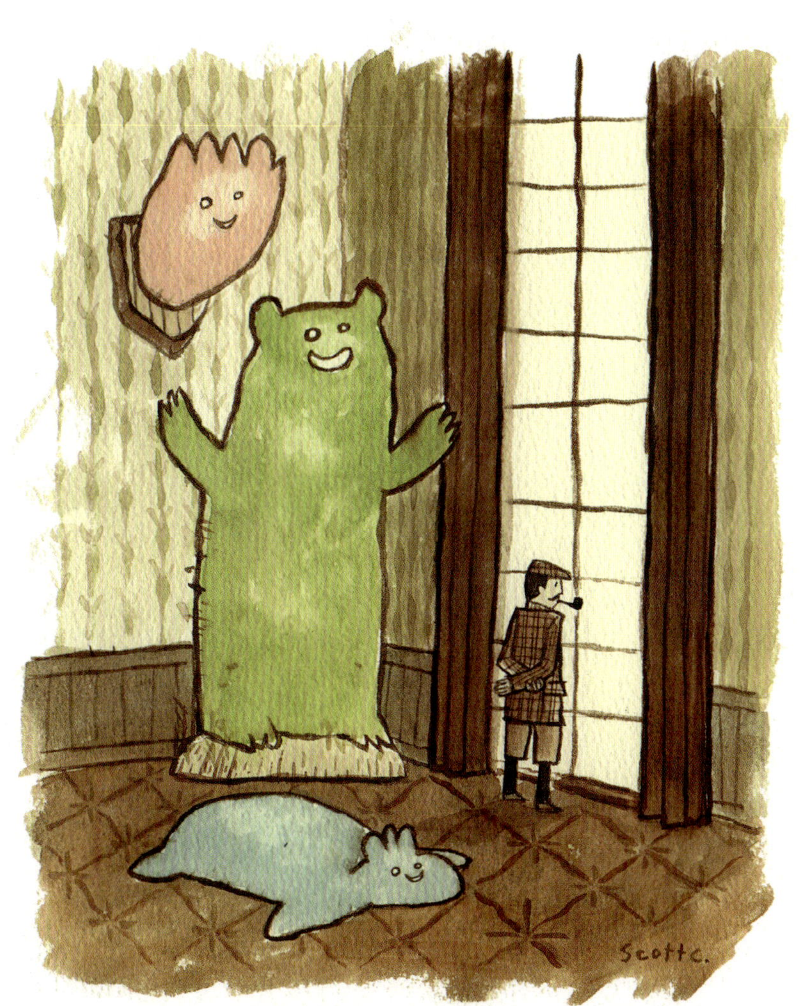

CUTE HUNTER LONGINGLY
watercolor
8" x 10"
2008

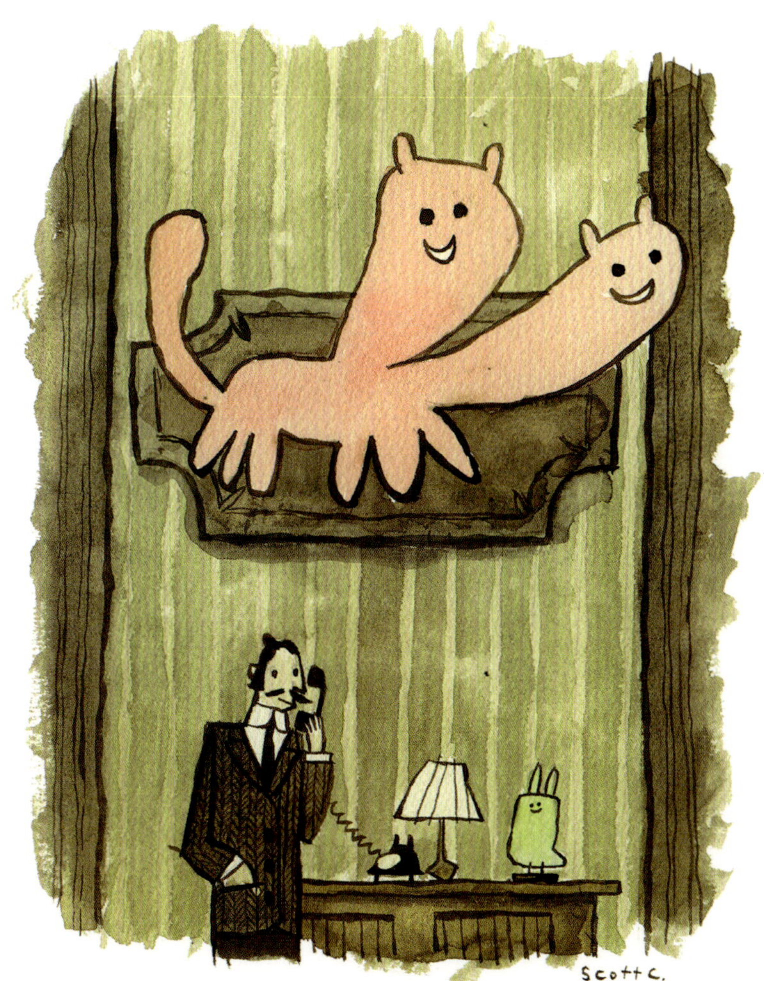

CUTE HUNTER TAKES A CALL
watercolor
8" x 10"
2008

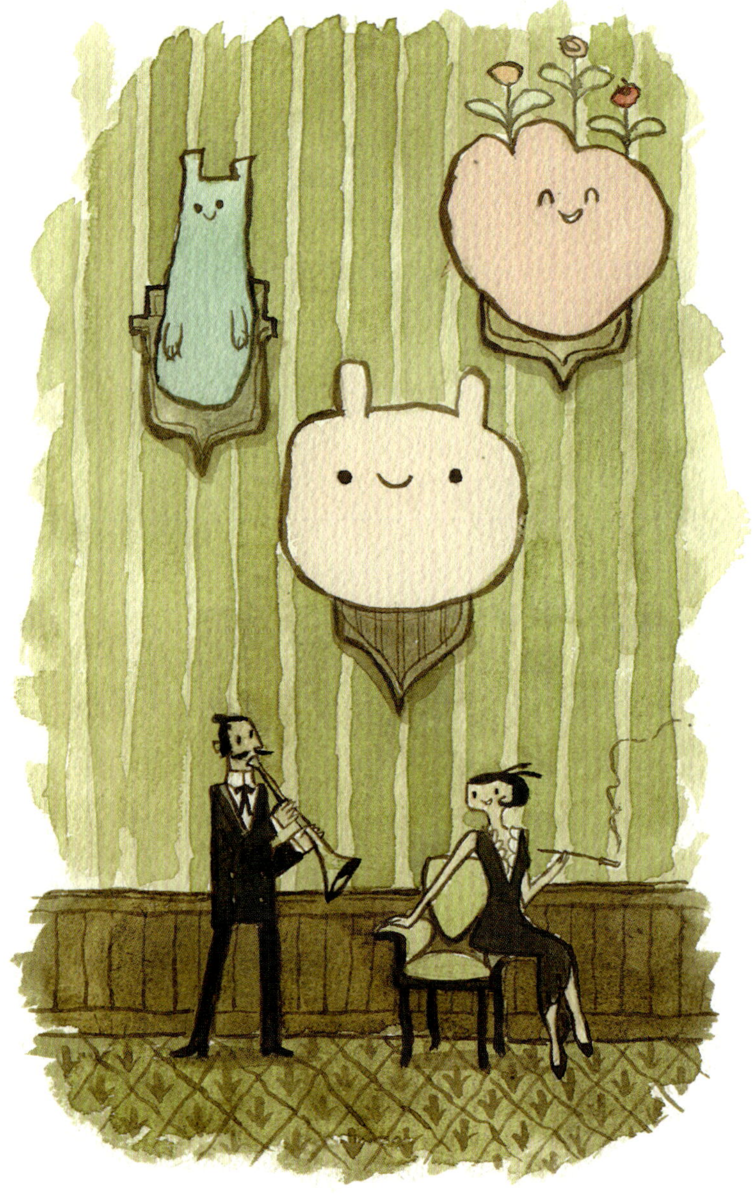

CUTE HUNTER WOOS LADY
watercolor
8" x 10"
2008

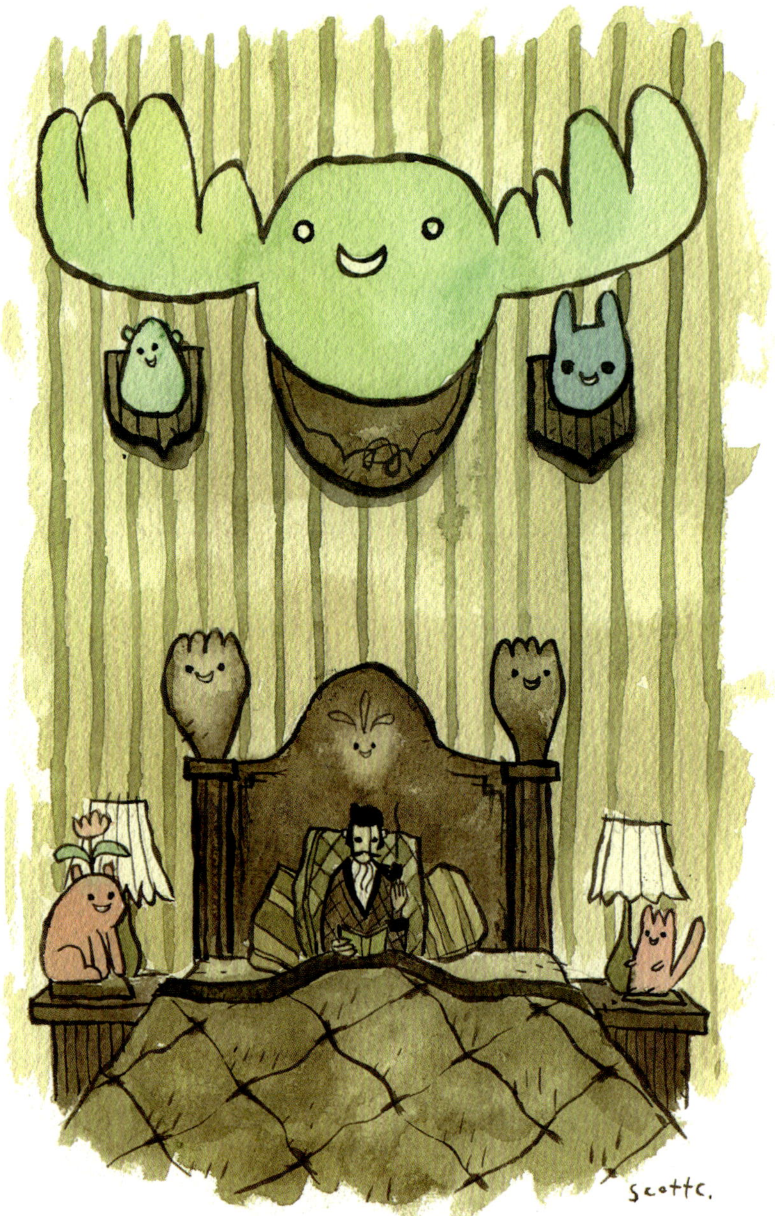

CUTE HUNTER RETIRES
watercolor
8" x 10"
2008

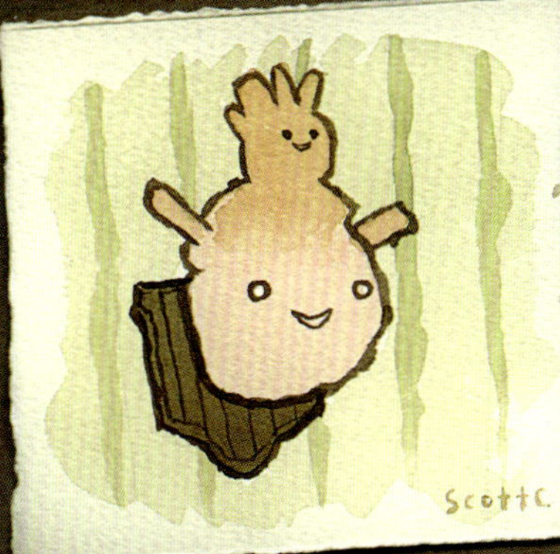
scottc.
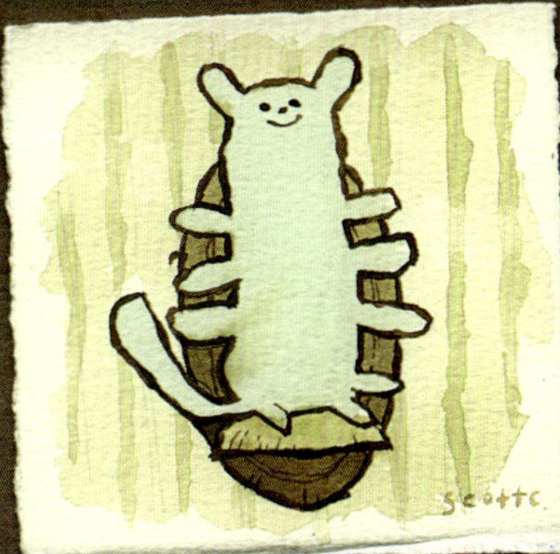
scottc.
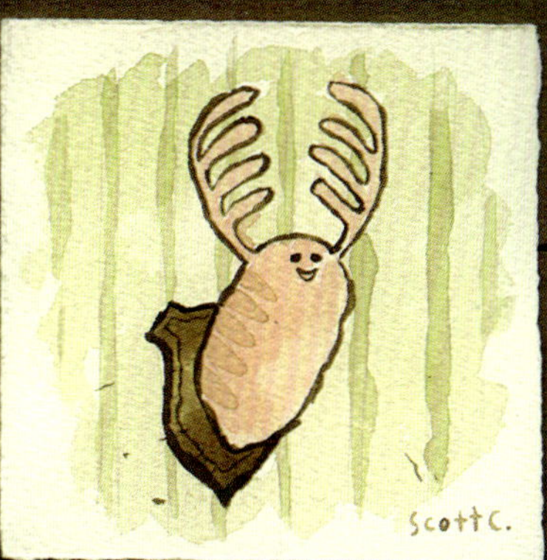
scottc.
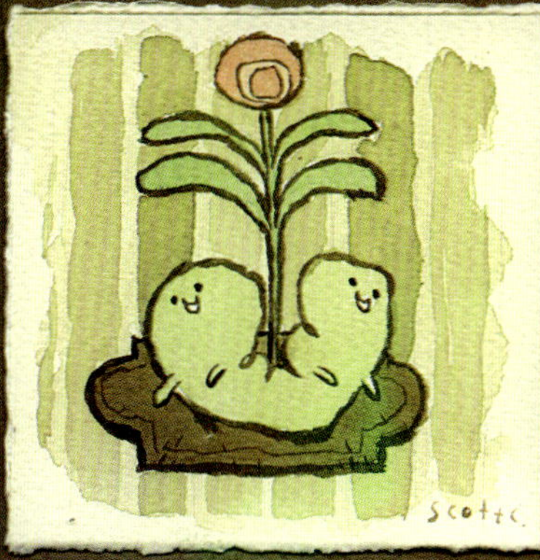
scottc.
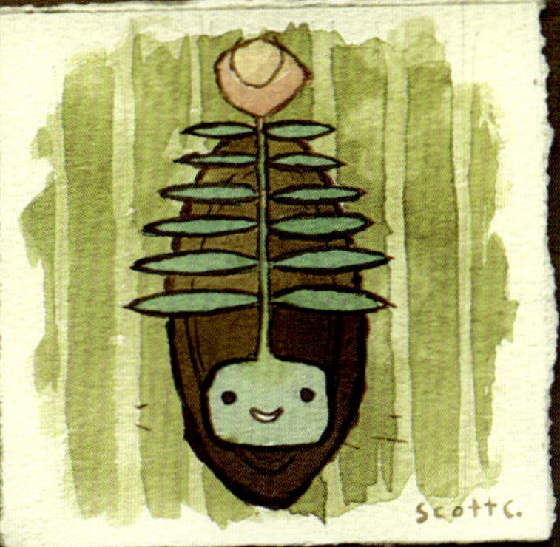
scottc.
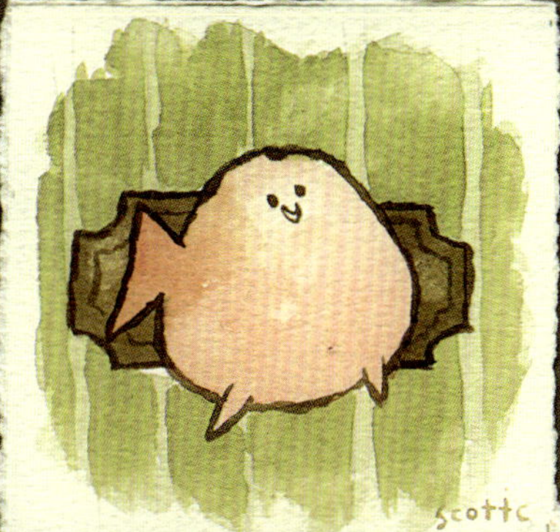
scottc.
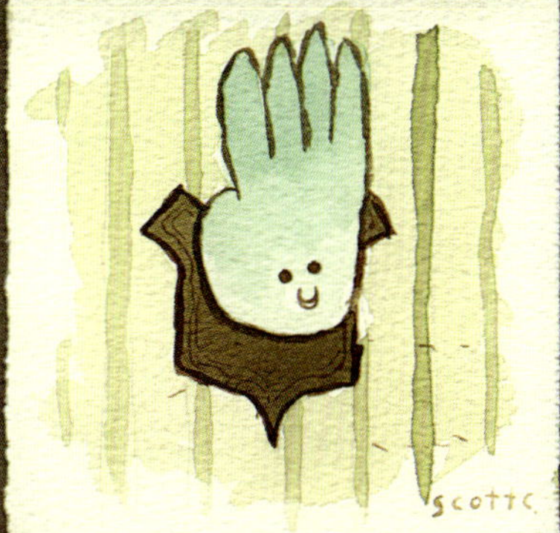
scottc.
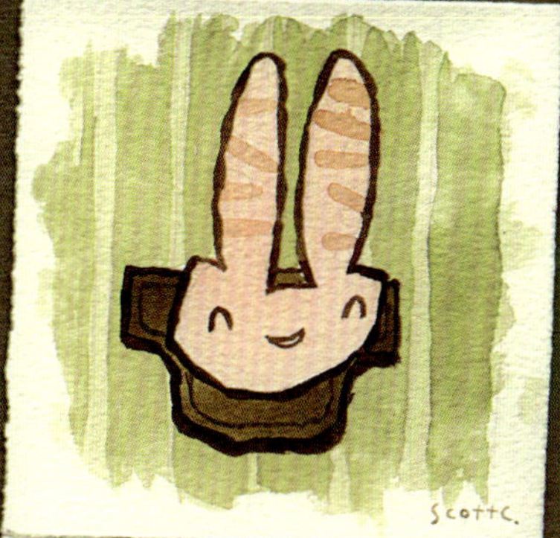
scottc.
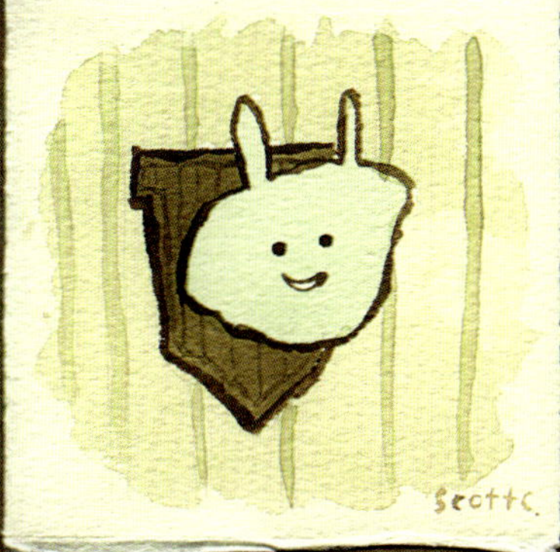
scottc.
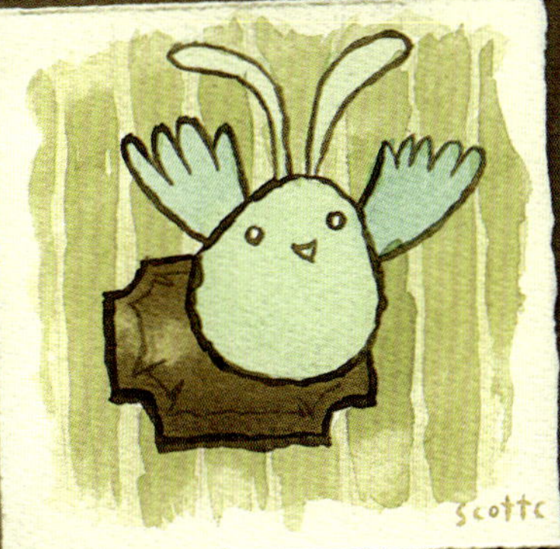
scottc.
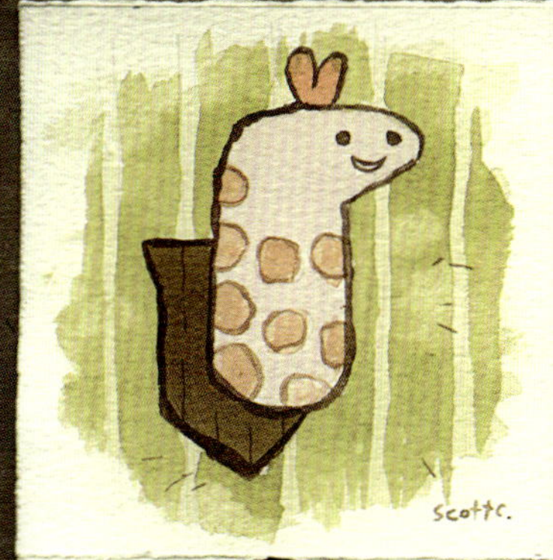
scottc.
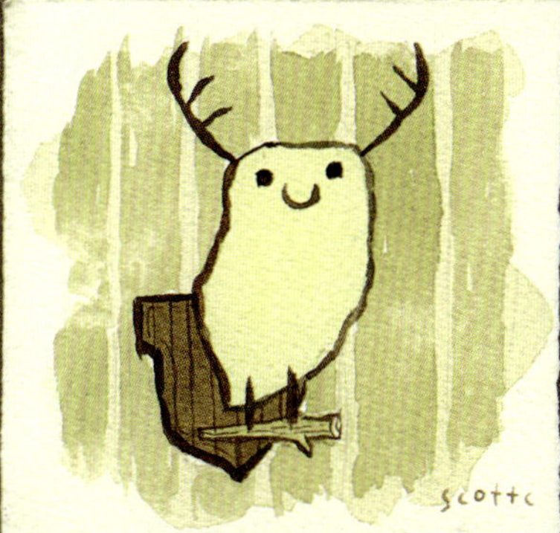
scottc.
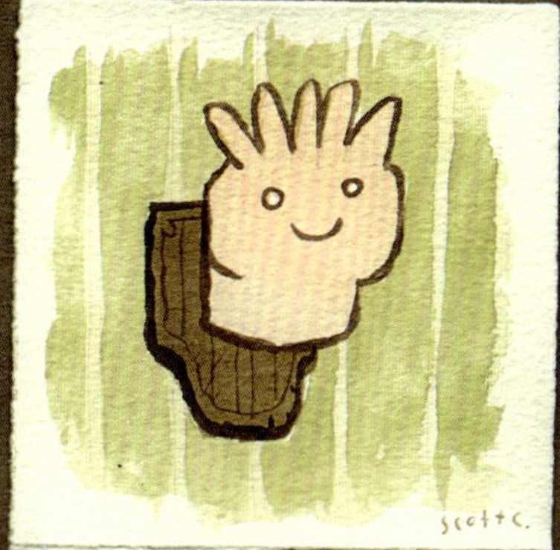
scottc.
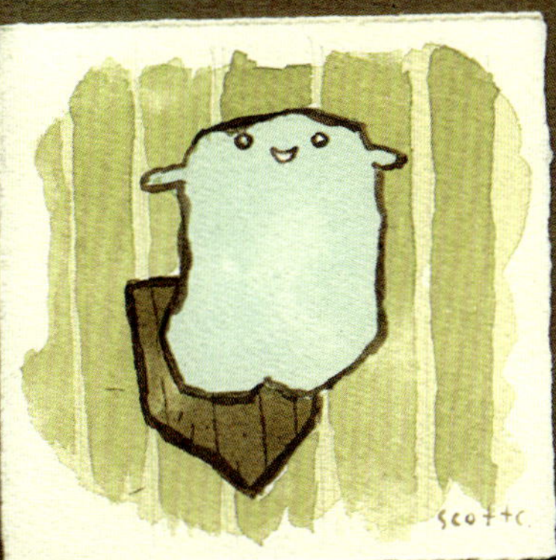
scottc.
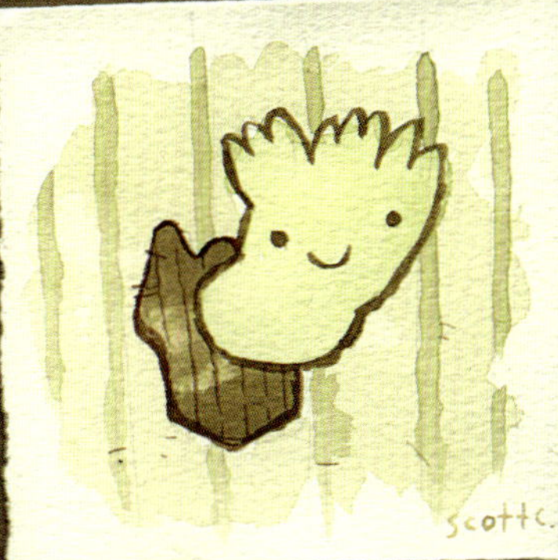
scottc.
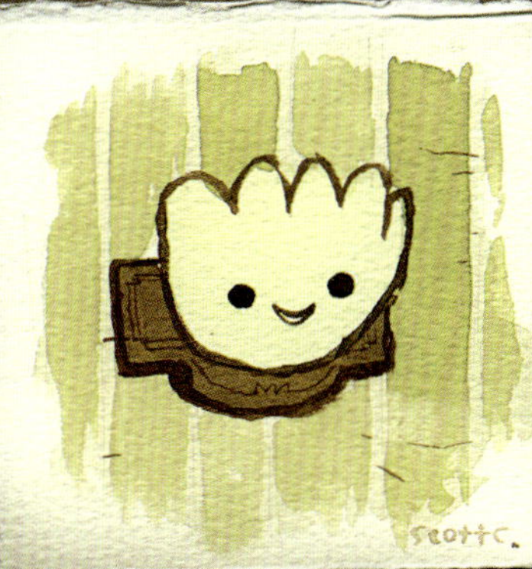
scottc.
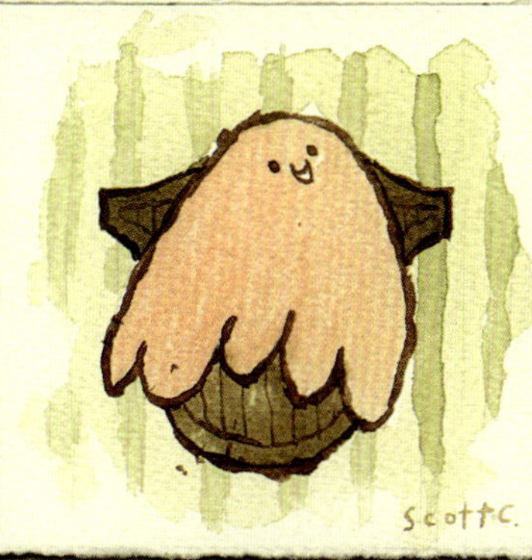
scottc.
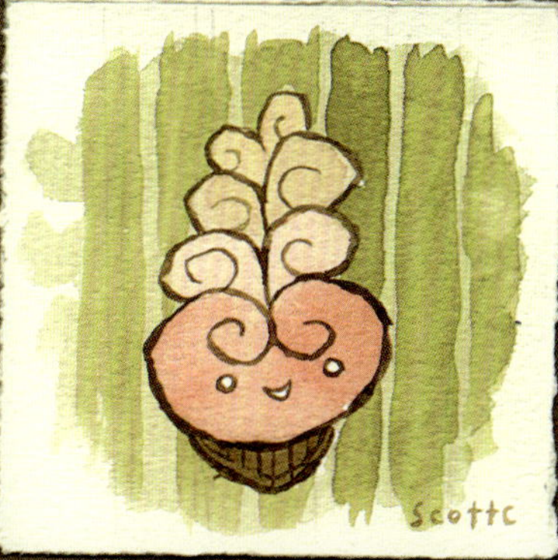
scottc.
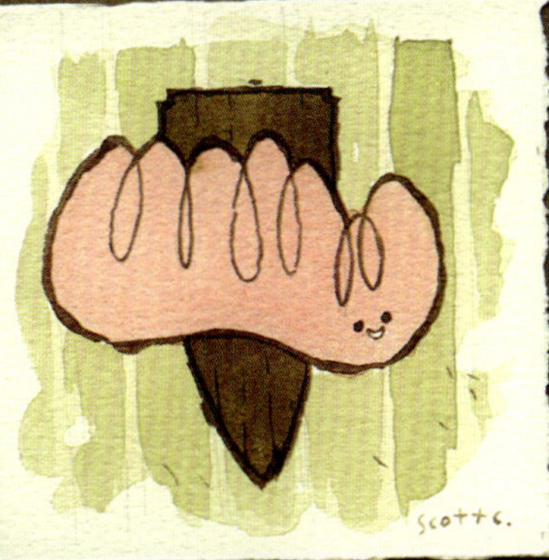
scottc.
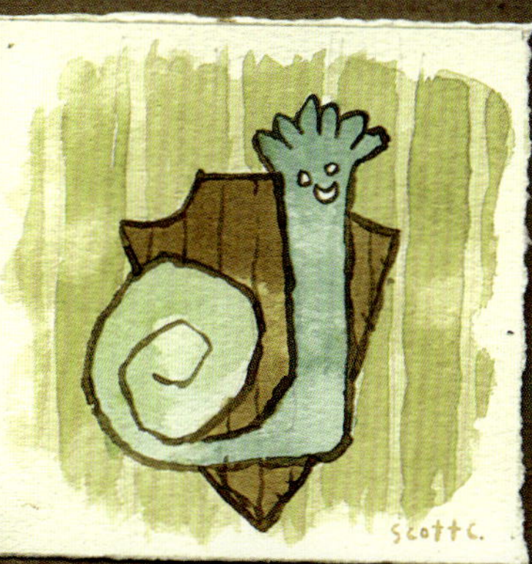
scottc.

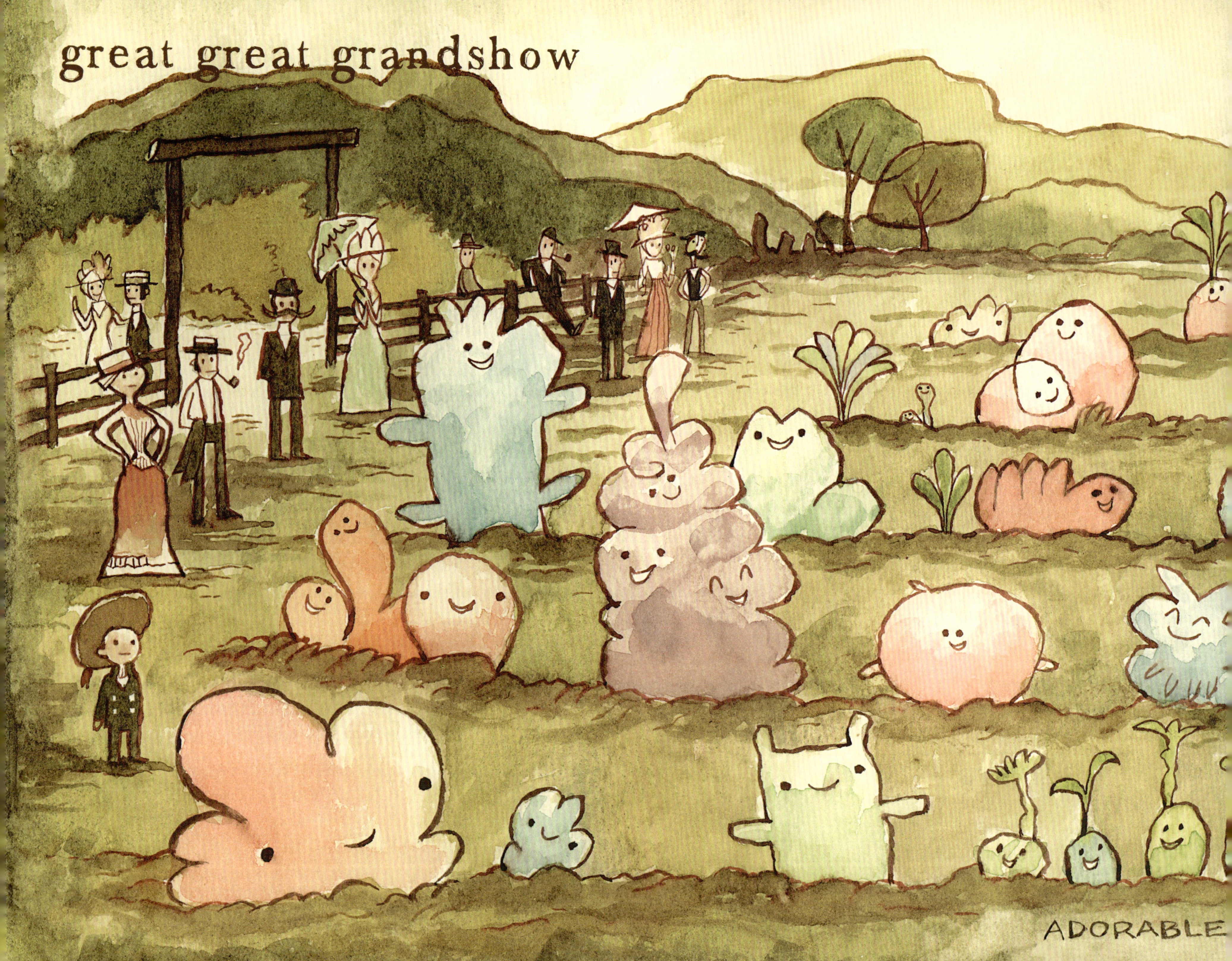
great great grandshow
ADORABLE

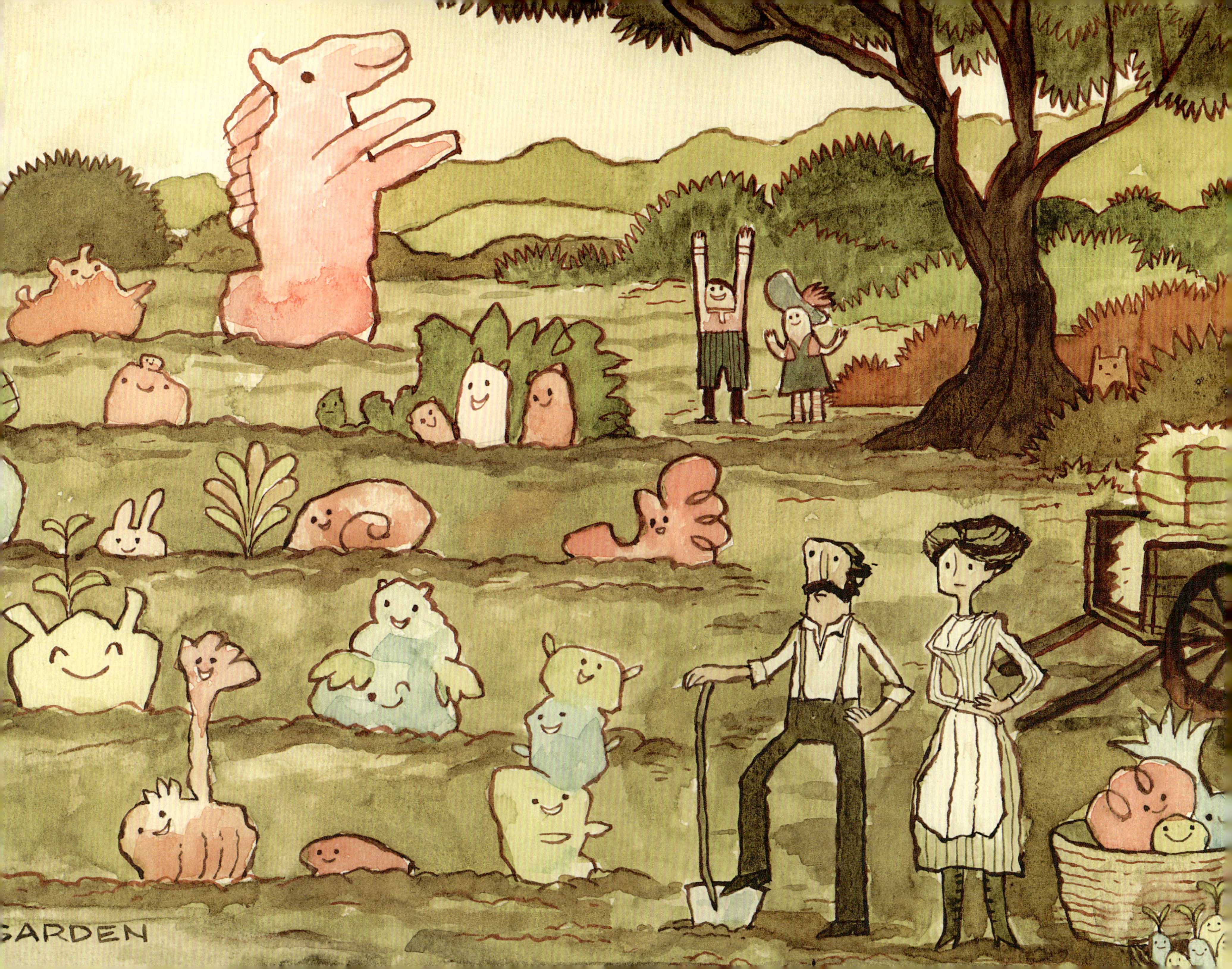
GARDEN

<< [section opener] ADORABLE GARDEN | watercolor on paper | 23" x 10"

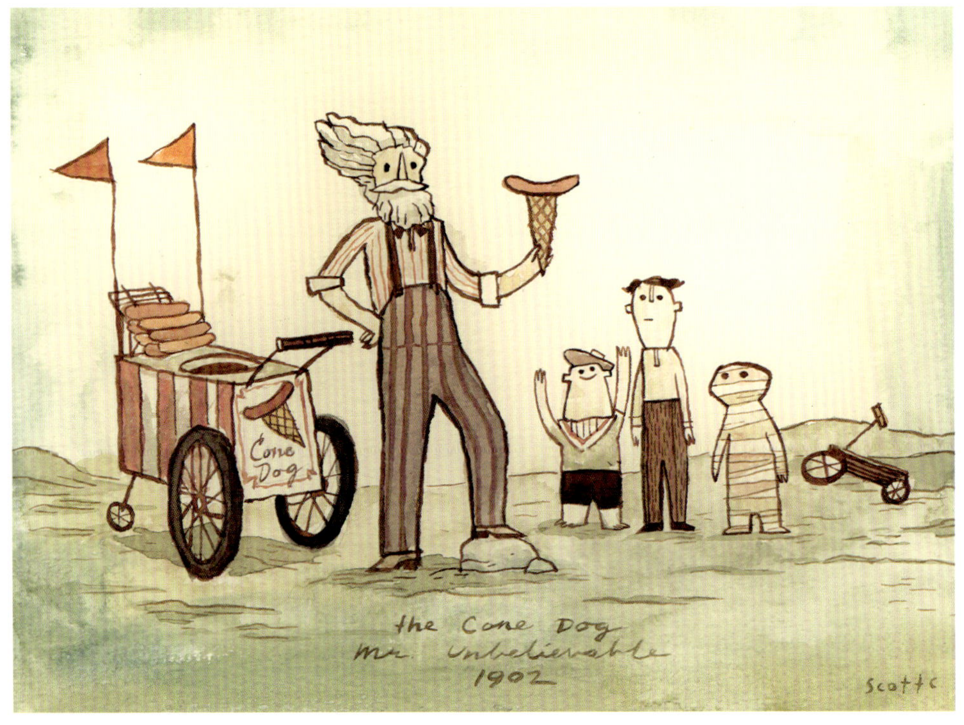

CONE DOG
watercolor
11" x 7"
2008

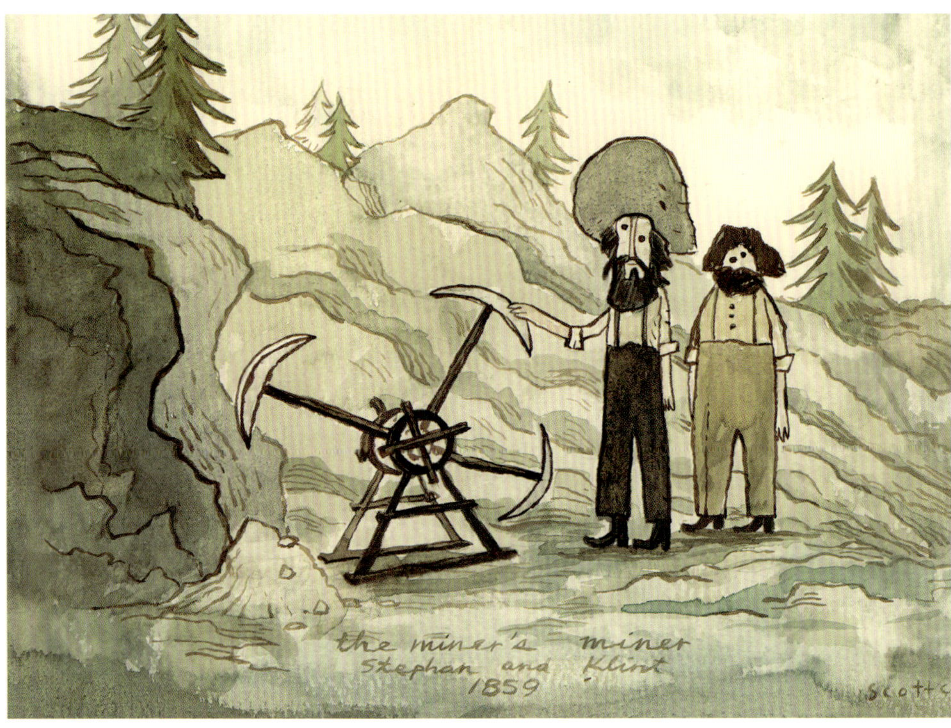

THE MINER'S MINER
watercolor
11" x 8.5"
2008

This series explores the many inventions that were too amazing for our world to handle. I did extensive research on the origins of things for this series. The hot dog, for example, emerged from the need for something in which to hold your hot sausage at the World's Fair. Everyone was burning their hands, so they just put them onto buns. Thus, the hot dog. But I am sure they tried other "holding devices," such as the ice-cream cone. Also I am sure there were some people who were so crazy excited about the new invention, "the Radio," they wanted to carry it everywhere they went, tuning in to all kinds of interesting stations for passersby from the comfort of their shirts.

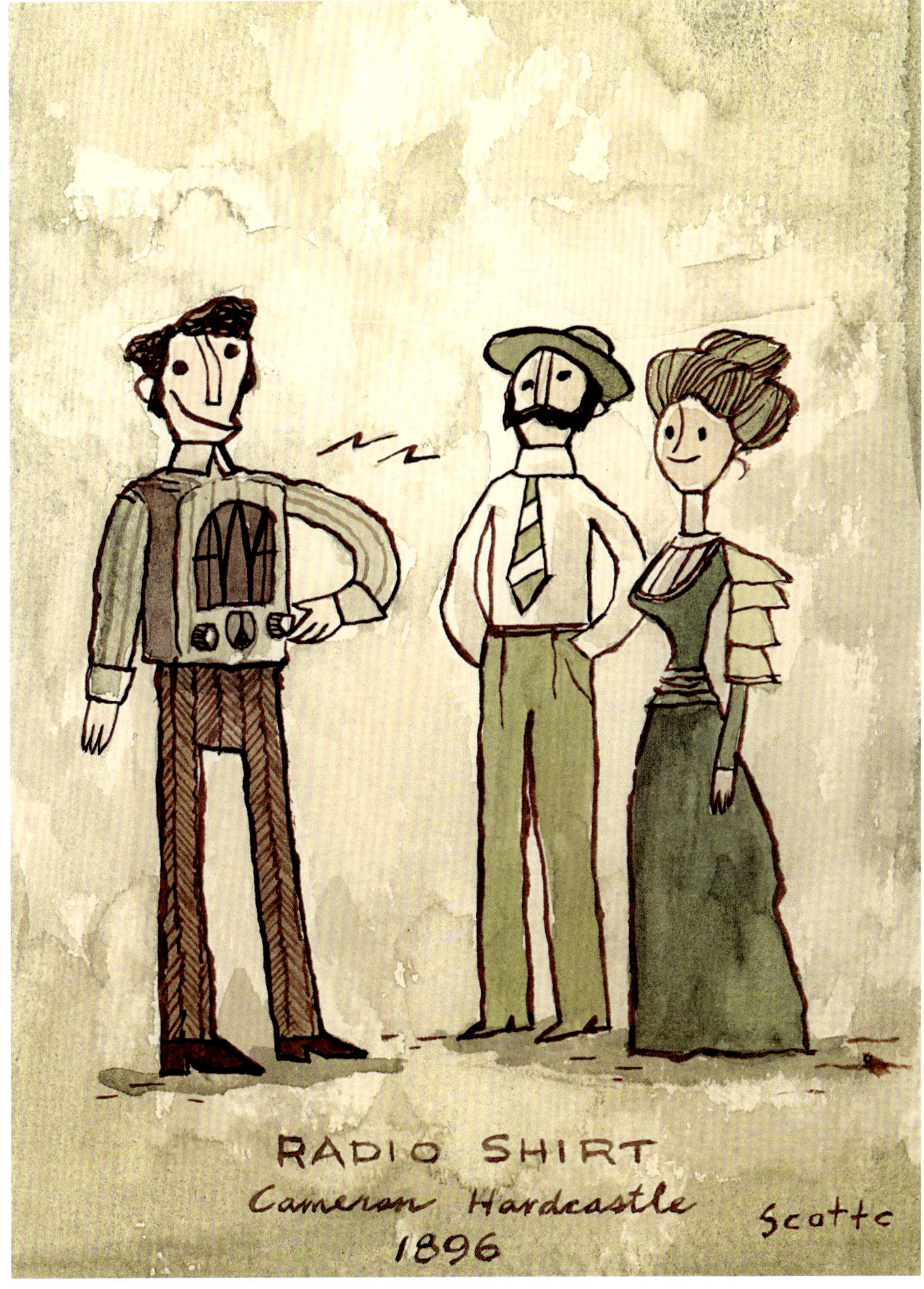

RADIO SHIRT
watercolor
5" x 7"
2008

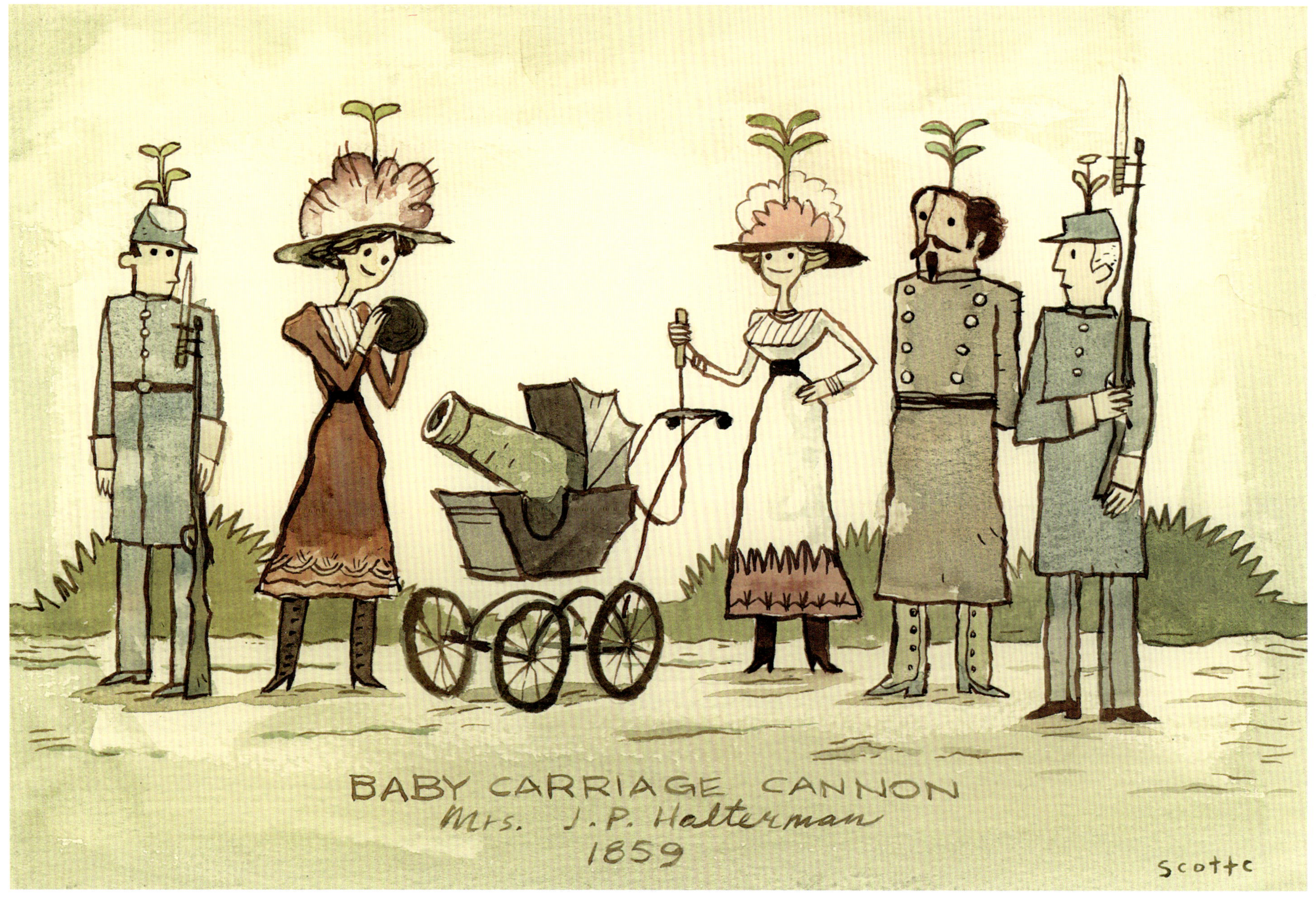

BABY CARRIAGE CANNON
watercolor
11" x 8.5"
2008

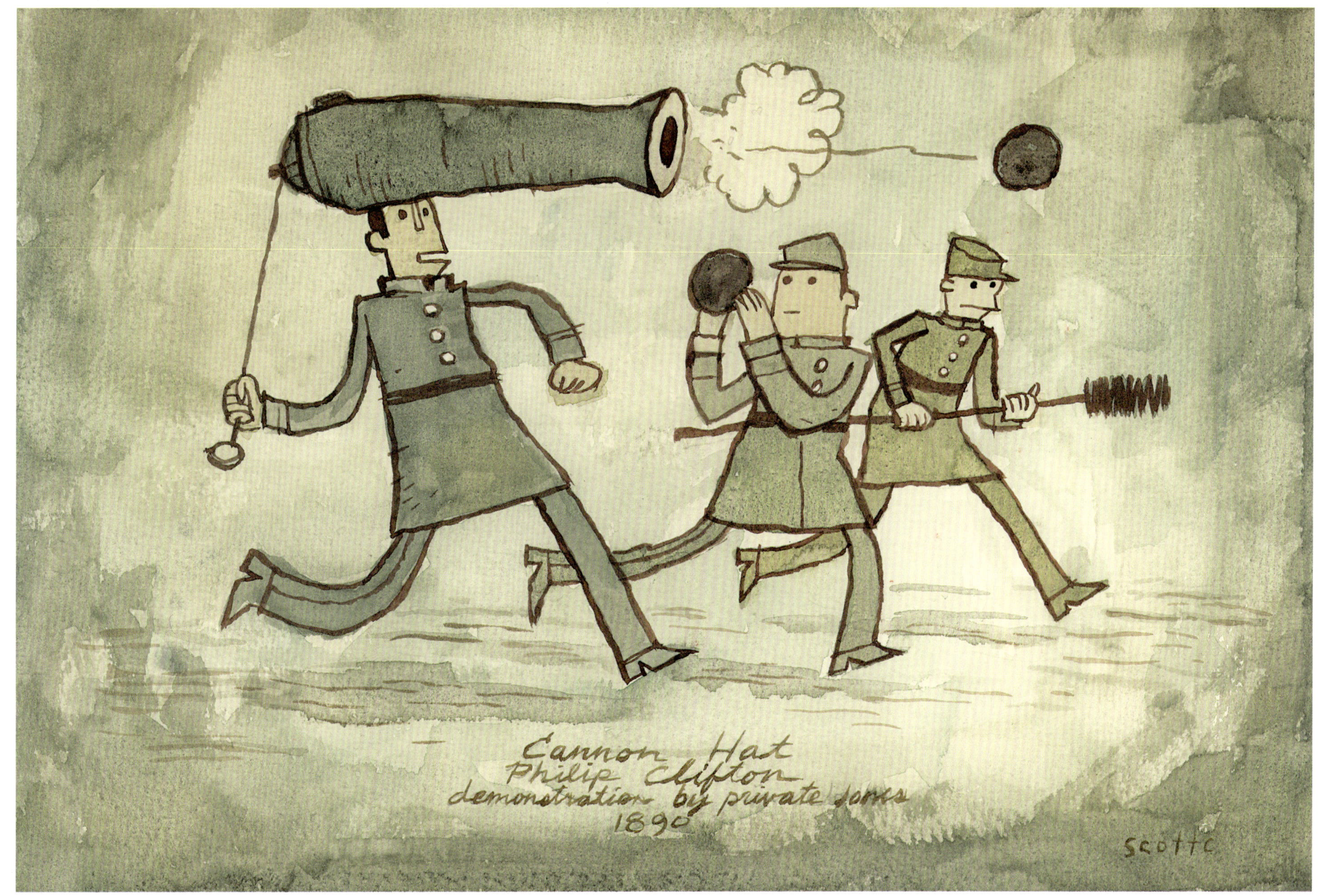

CANNON HAT
watercolor
11" x 8.5"
2008

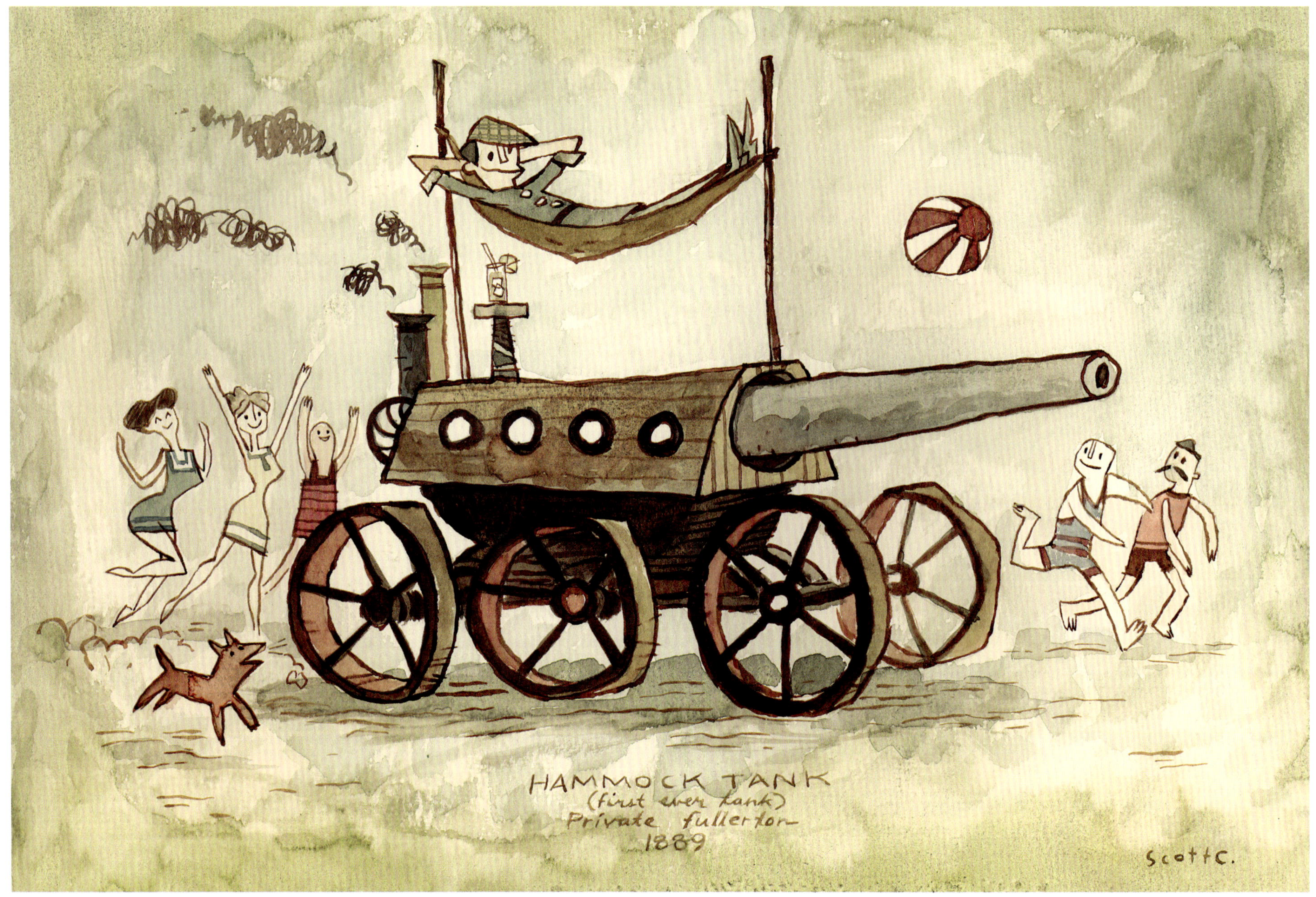

HAMMOCK TANK
watercolor
13" x 9"
2008

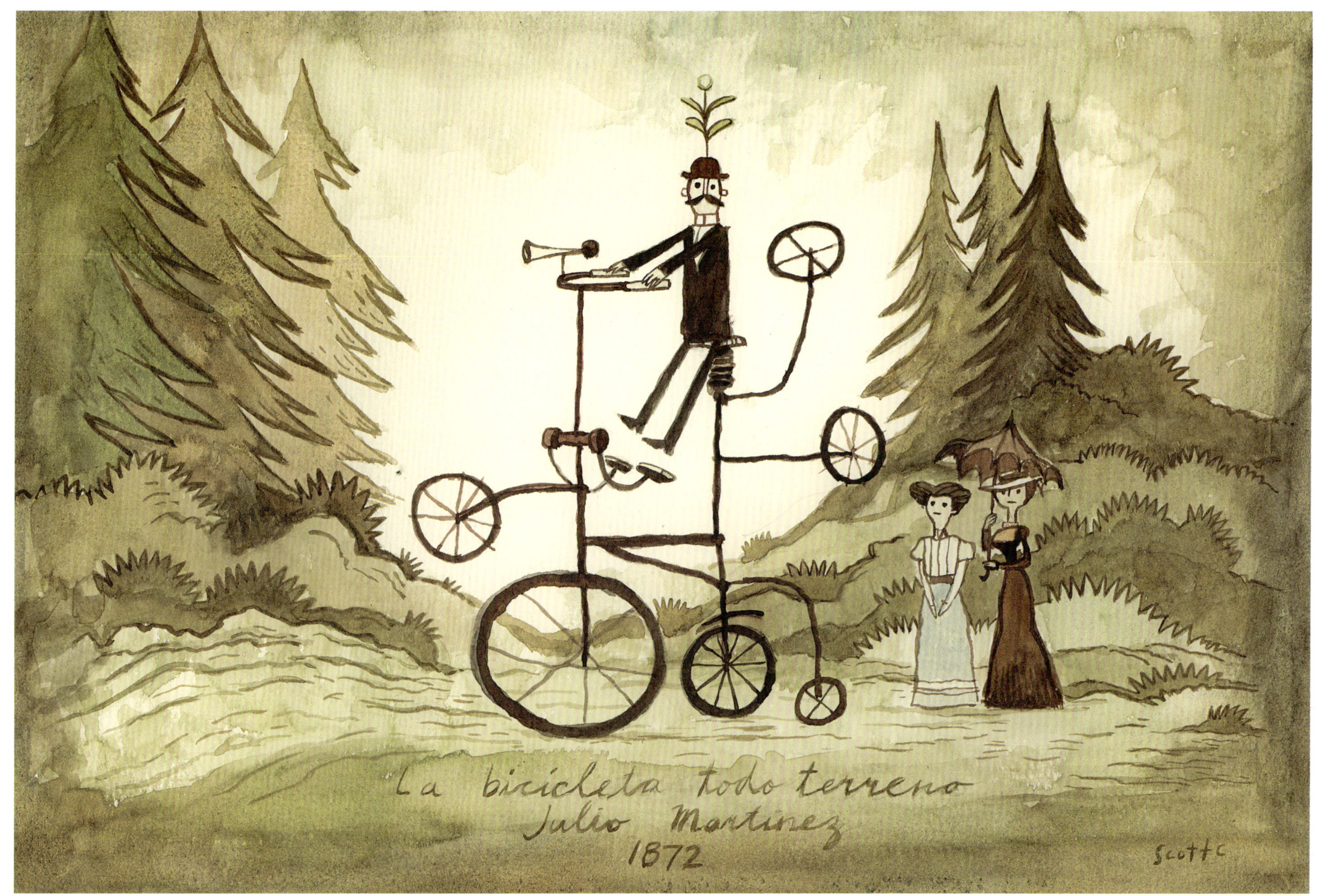

LA BICICLETA TODO TERRENO
watercolor
13" x 9"
2008

THE FLYING SWING | watercolor | 14" x 9.5" | 2008 >>

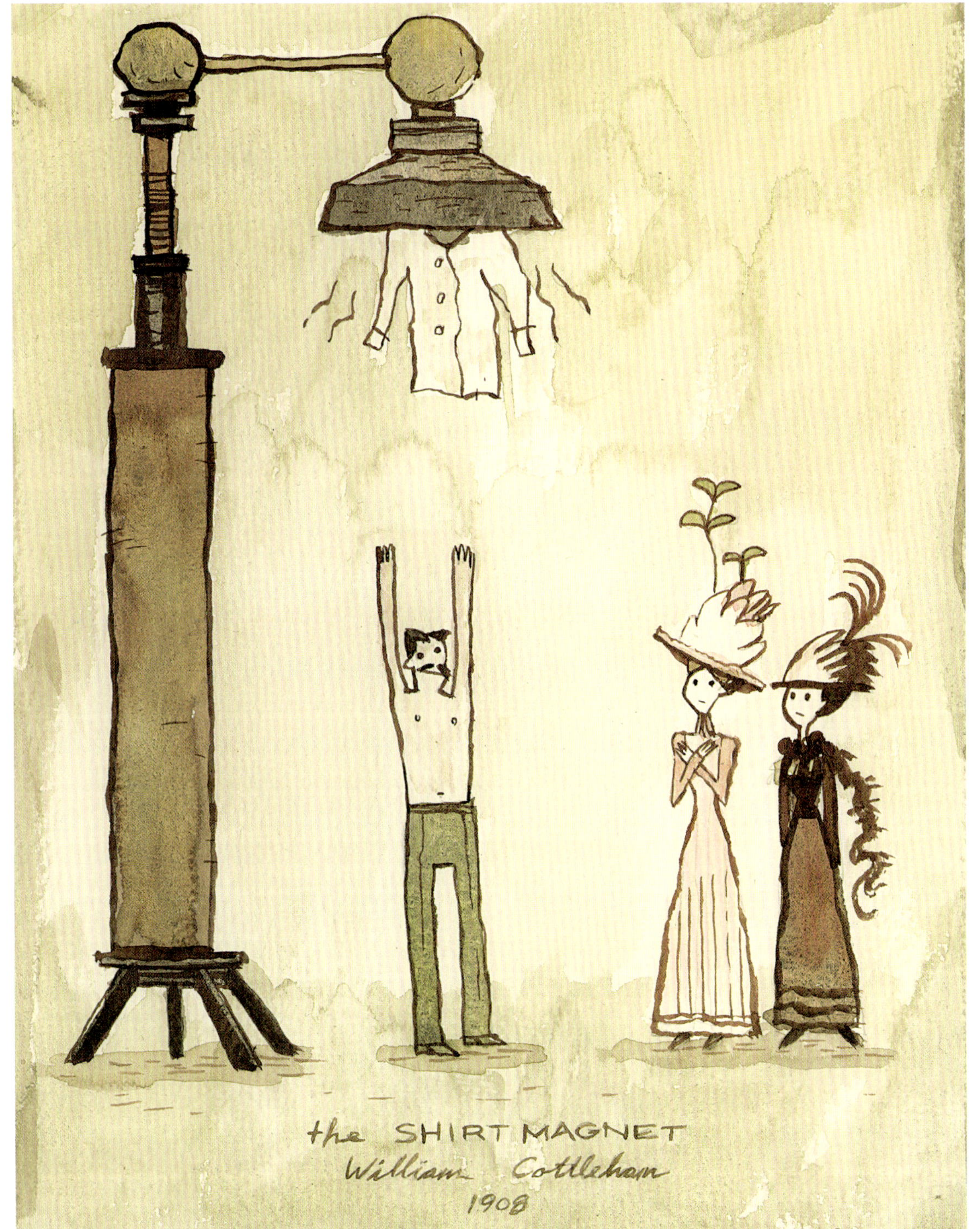

SHIRT MAGNET
watercolor
8" x 10"
2008

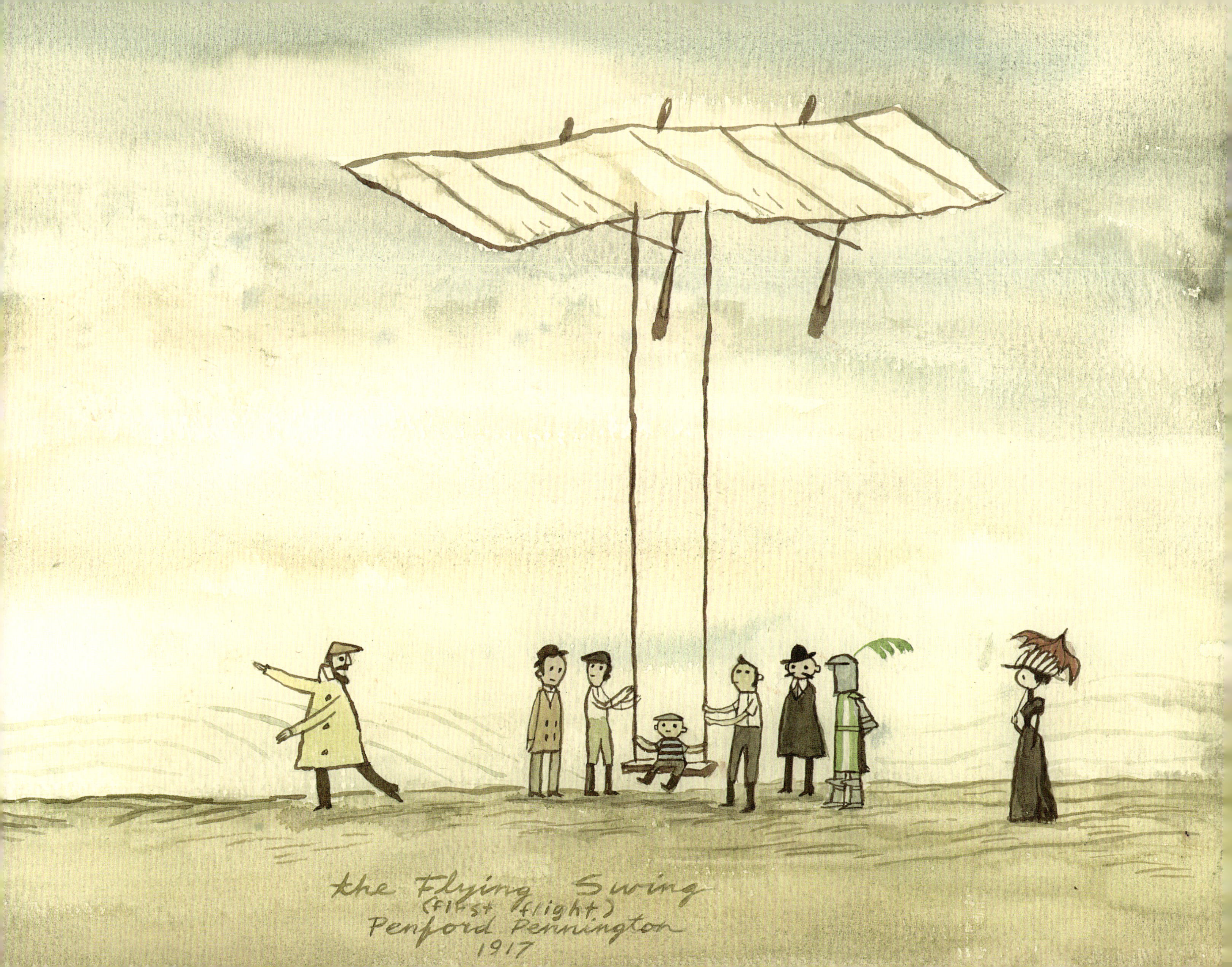
the Flying Swing
(first flight)
Penford Pennington
1917

home slices

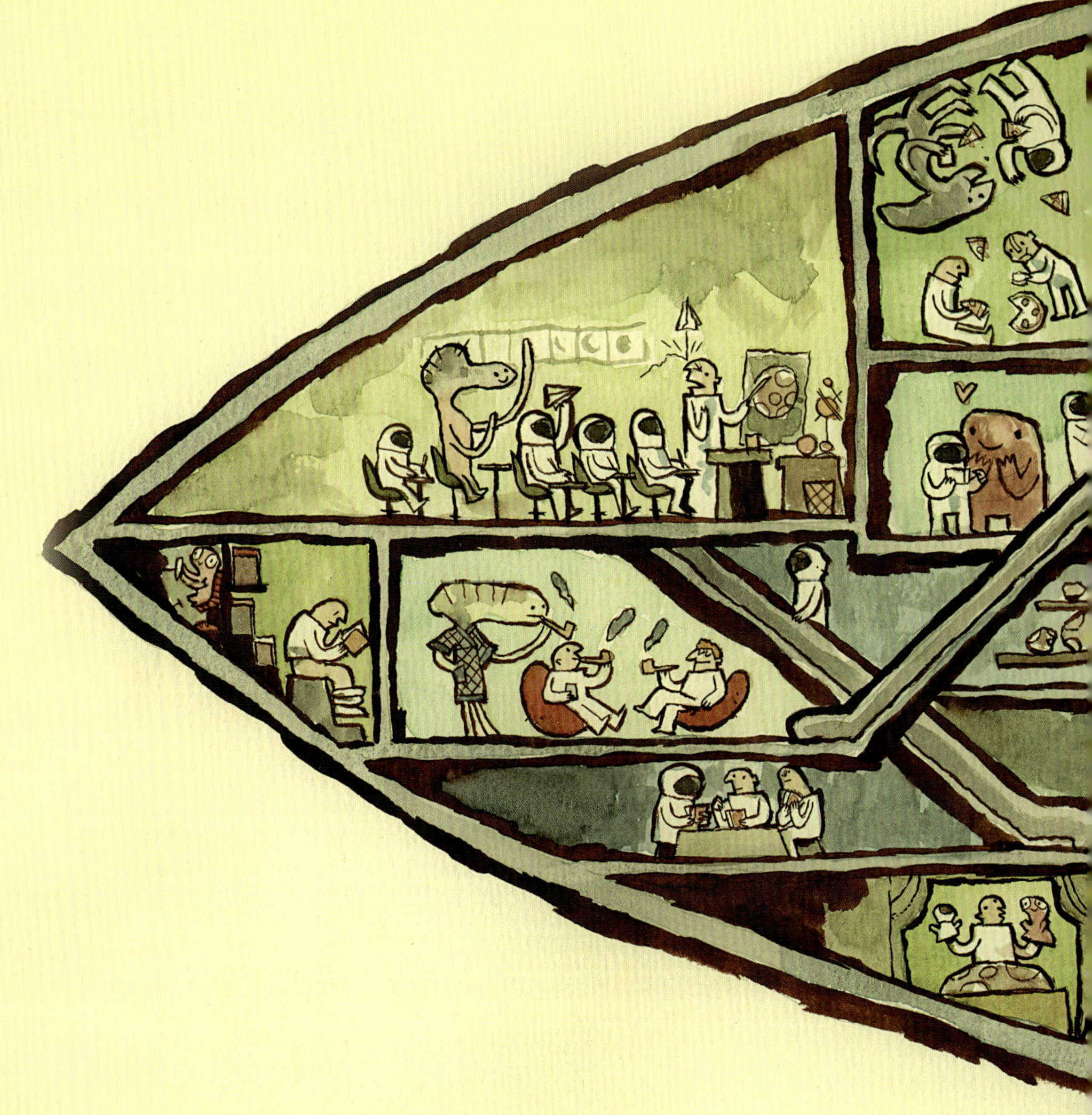

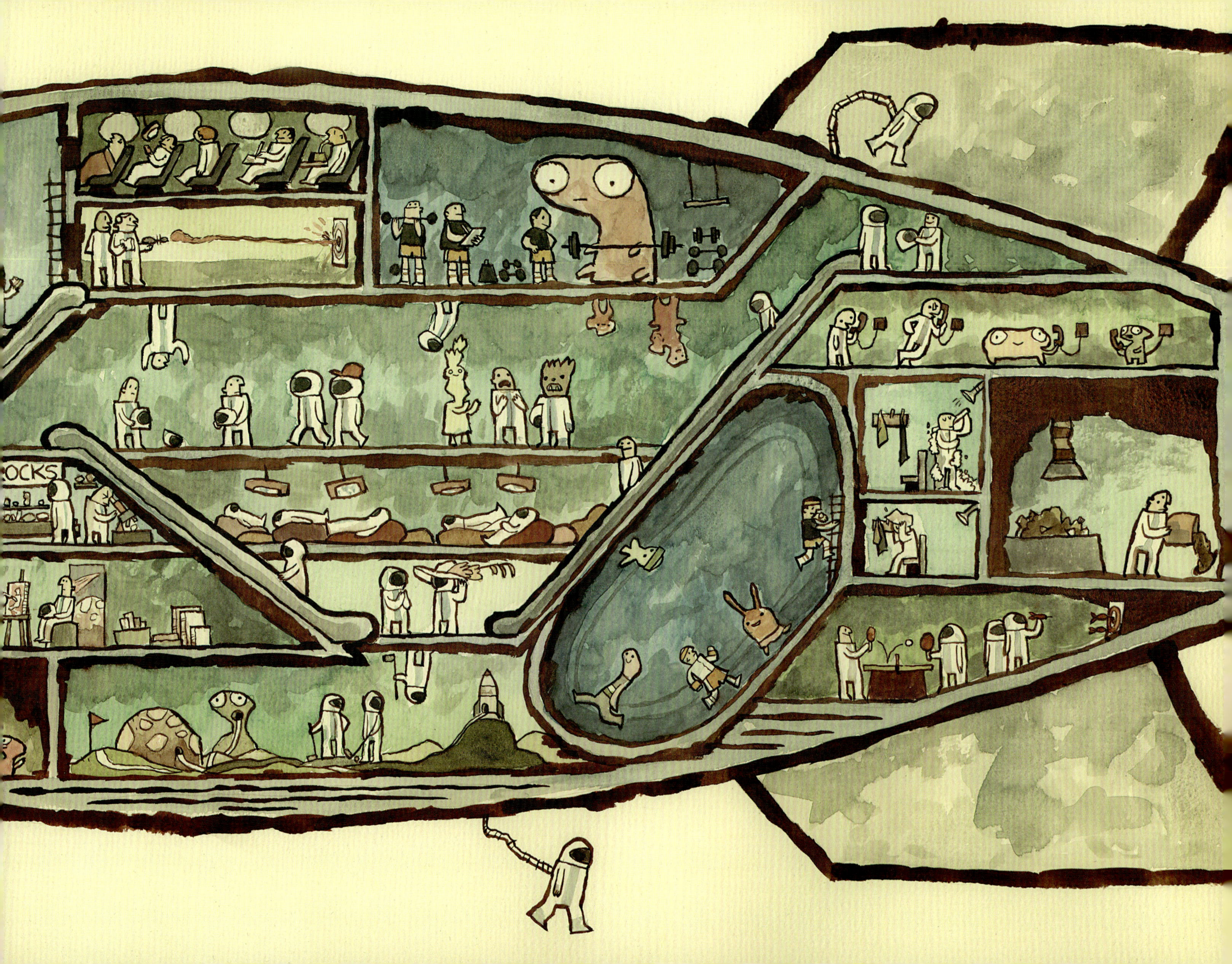
OCKS

<< [section opener] ROCKET HOUSE | watercolor | 15" x 9" | 2009

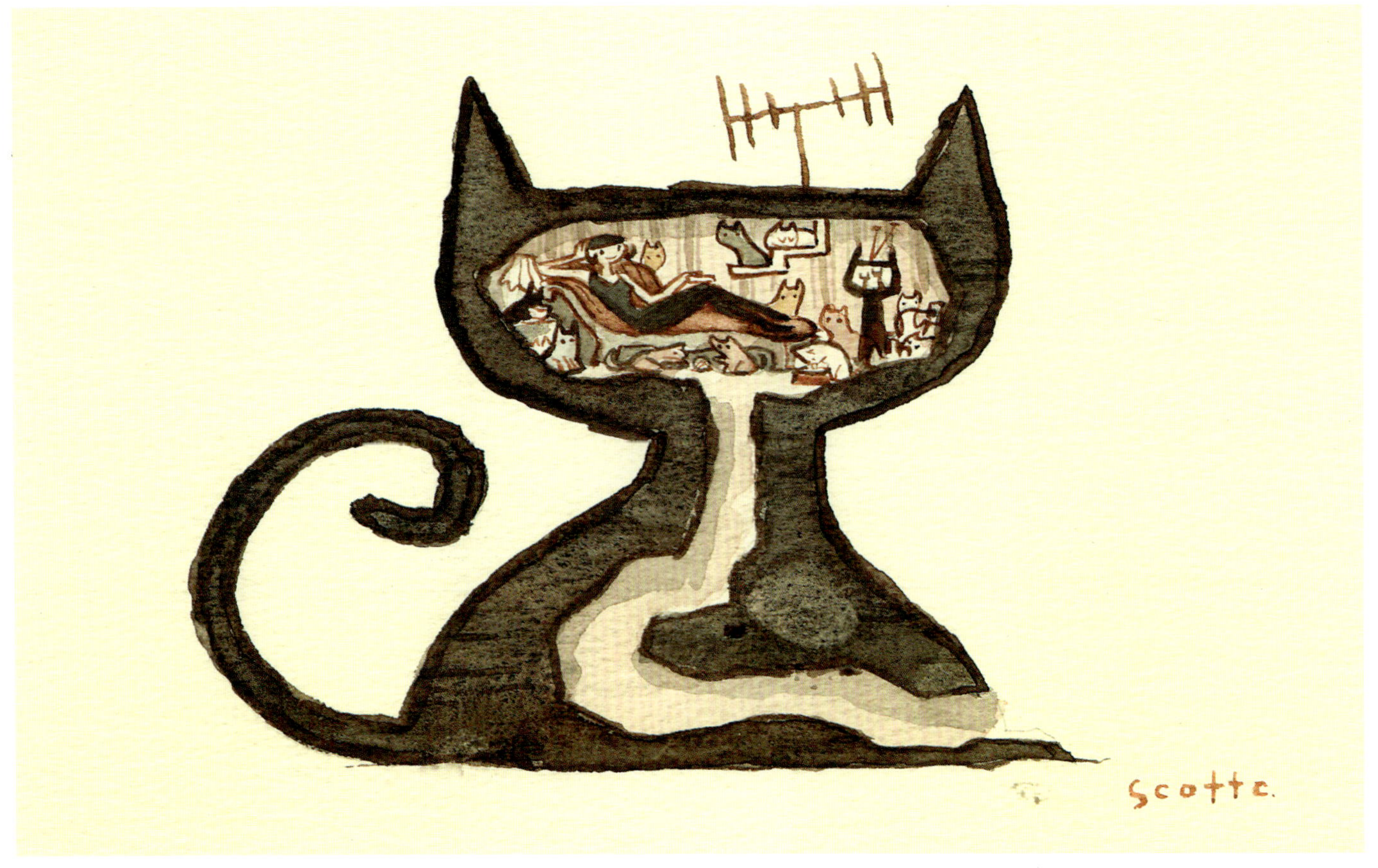

CAT HOUSE
watercolor
7" x 5"
2009

CRAB HOUSE
watercolor
10" x 8"
2009

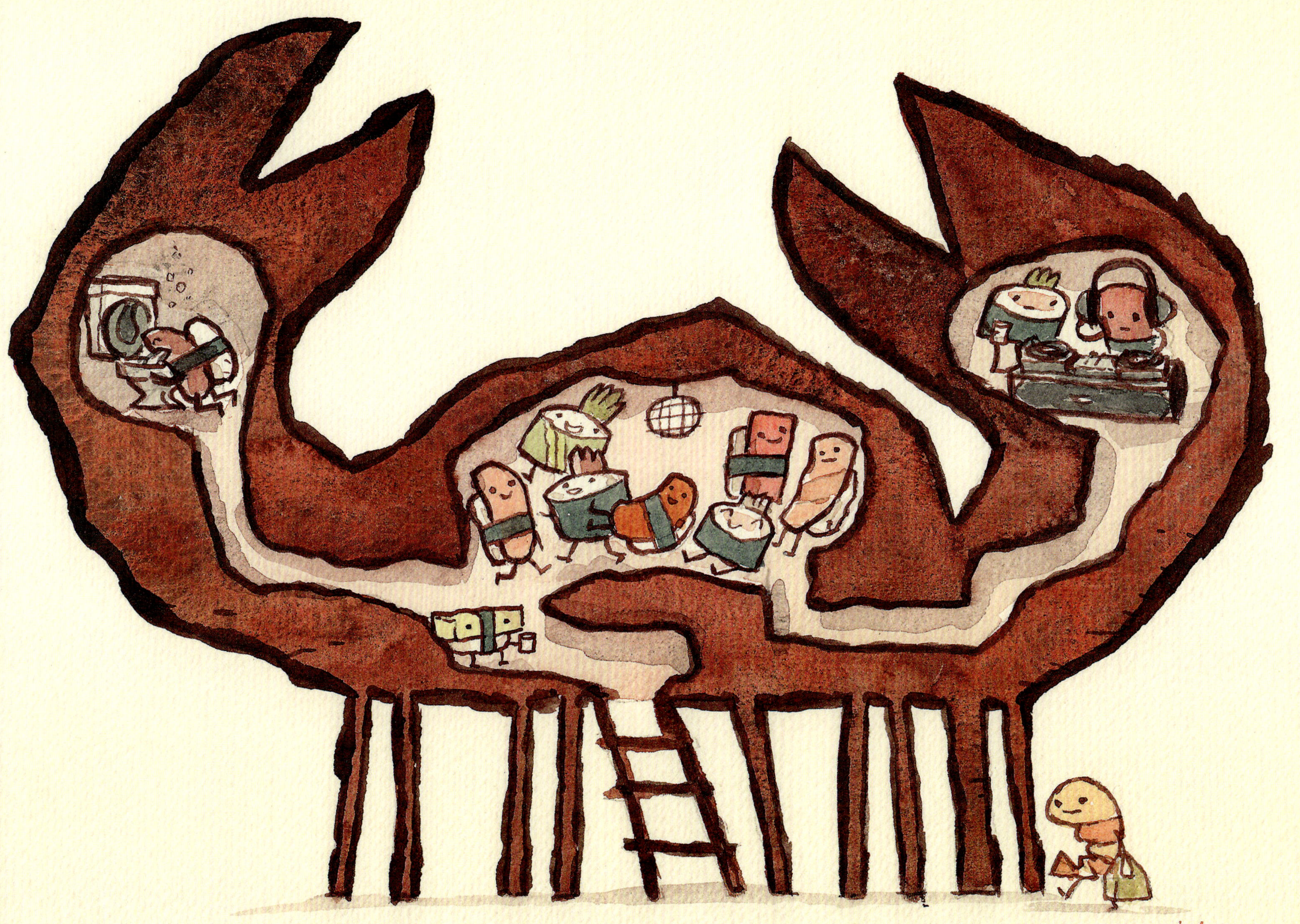
scott c.

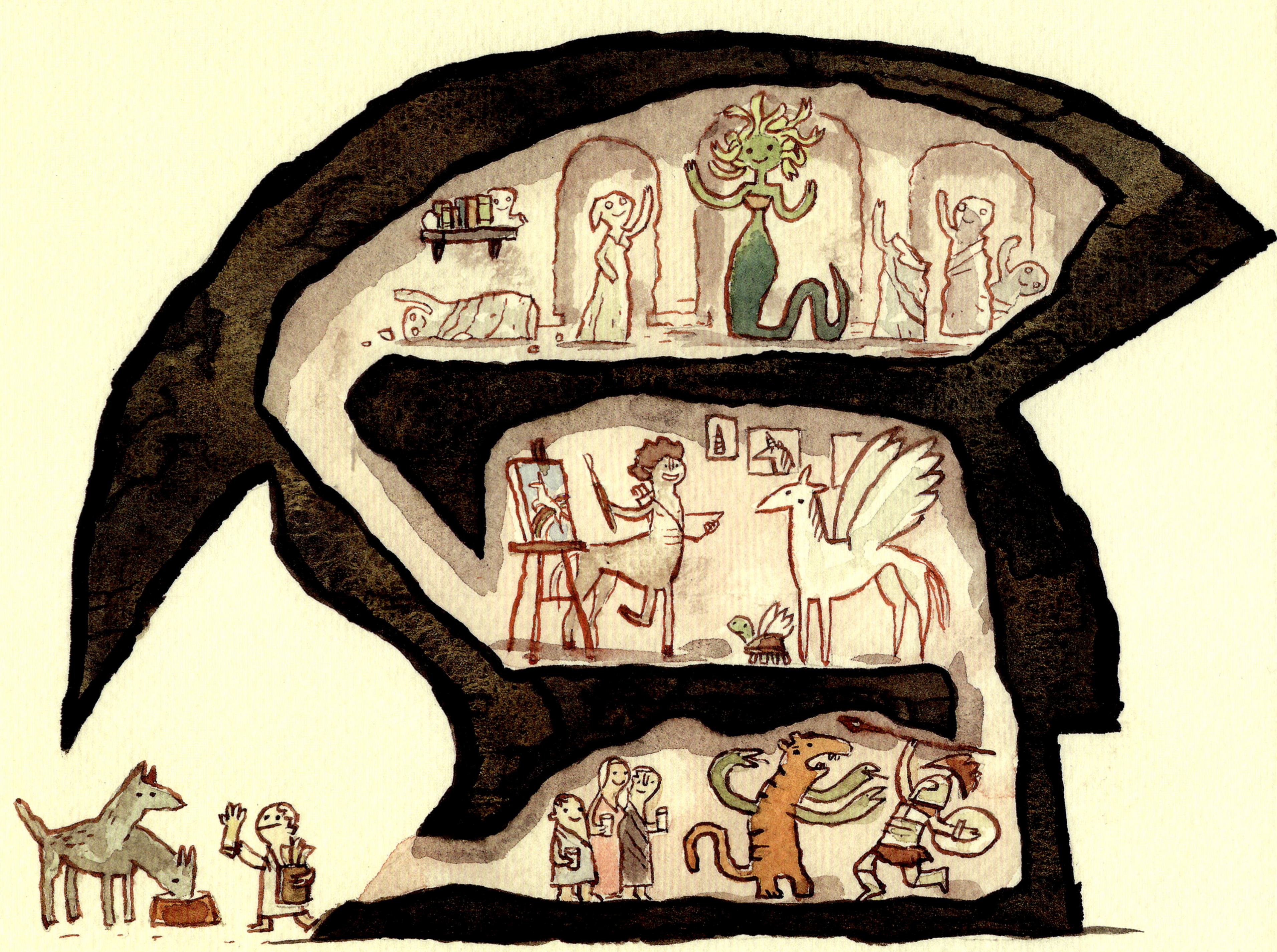

scott c.

<< HOUSE OF MYTH AND LEGEND | watercolor | 10" x 8" | 2009

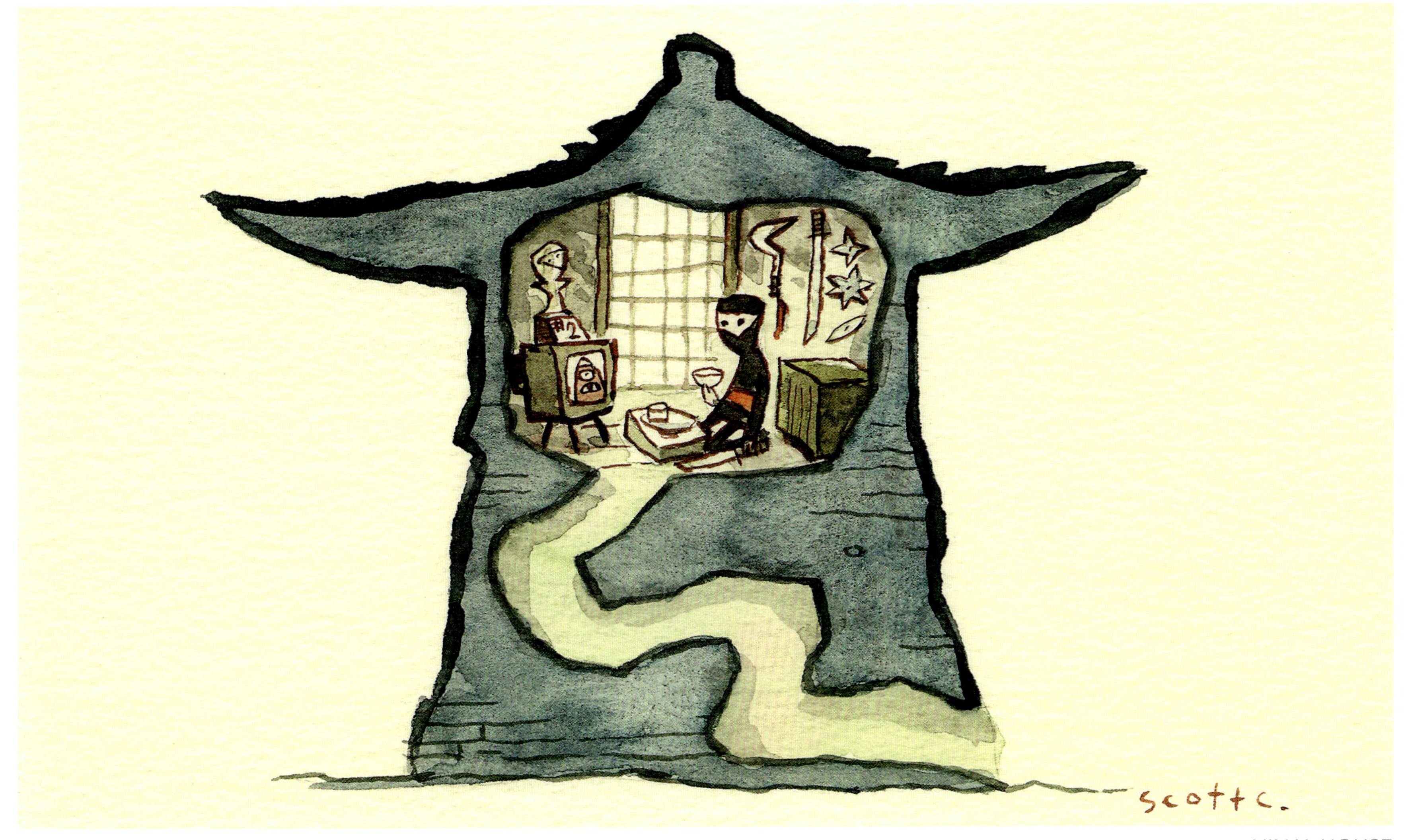

NINJA HOUSE
watercolor
7" x 5"
2009

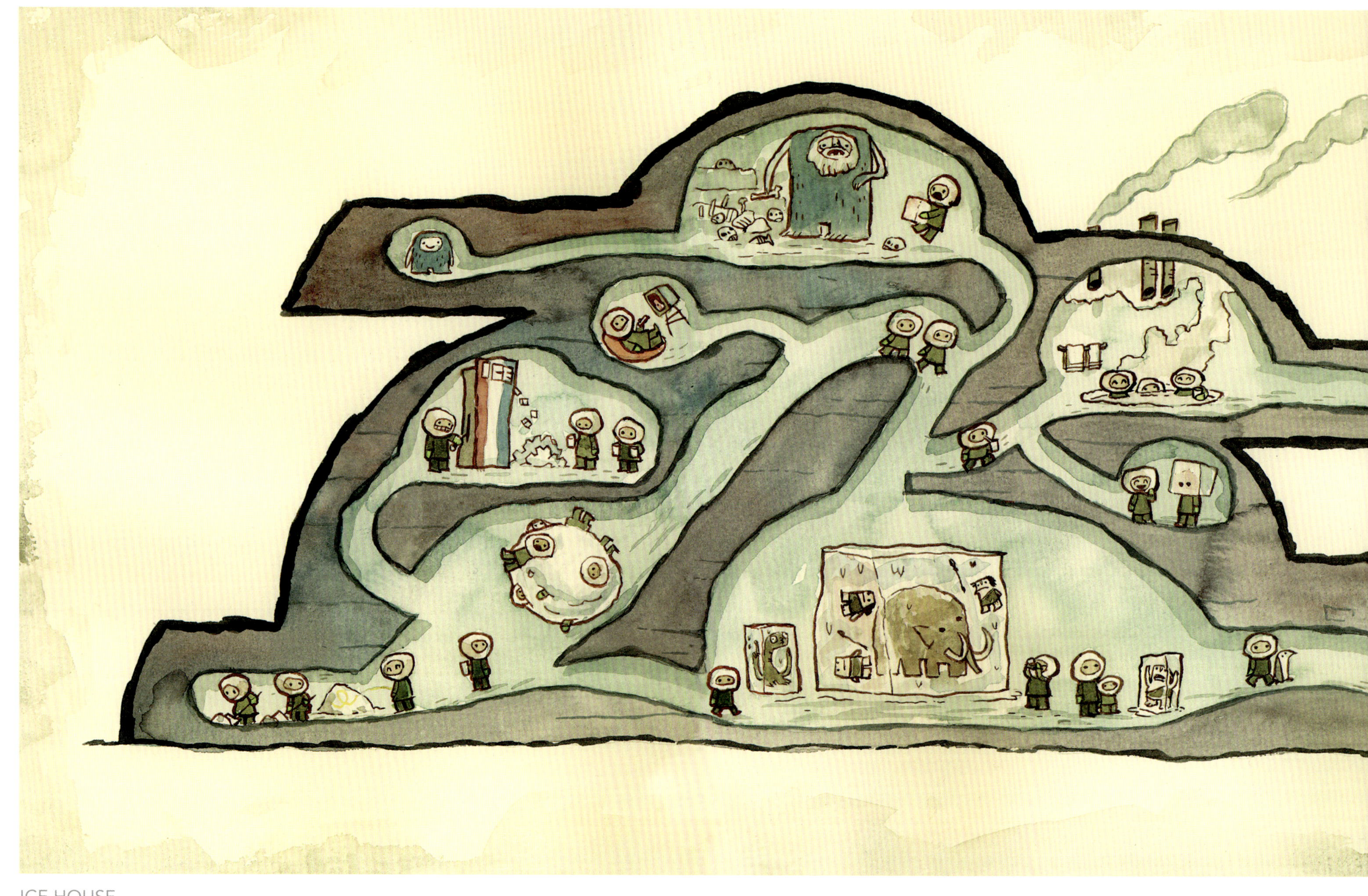

ICE HOUSE
watercolor
22" x 11"
2009

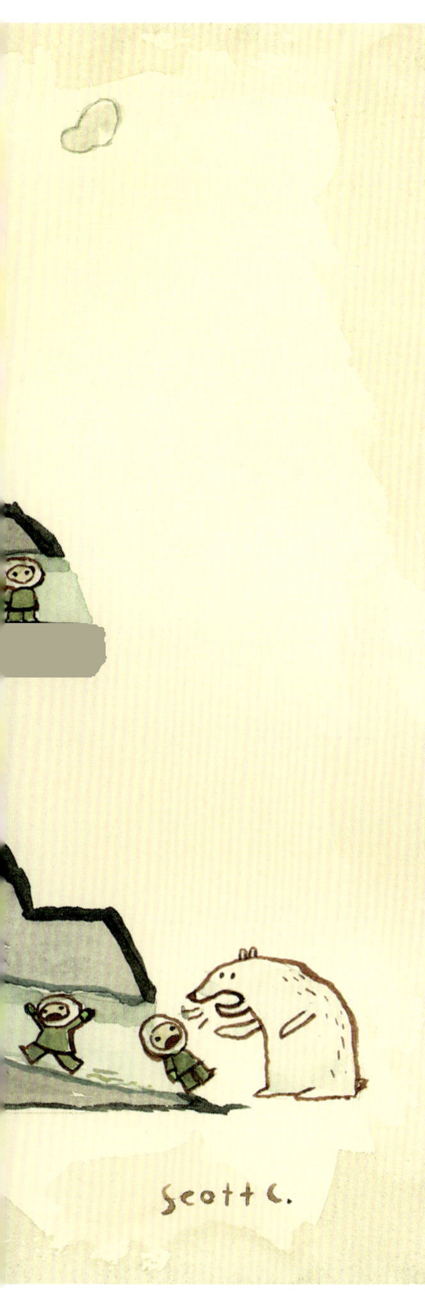

BODY HOUSE
watercolor
20" x 30"
2009

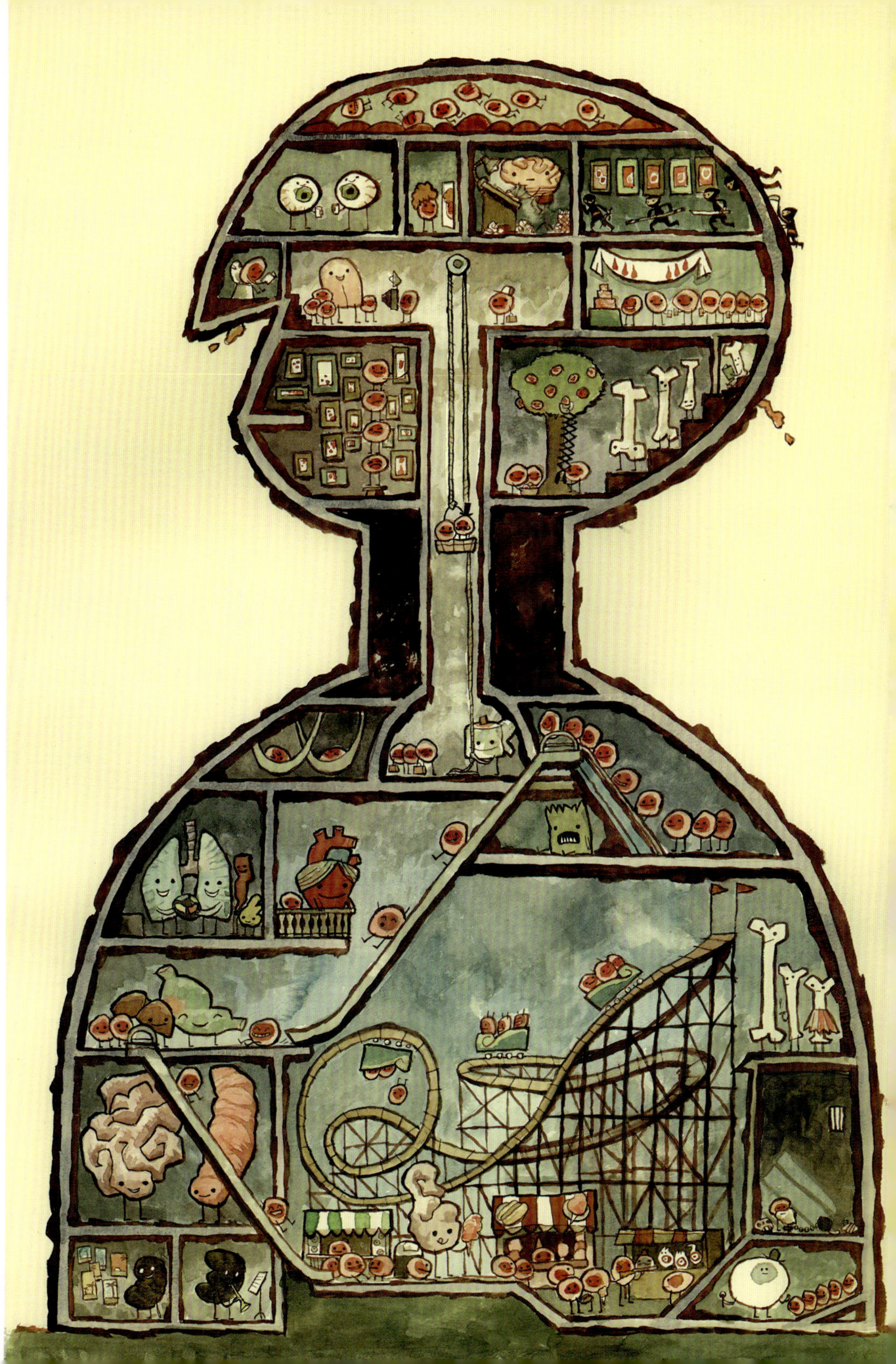

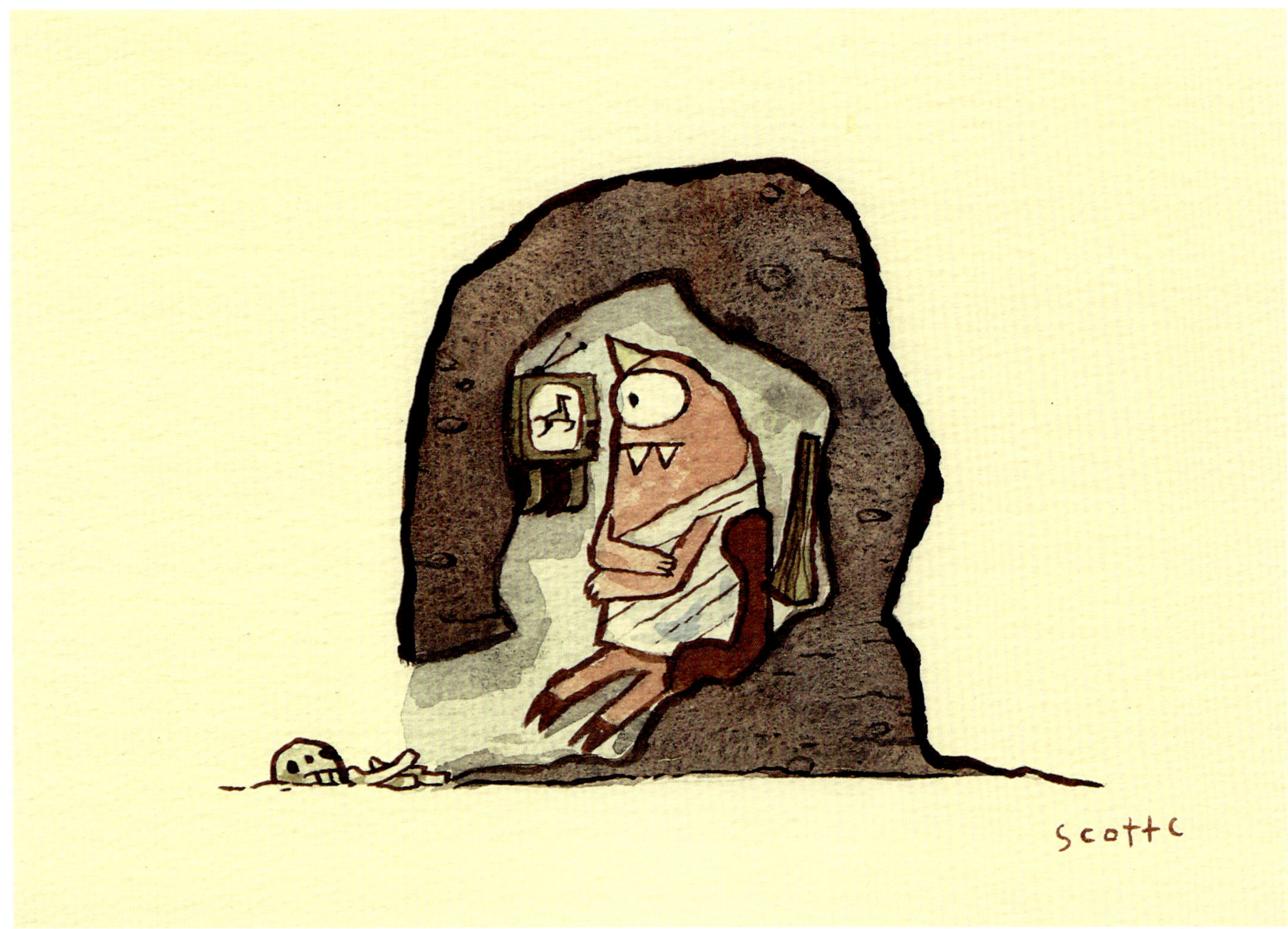

CYCLOPS HOUSE
watercolor
7" x 5"
2009

PYRAMID HOUSE | watercolor | 30" x 20" | 2009 >>

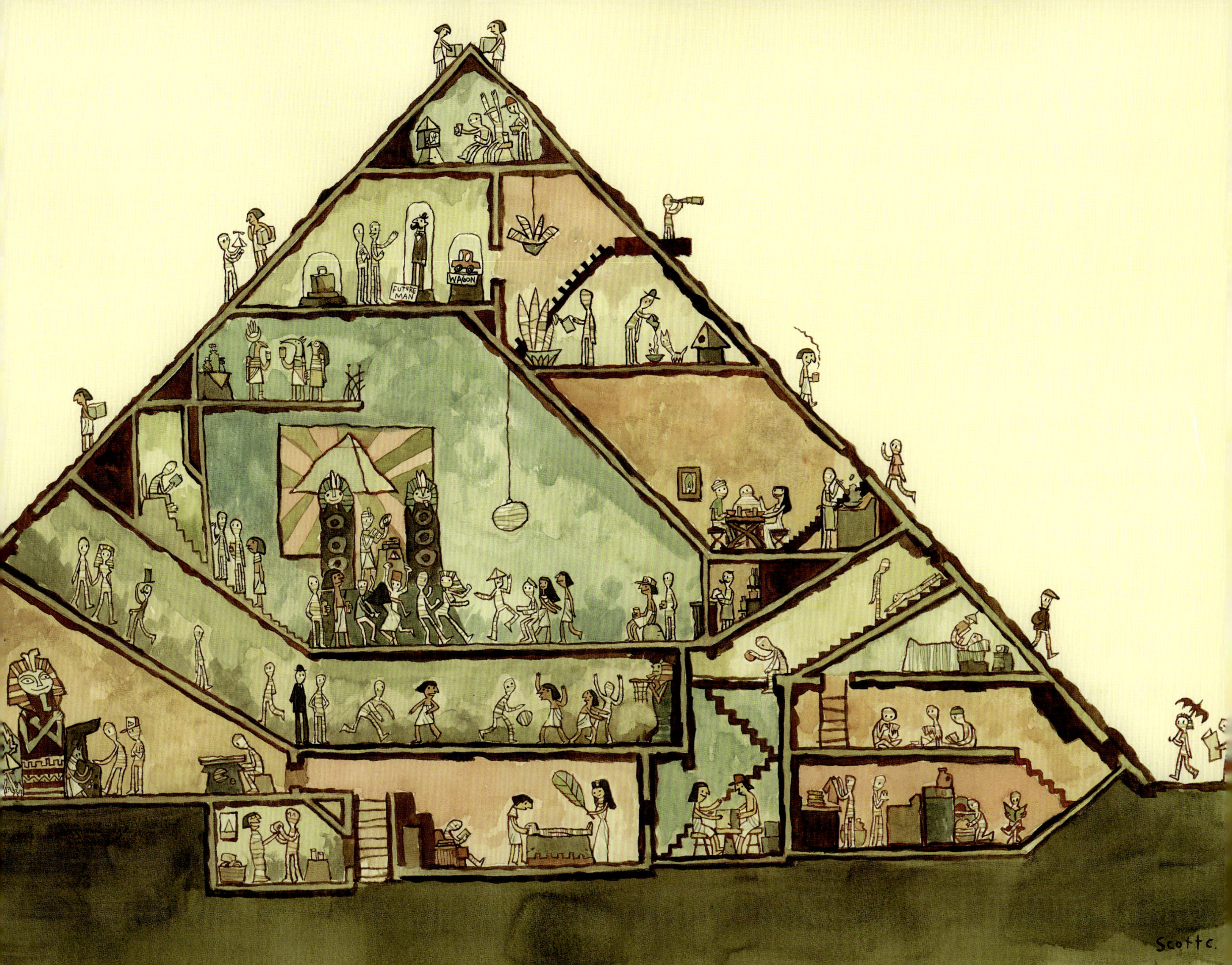
FUTURE MAN
WAGON
Scott C.

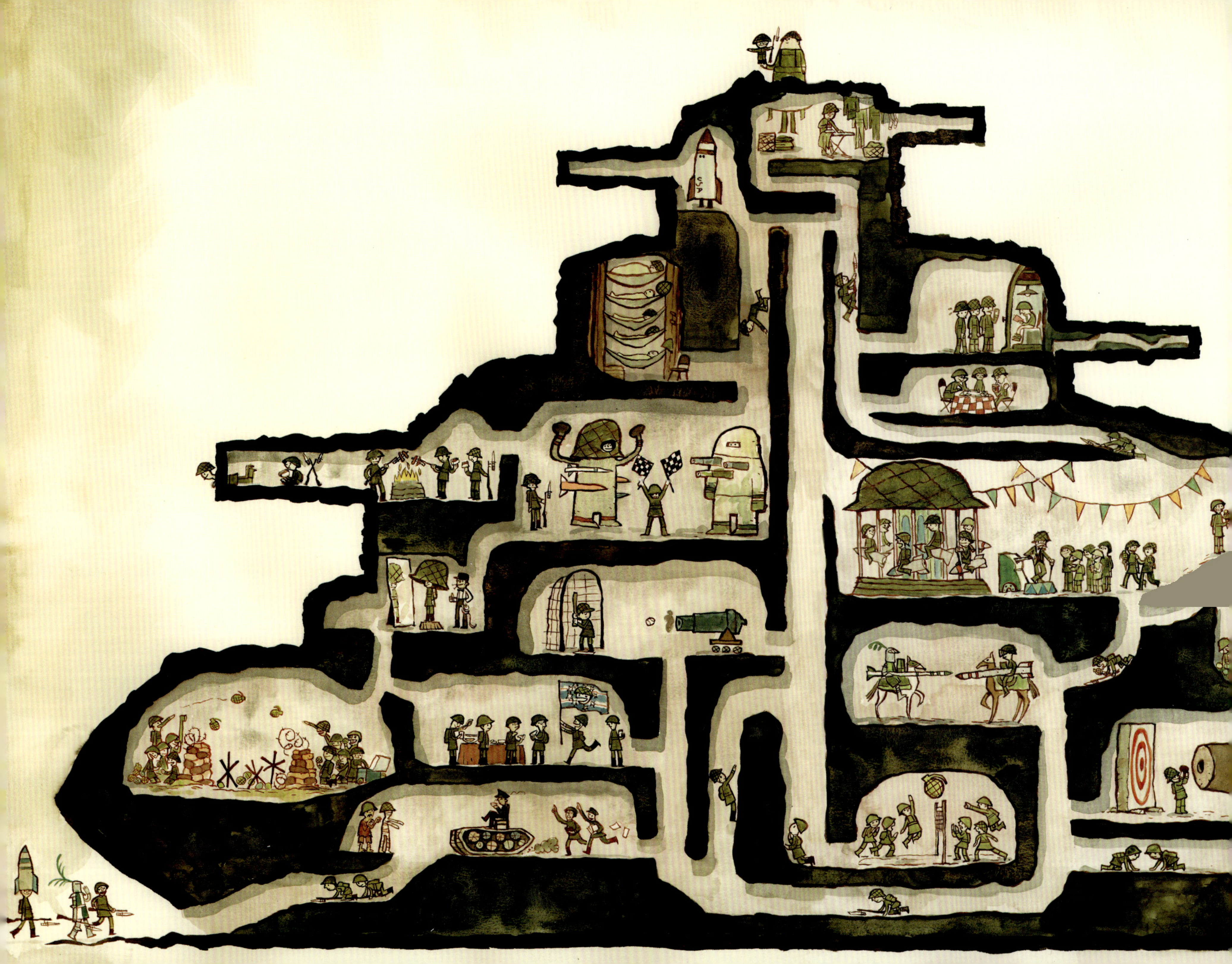
USA

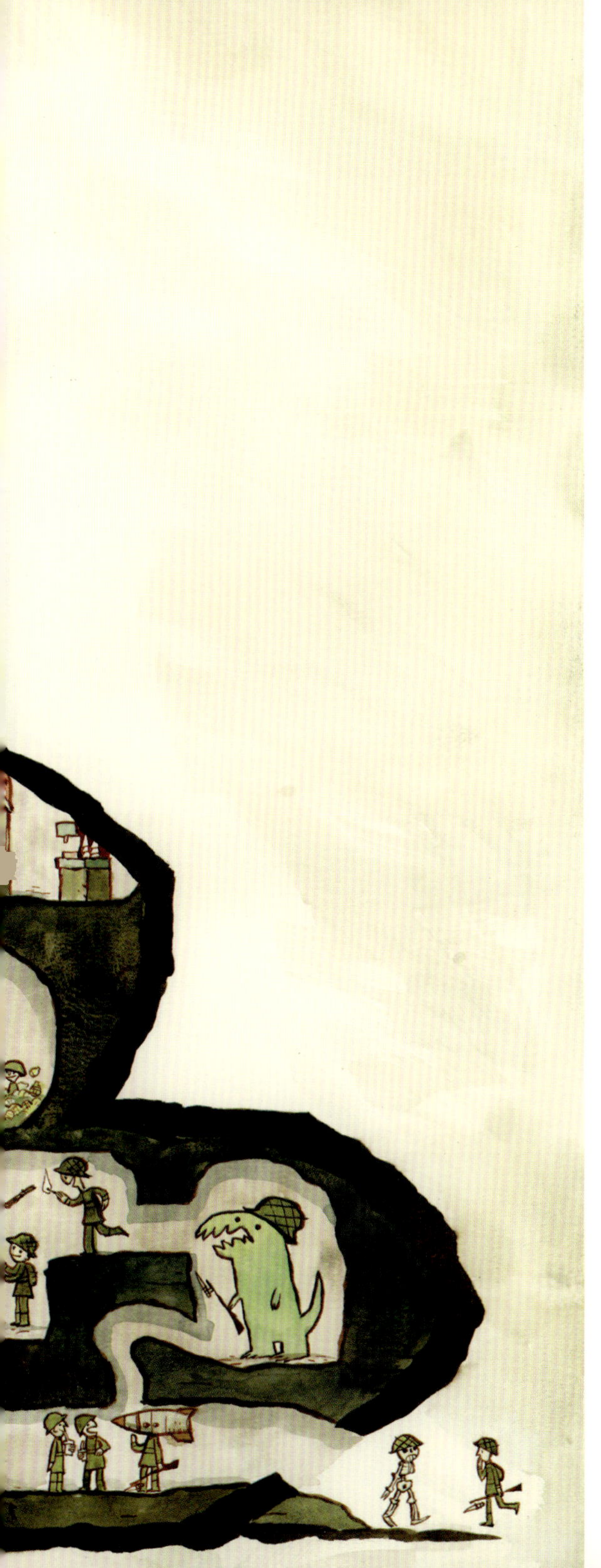

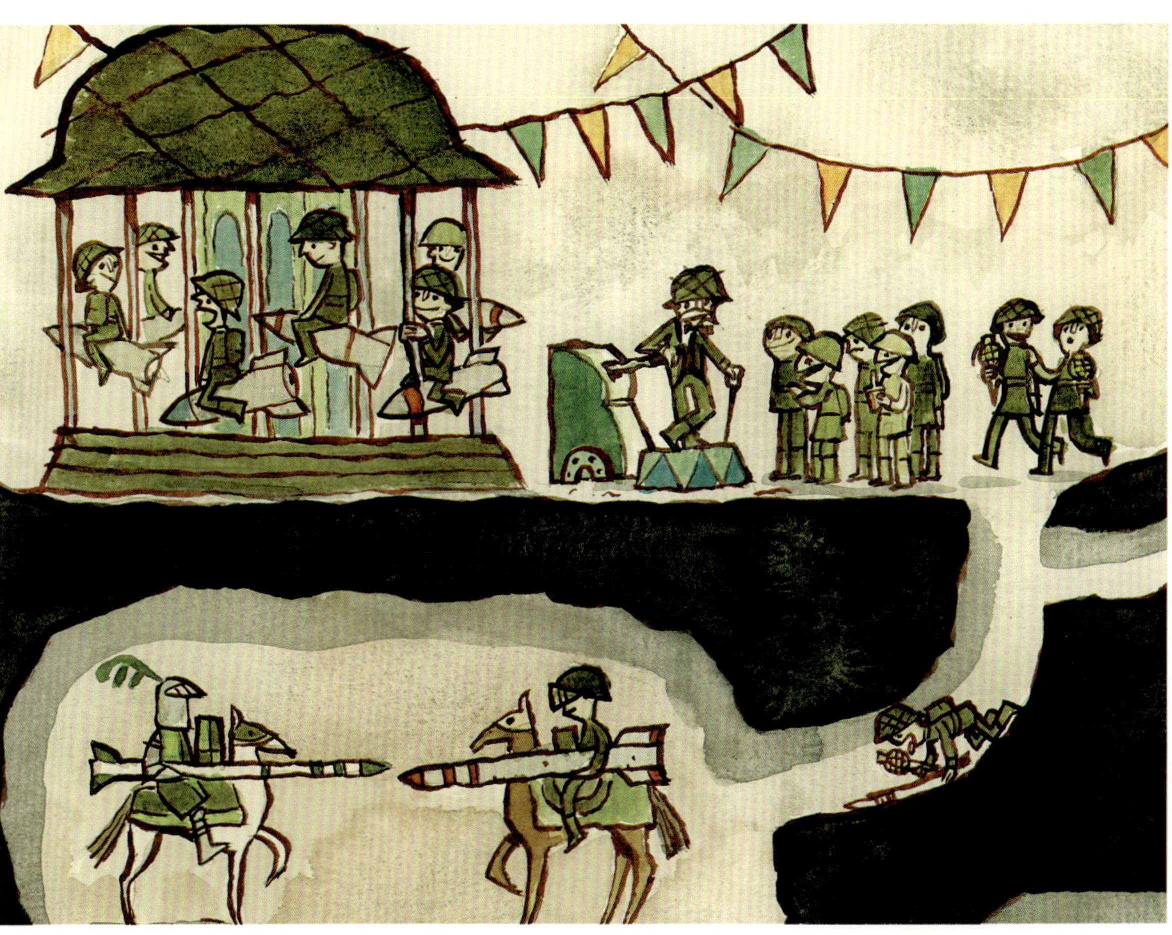

<< TANK HOUSE | watercolor | 44" x 30" | 2009

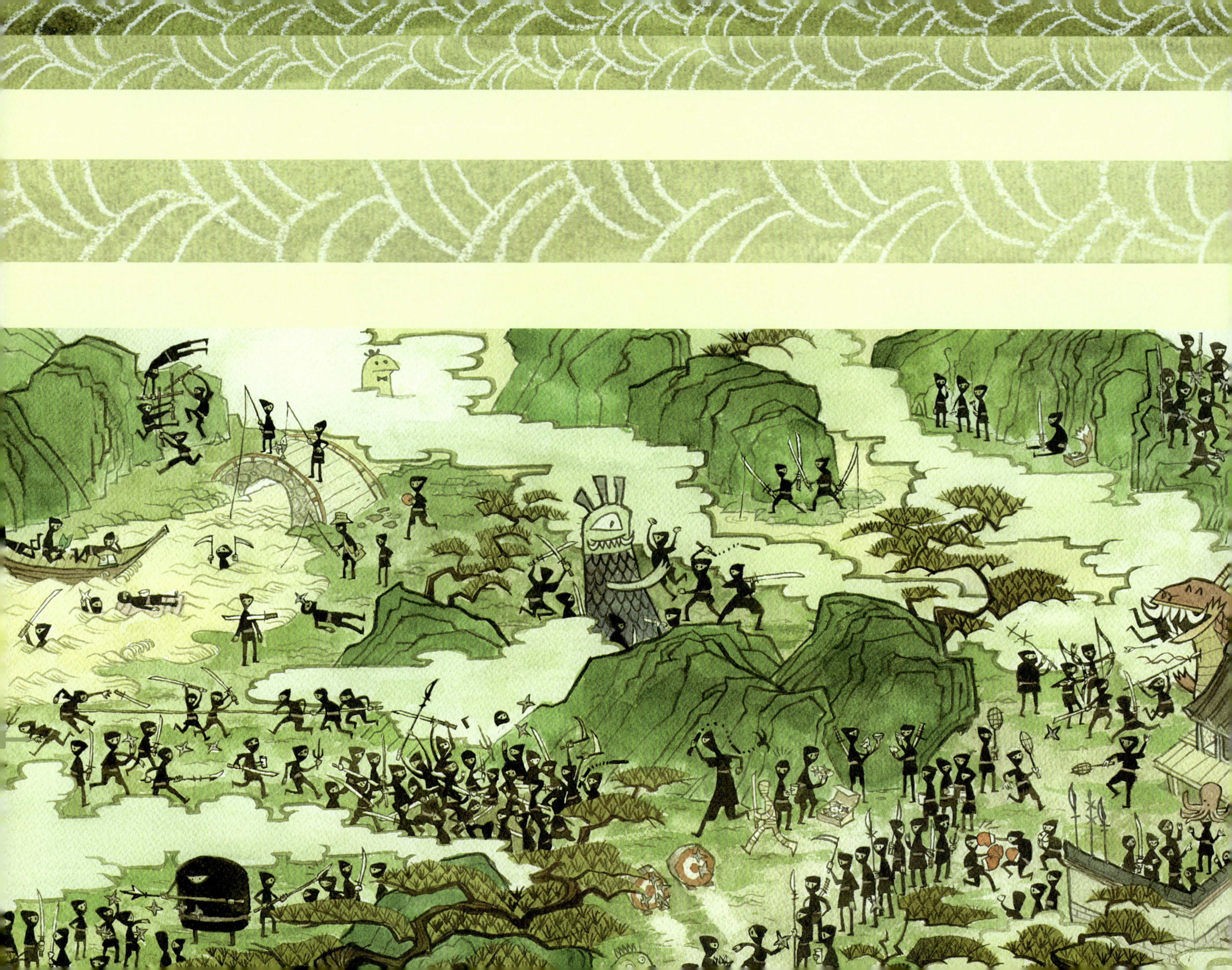

knights and warriors

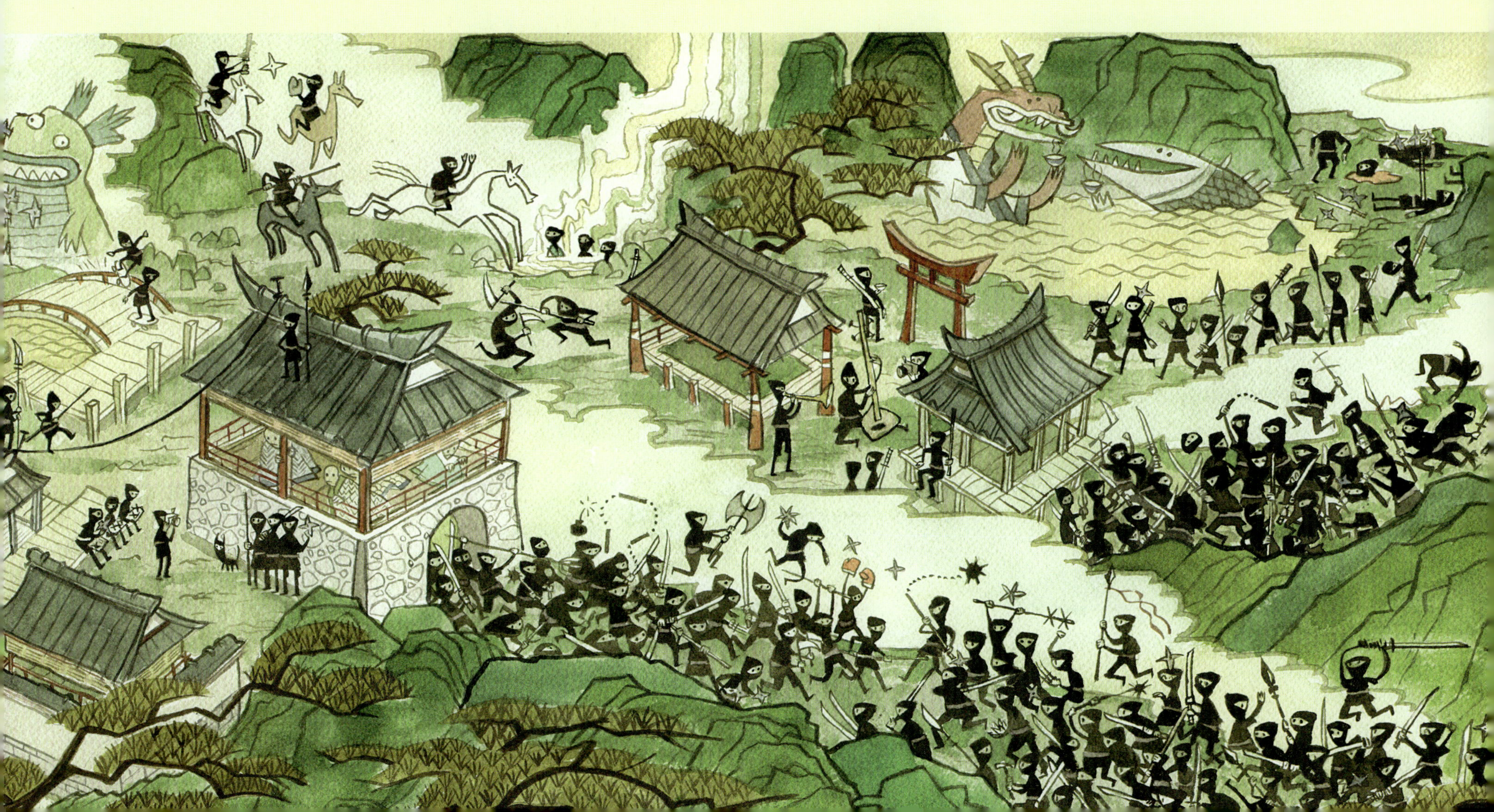

<< [section opener] NINJAS ALL OVER THE PLACE | watercolor | 40" x 11" | 2007

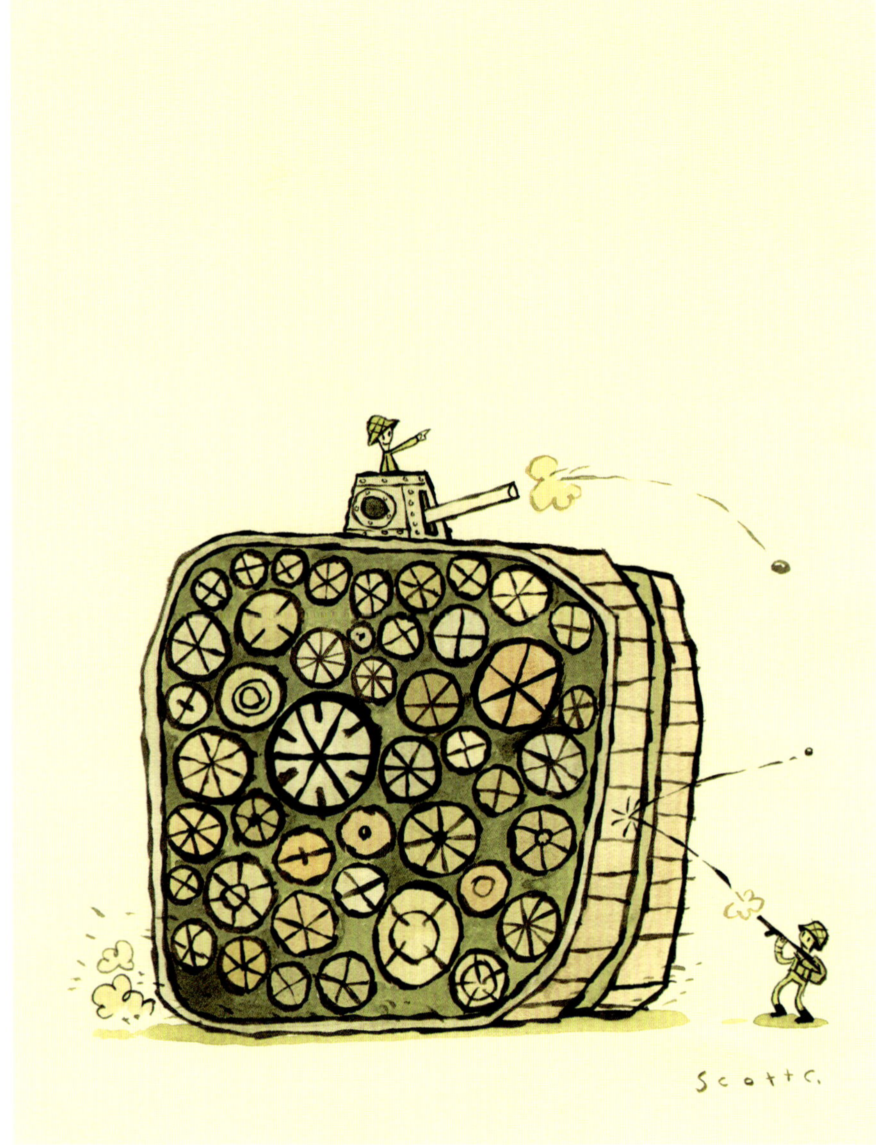

ULTIMATE TANK #1
watercolor
9" x 11"
2006

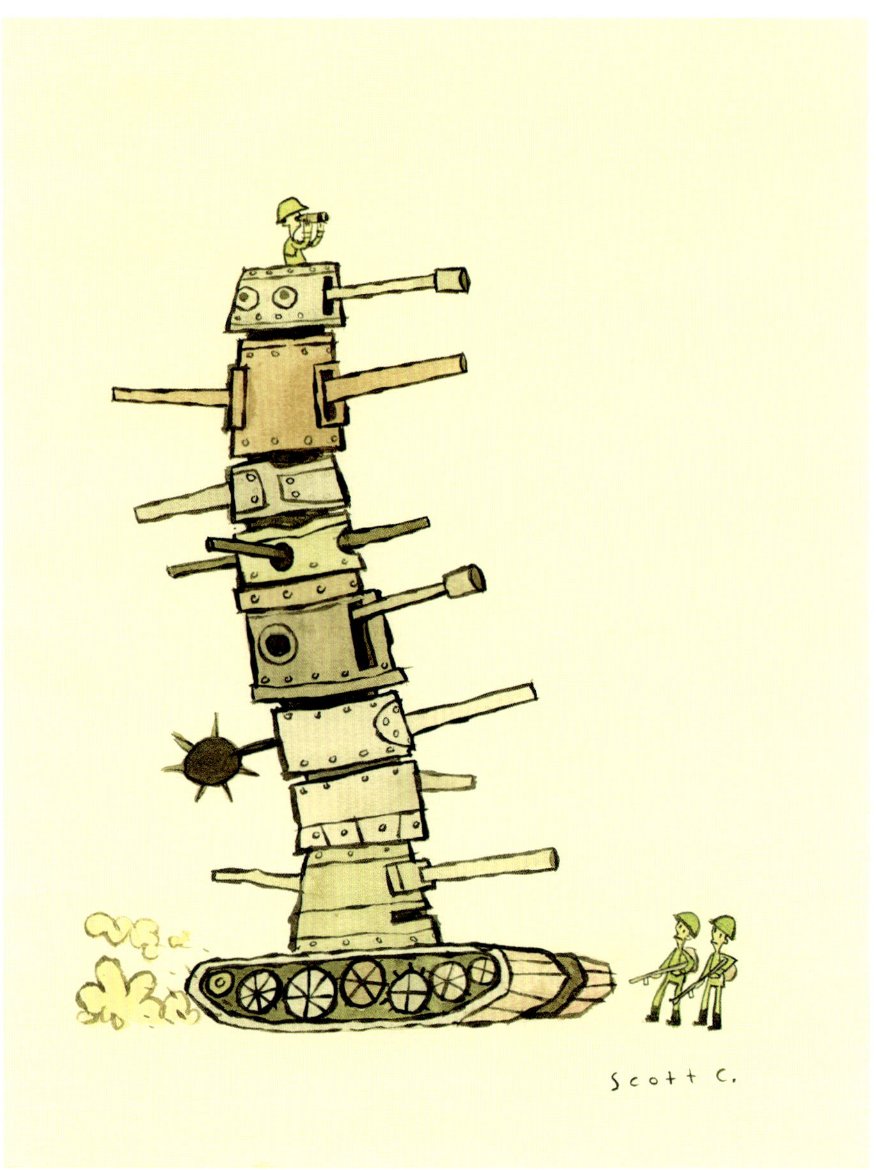

ULTIMATE TANK #2
watercolor
9" x 11"
2006

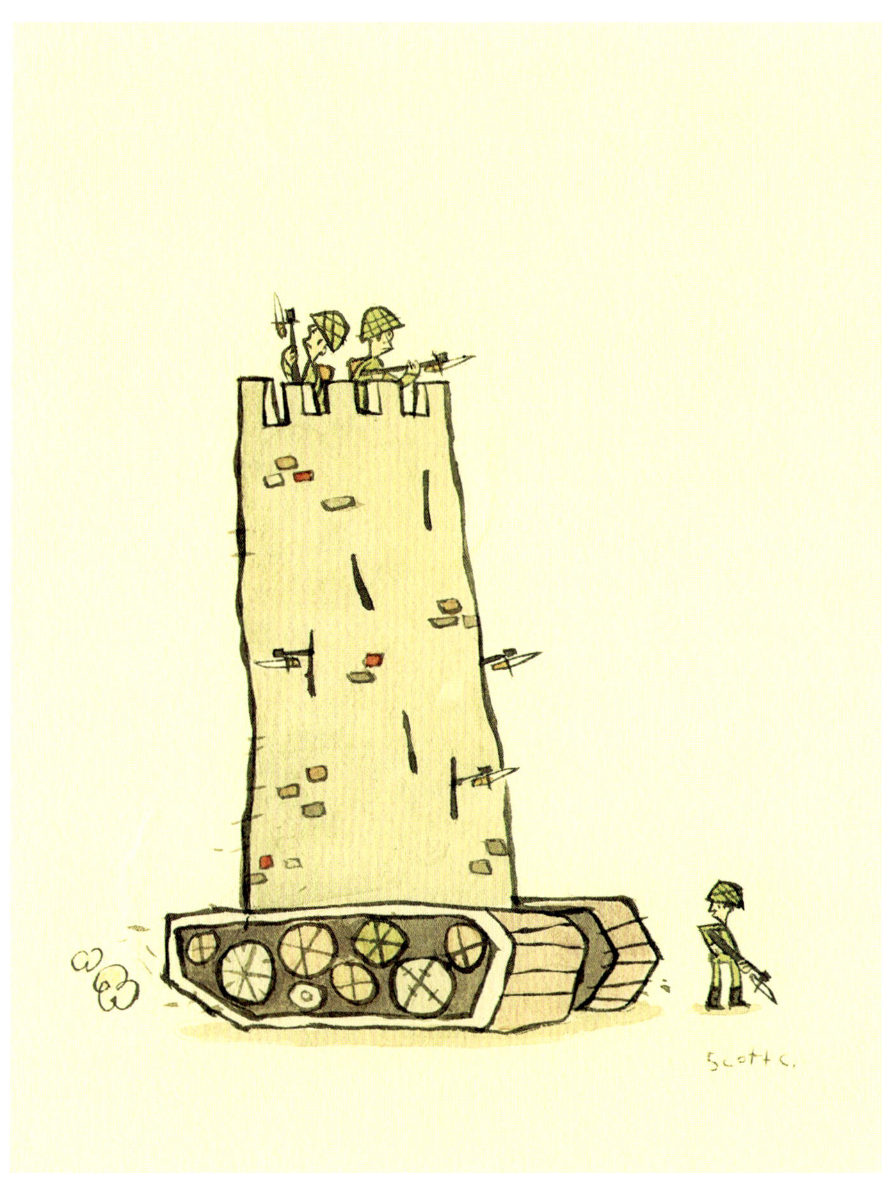

ULTIMATE TANK #3
watercolor
6" x 8"
2006

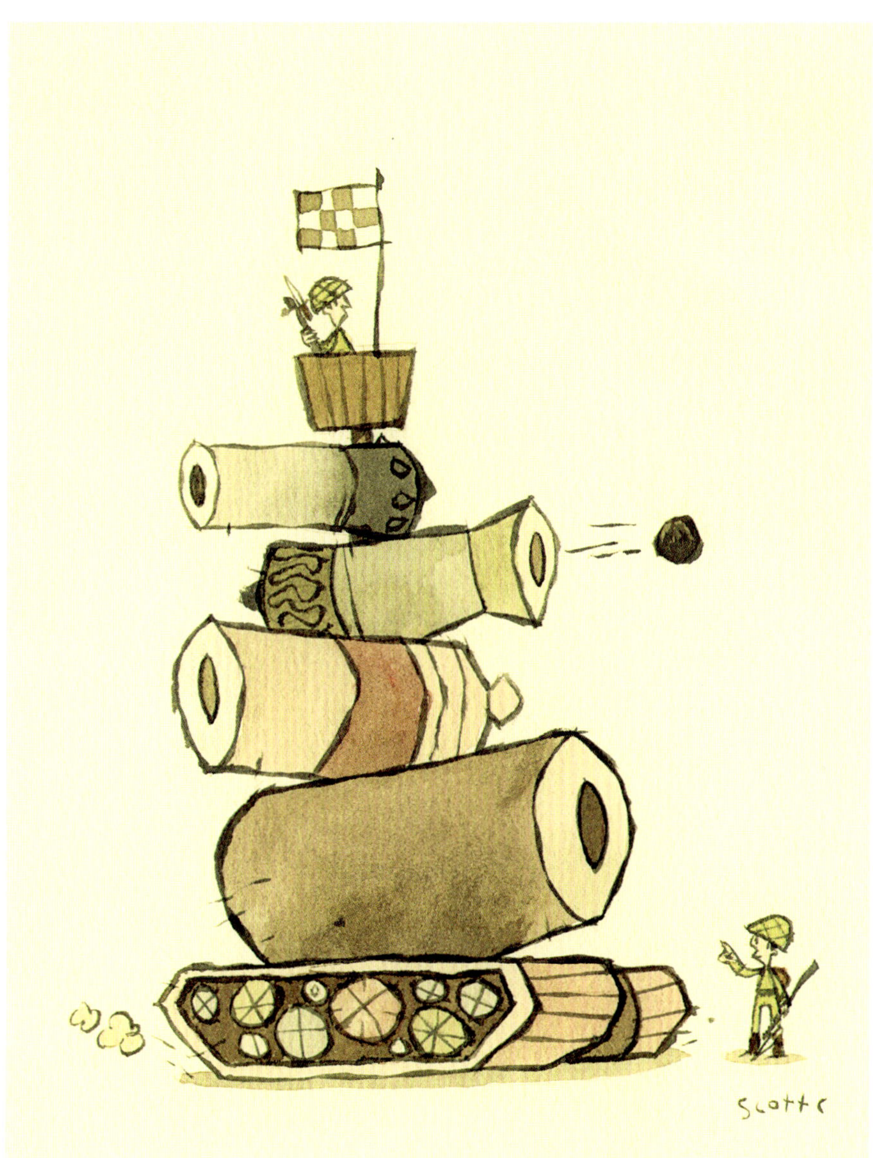

ULTIMATE TANK #4
watercolor
6" x 8"
2006

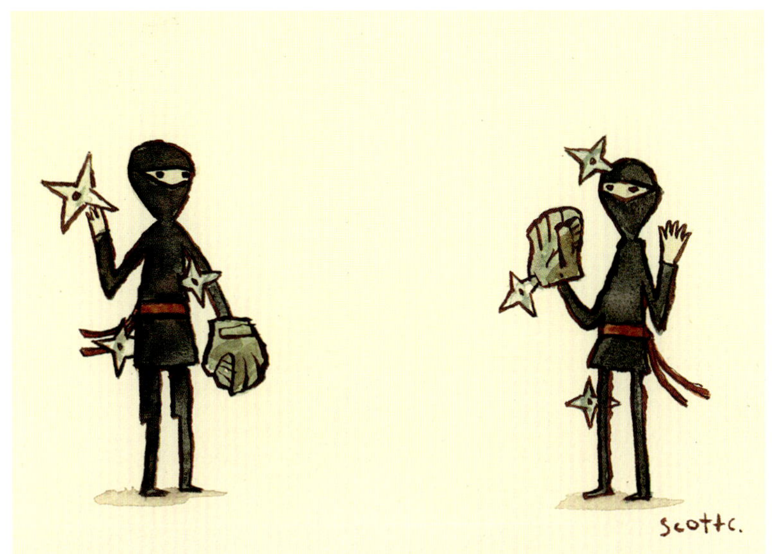

NINJA CATCH
watercolor
7" x 5"
2009

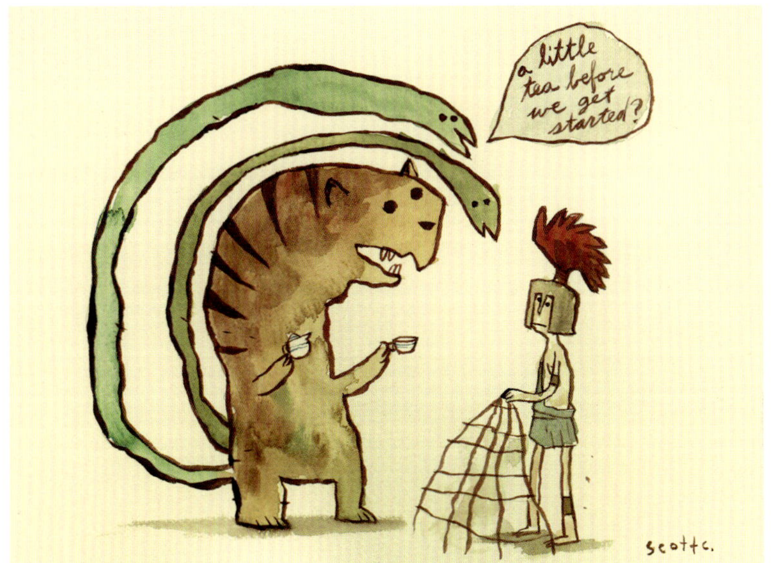

PRE BATTLE TEA
watercolor
10" x 8"
2009

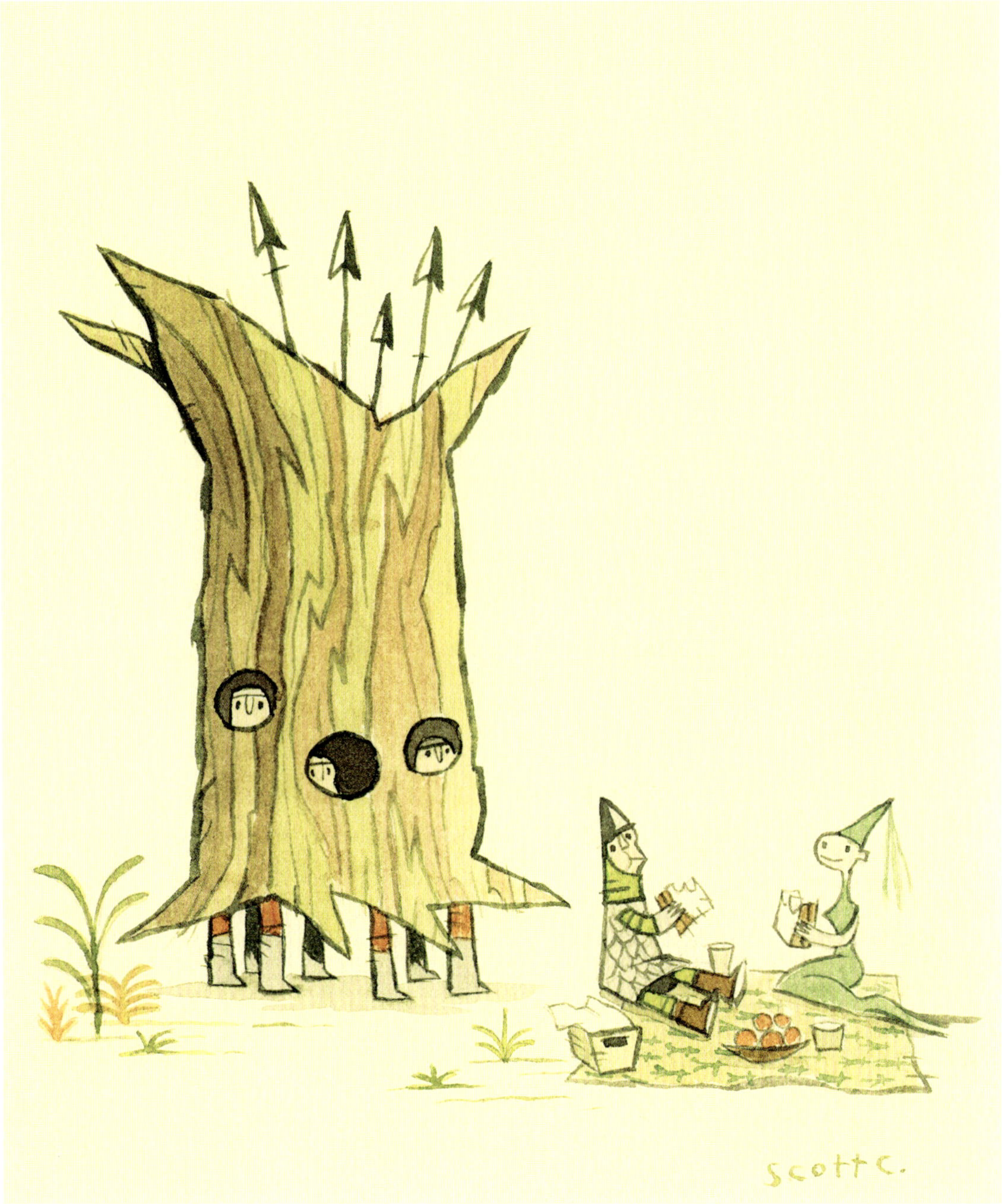

TREE DISGUISE
watercolor
6" x 8"
2007

clockwise from top left

ADORABLE BATTLE #1
watercolor
5" x 5"
2007

ADORABLE BATTLE #2
watercolor
5" x 5"
2007

ADORABLE BATTLE #3
watercolor
5" x 5"
2007

ADORABLE BATTLE #4
watercolor
5" x 5"
2007

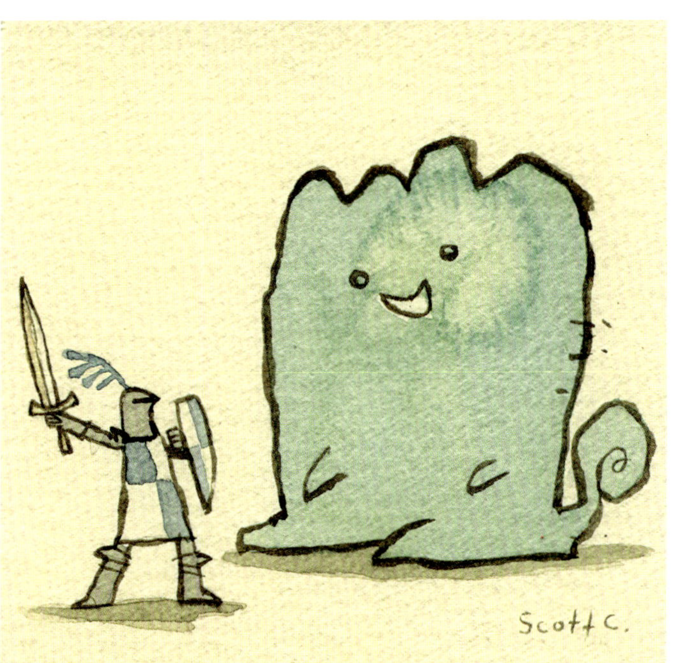

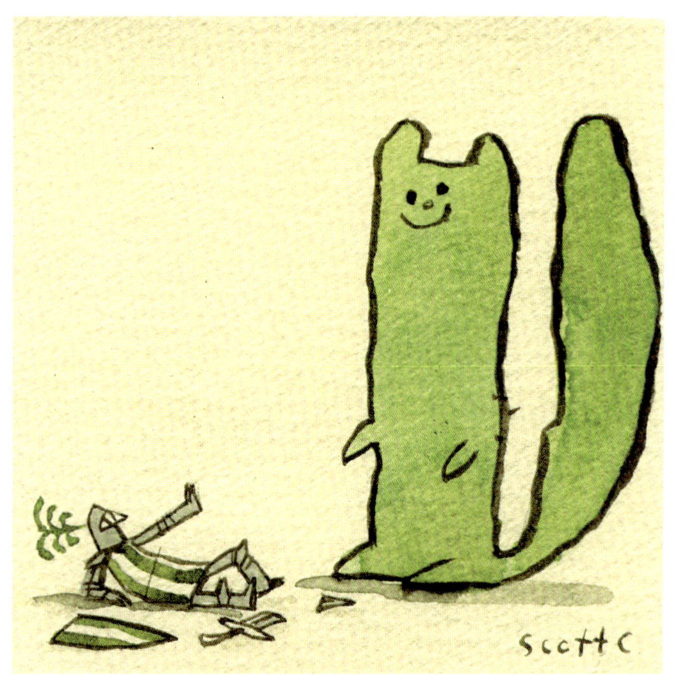

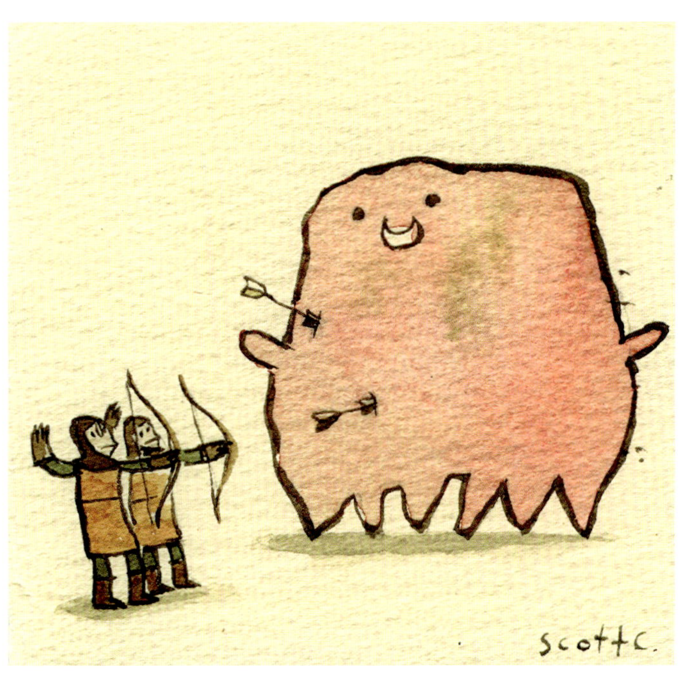

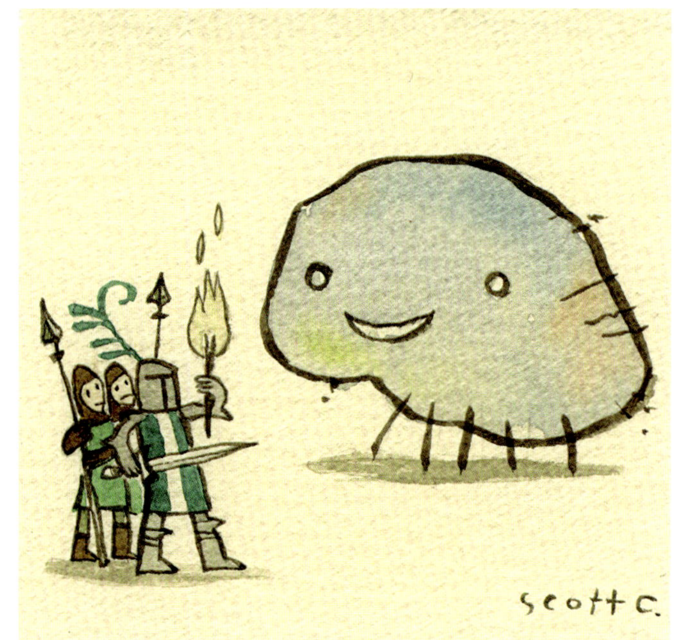

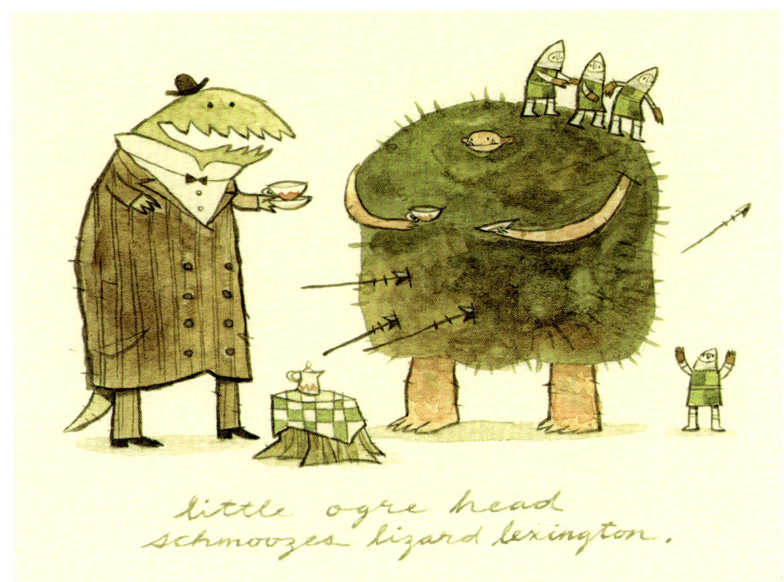

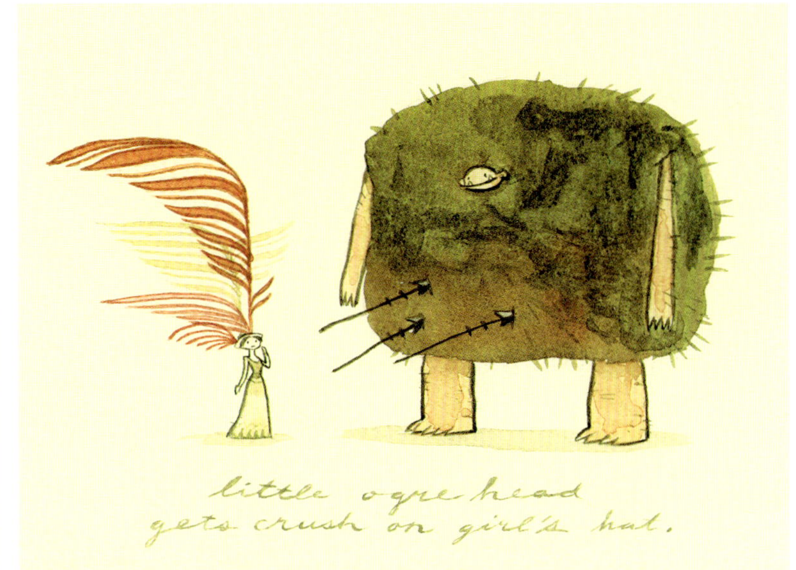

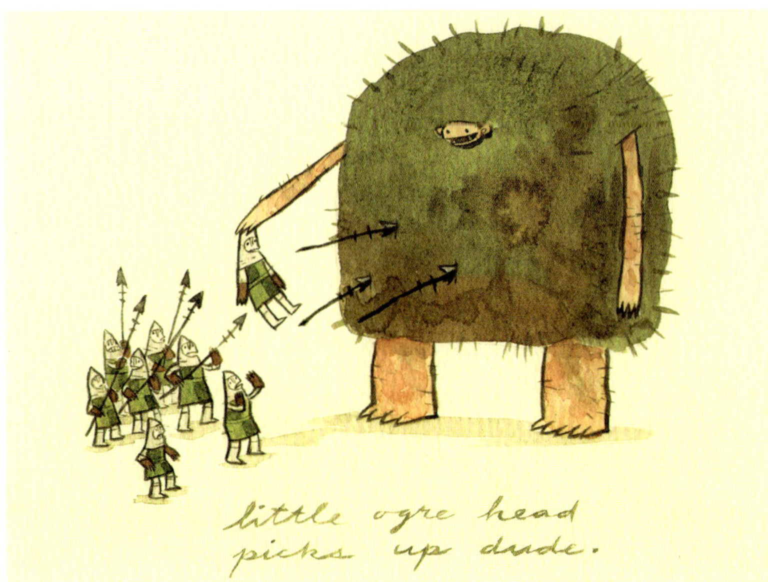

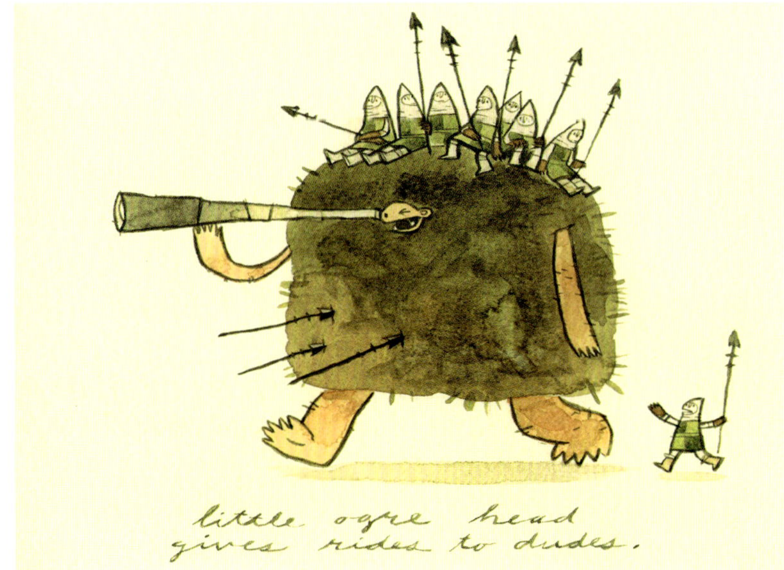

clockwise from top left

LITTLE OGRE HEAD SCHMOOZES
watercolor
7" x 7"
2007

LITTLE OGRE HEAD GETS CRUSH
watercolor
7" x 7"
2007

LITTLE OGRE HEAD GIVES RIDES
watercolor
7" x 7"
2007

LITTLE OGRE HEAD PICKS UP DUDE
watercolor
7" x 7"
2007

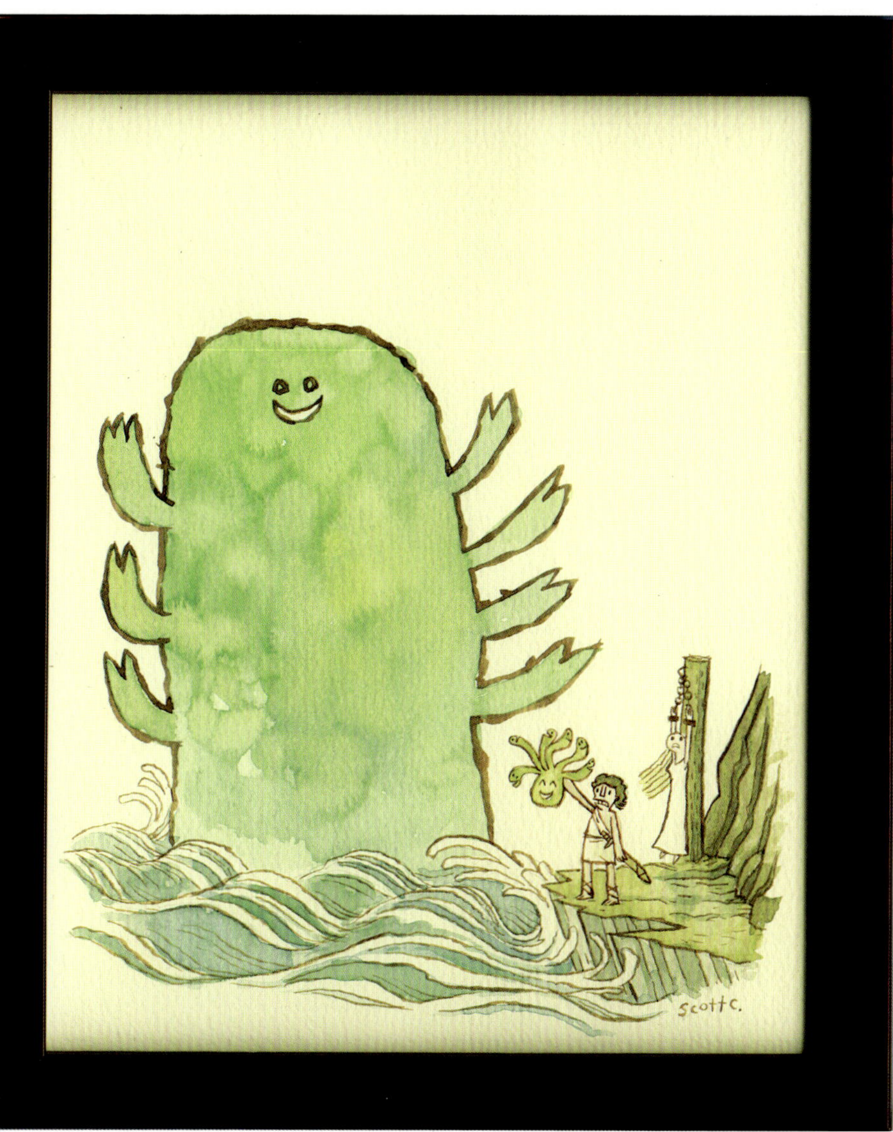

ADORABLE BATTLE (BY THE SEASIDE)
watercolor
8" x 10"
2008

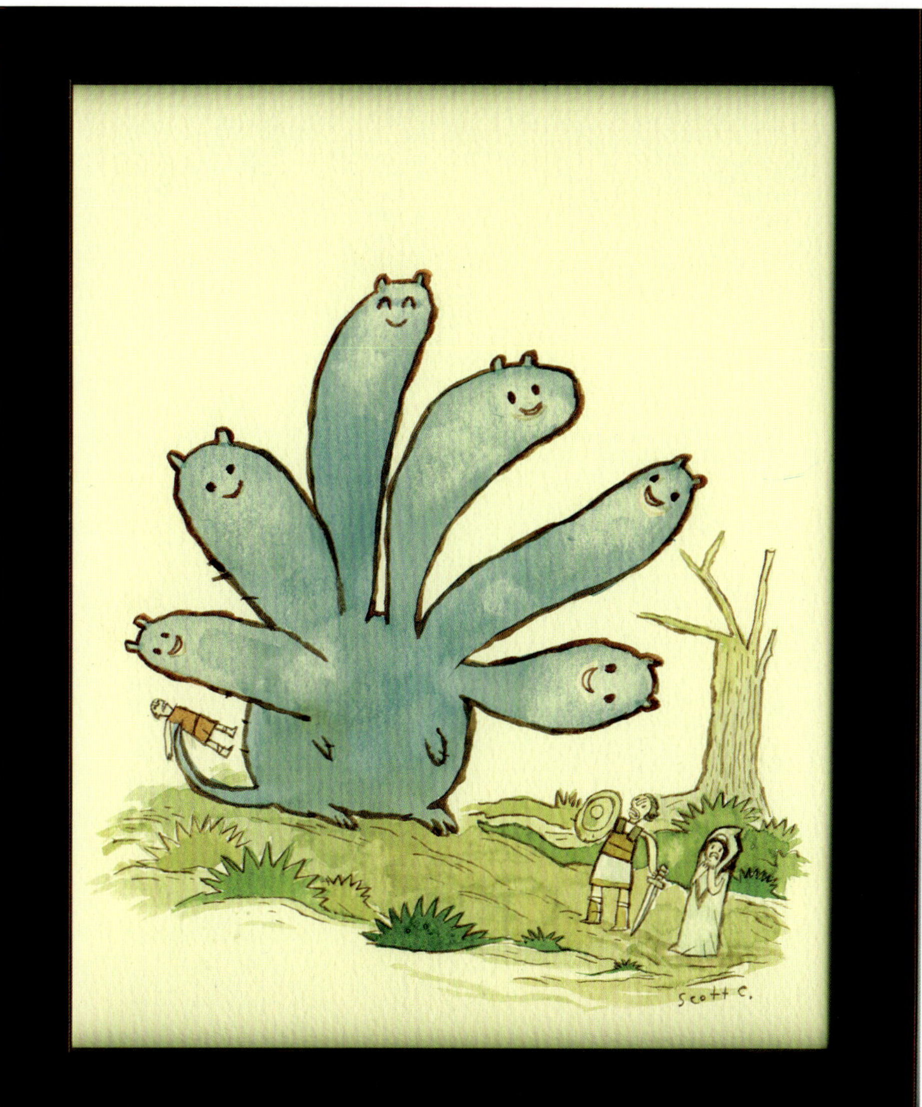

ADORABLE BATTLE (NEAR OLD TREE)
watercolor
8" x 10"
2008

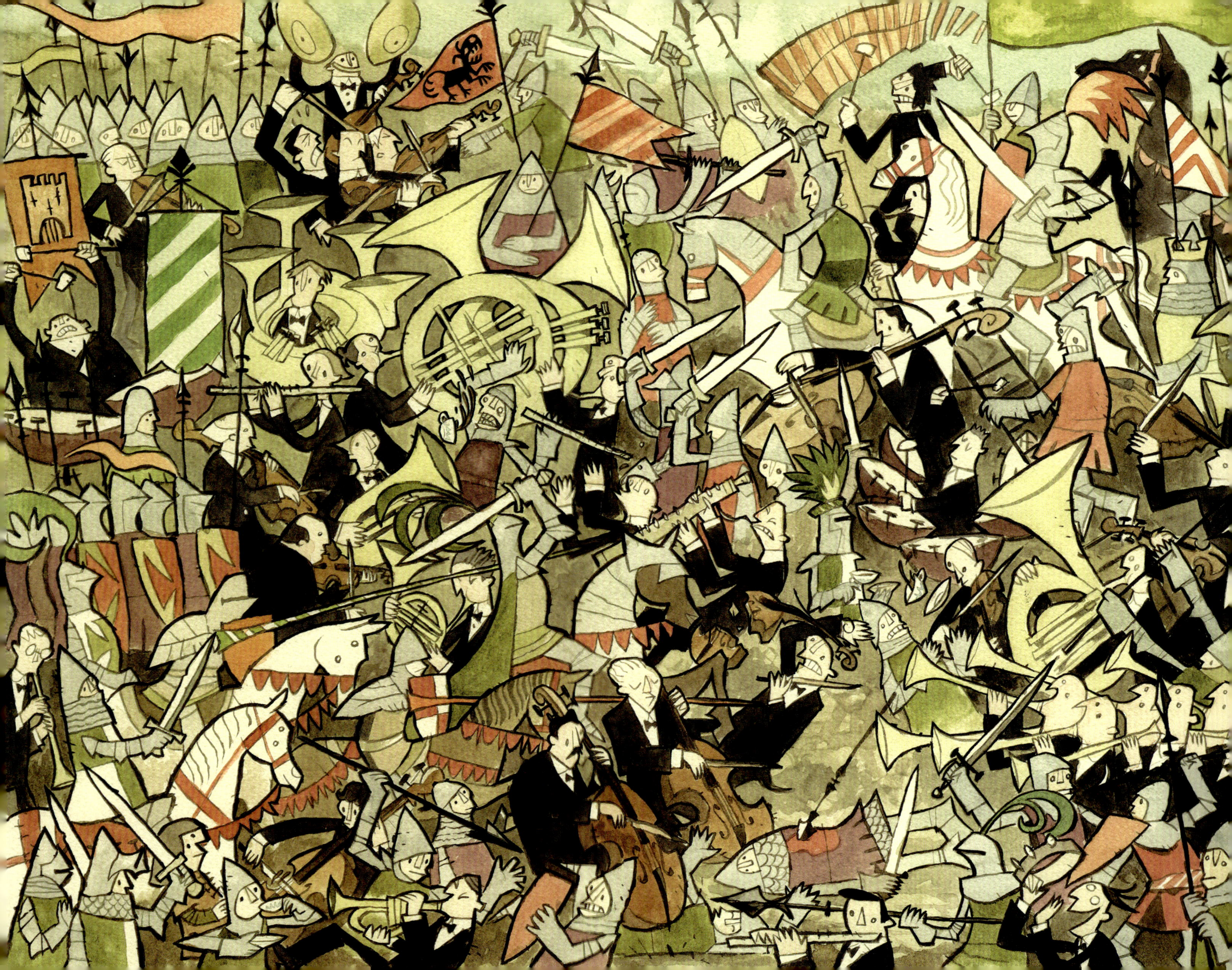

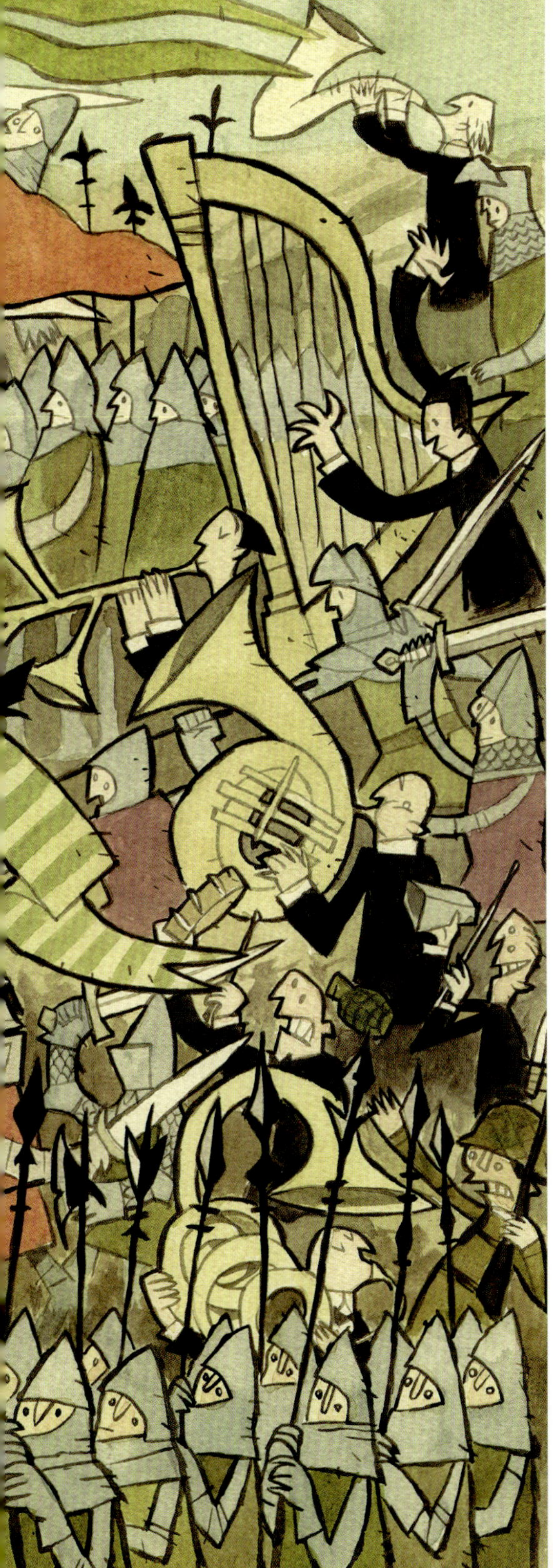

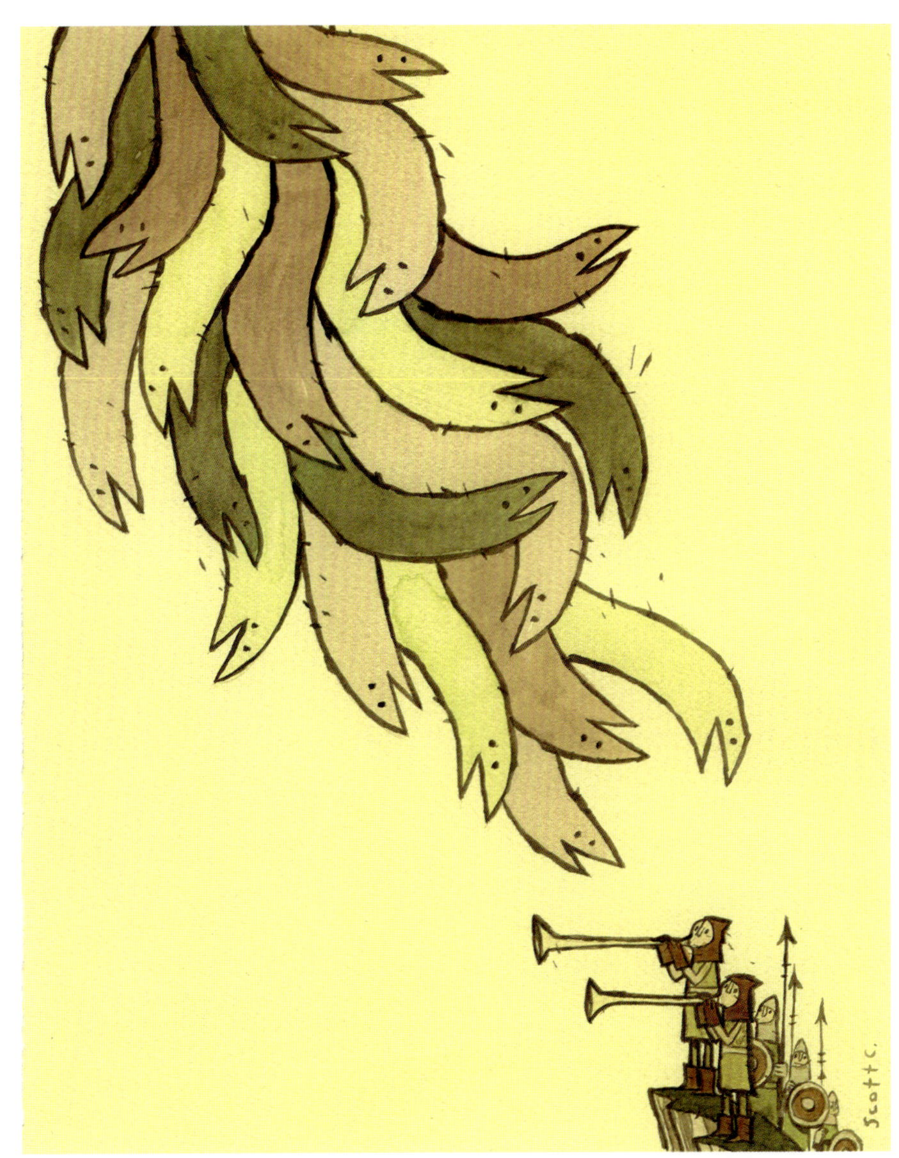

CALLING ON THE SERPENTS
watercolor
11" x 14"
2007

BATTLE SUPREME
watercolor
18" x 11"
2007

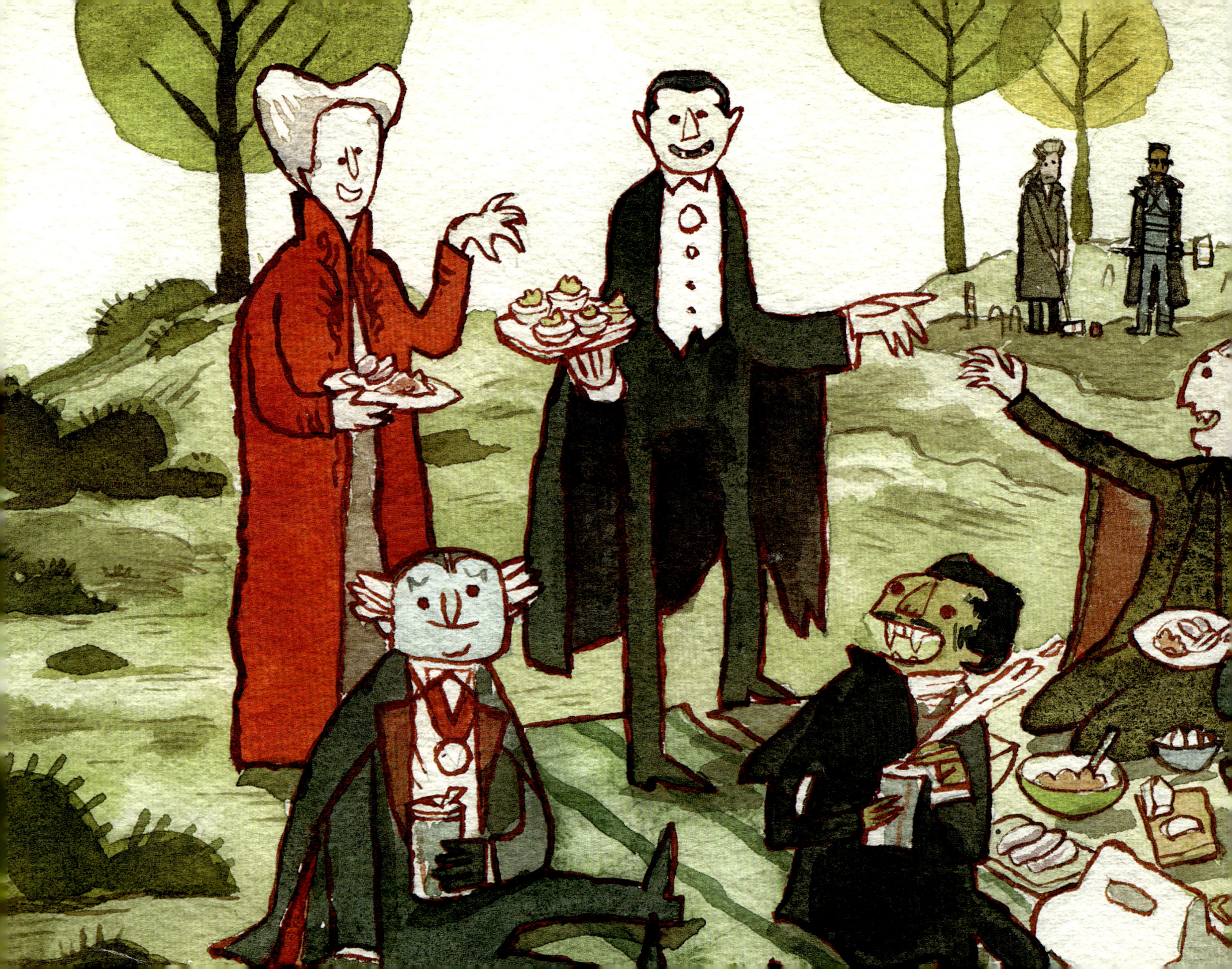

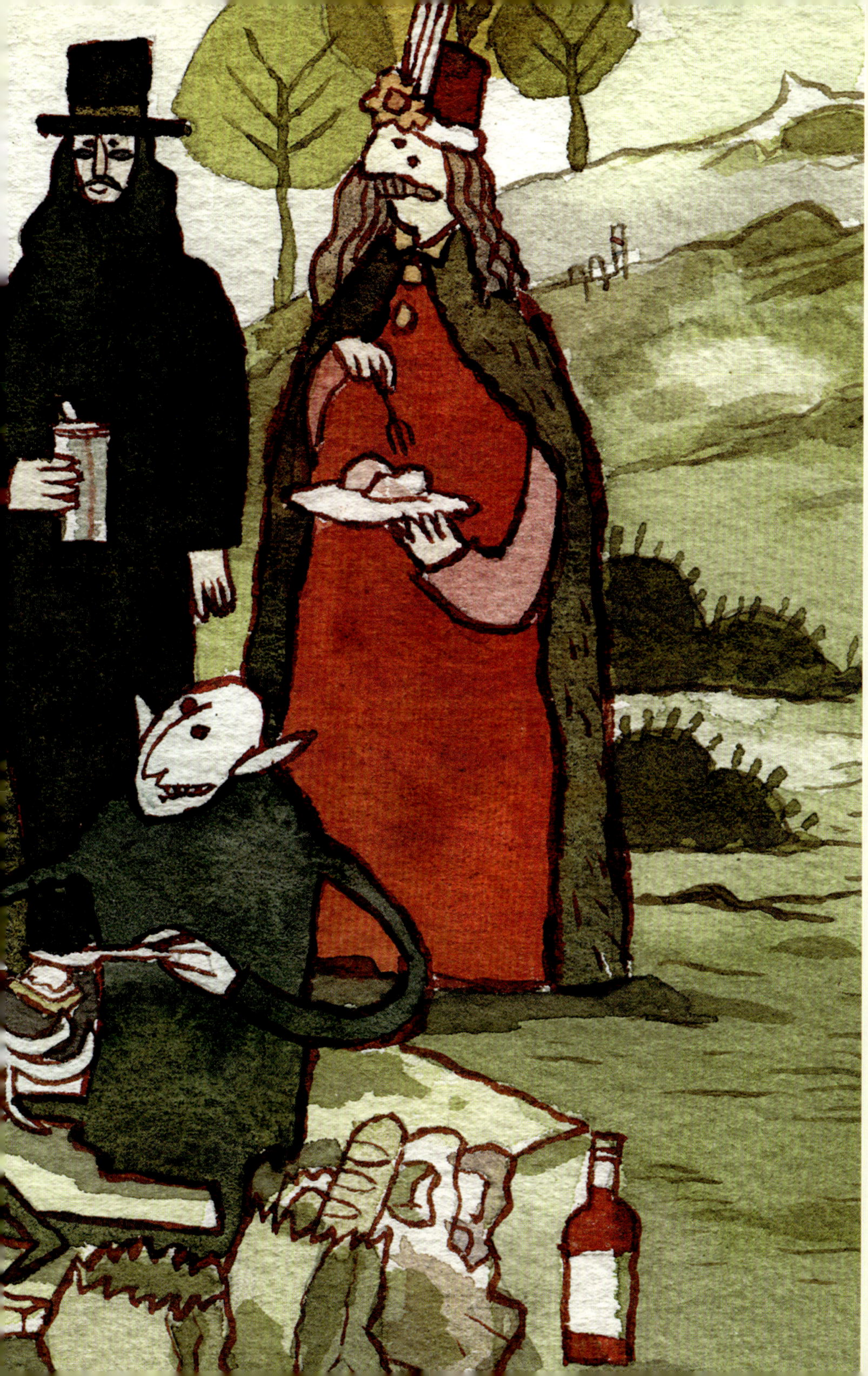

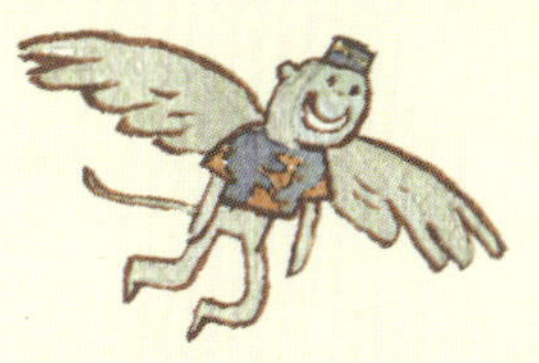

amicvs monstrvm

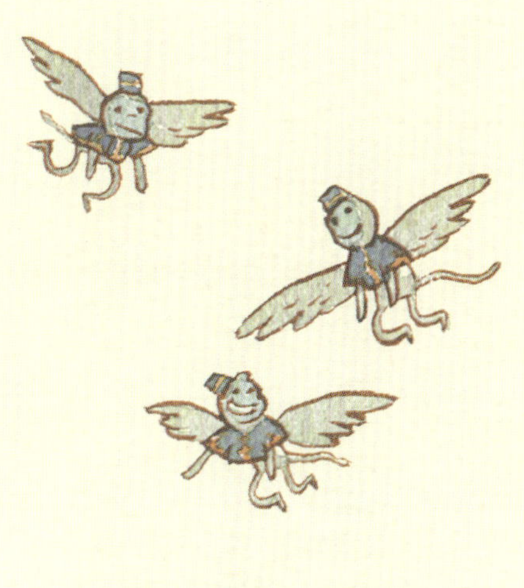

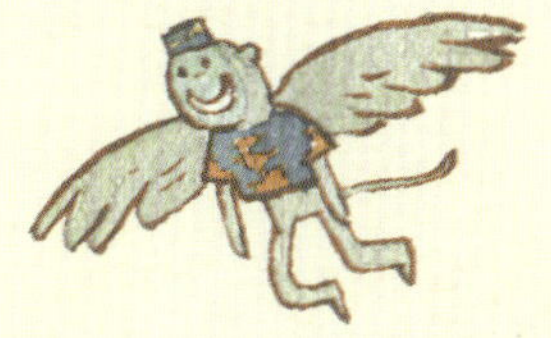

<< [section opener] PICNIC WITH THE DRACULAS | watercolor on paper | 12" x 9"

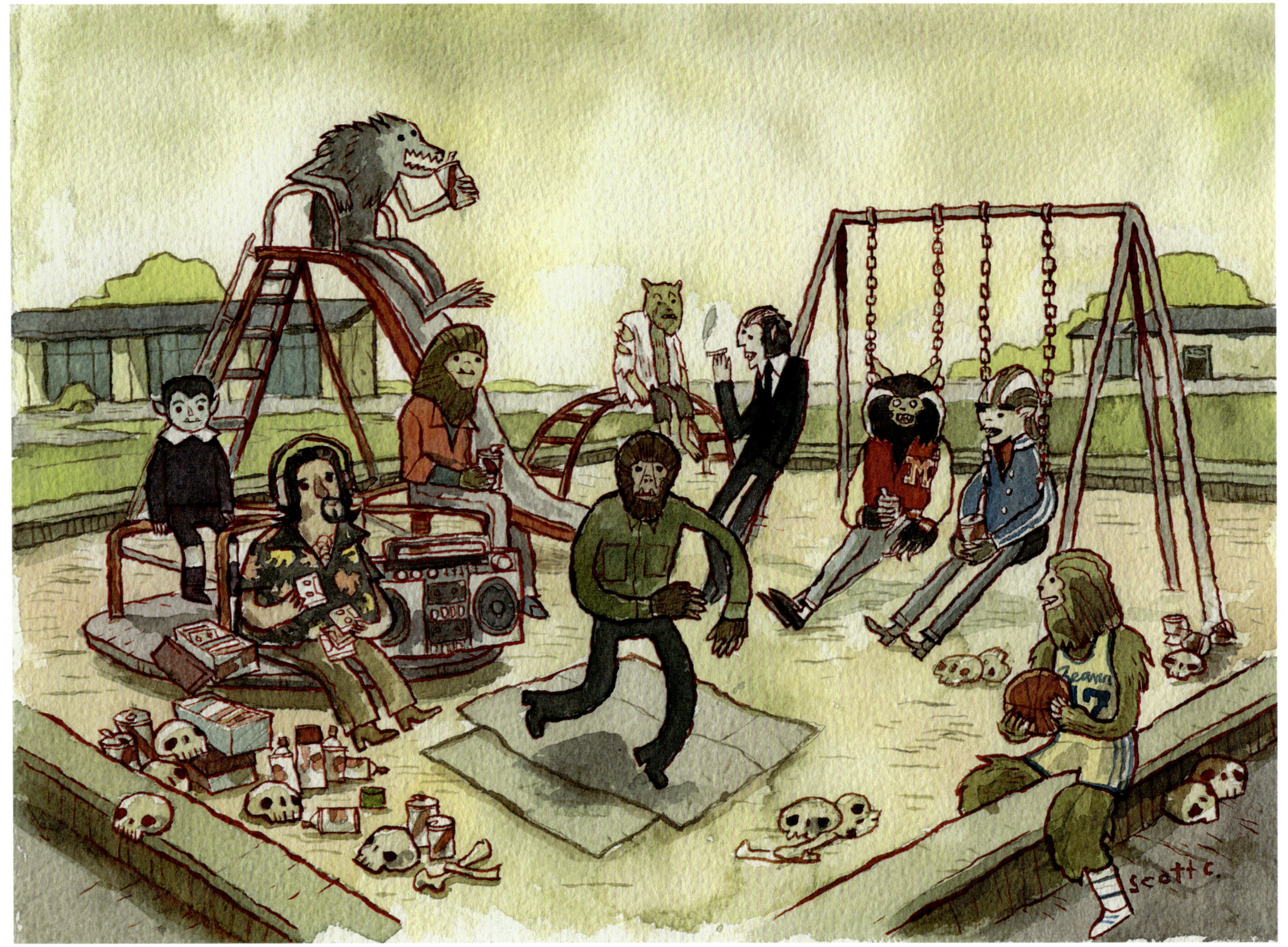

WOLFMANS ON SCHOOL GROUNDS
watercolor
10" x 8"
2010

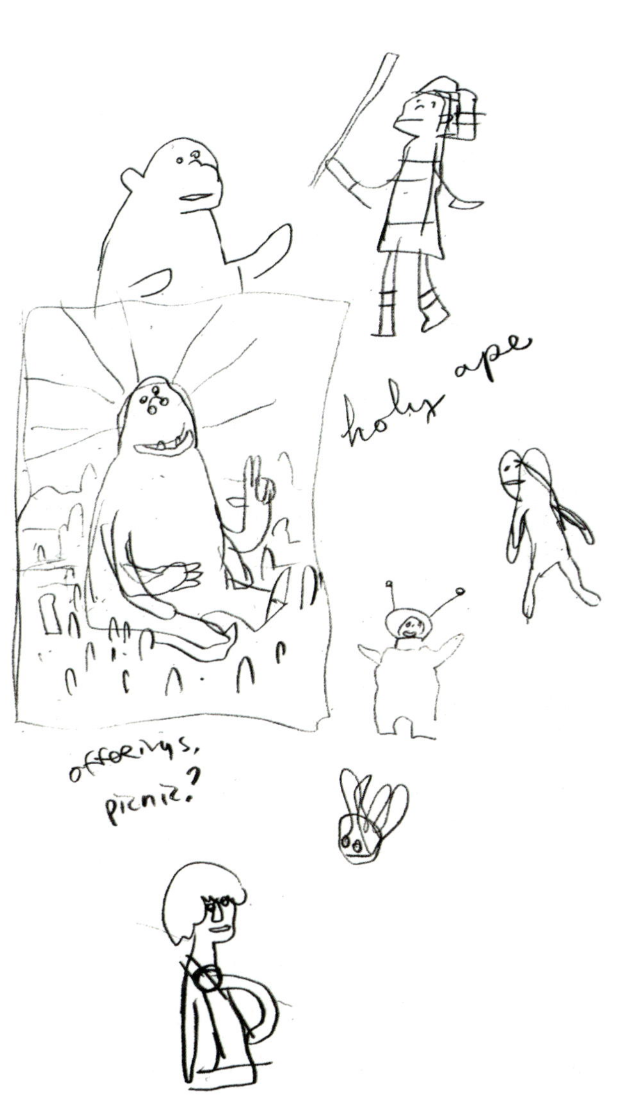

APE AMONGST APES
watercolor
9" x 12"
2010

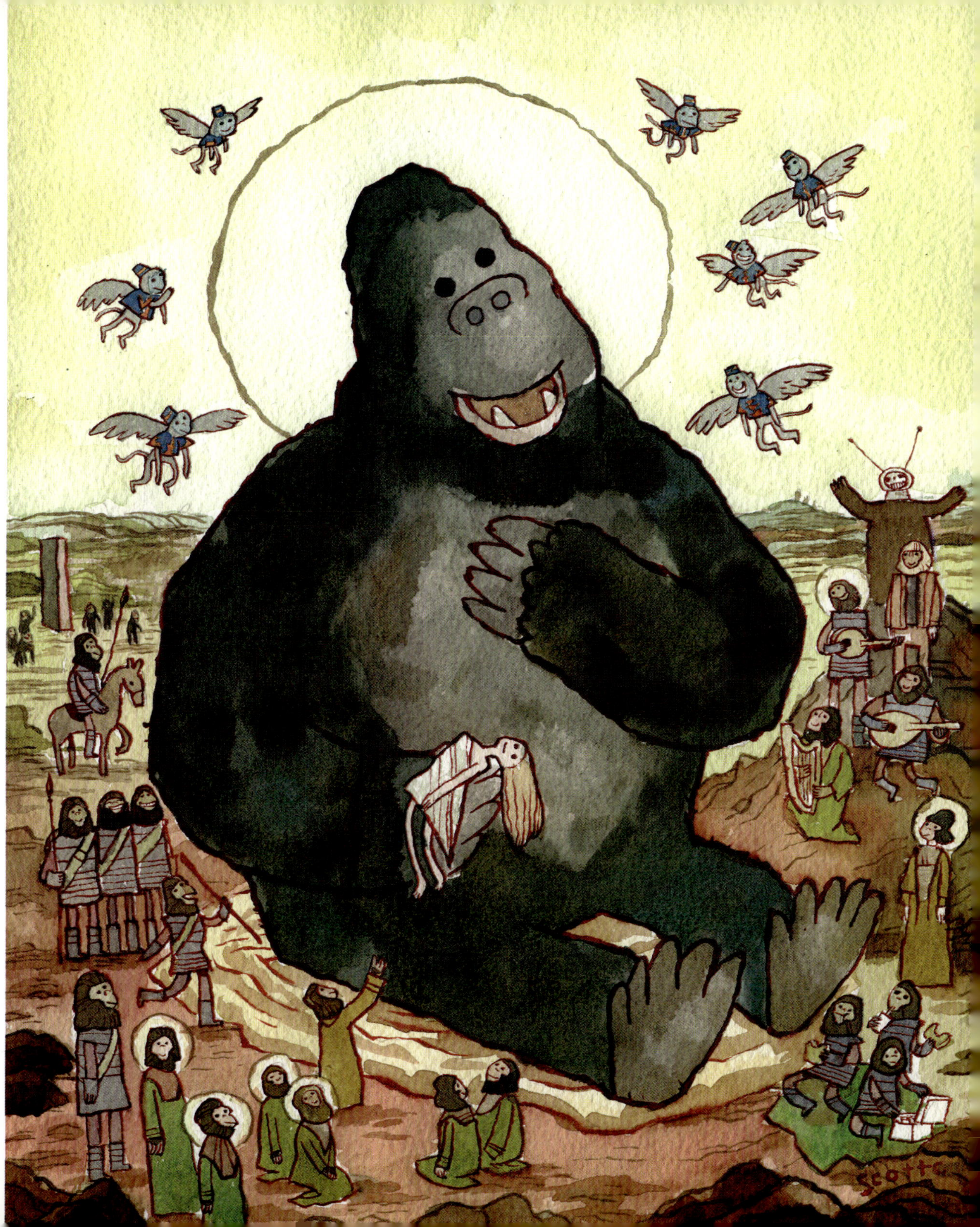

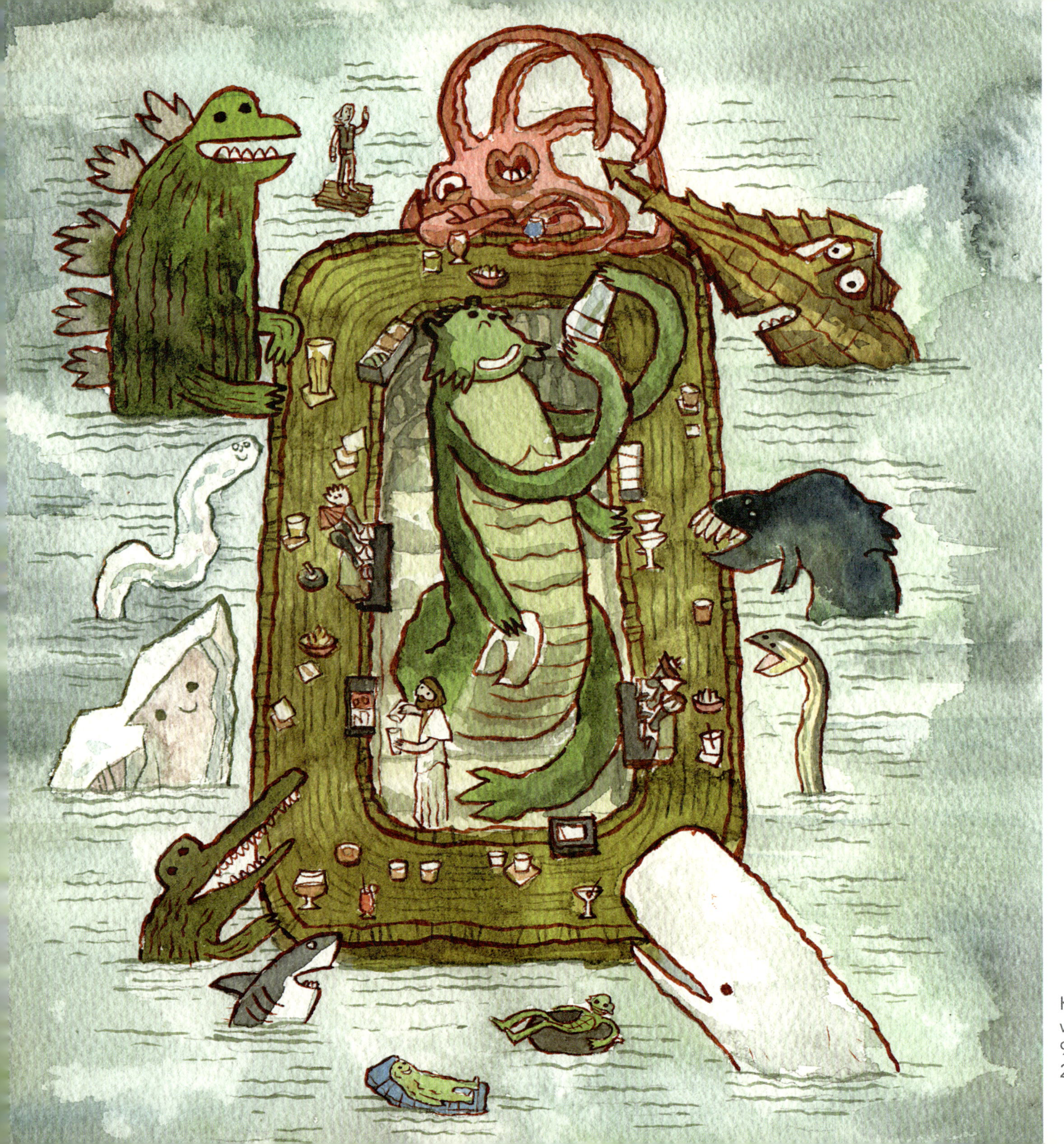

KRAKEN'S FLOATING BAR
watercolor
9" x 12"
2010

Phantom's paintings are full of deep meaning, and he is often found explaining them to patrons. There is rarely an exhibition that Phantom is not found explaining things. The ocean, on the other hand, is dominated by the Kraken and his sweet floating bar. Kraken is a reknowned mixologist.

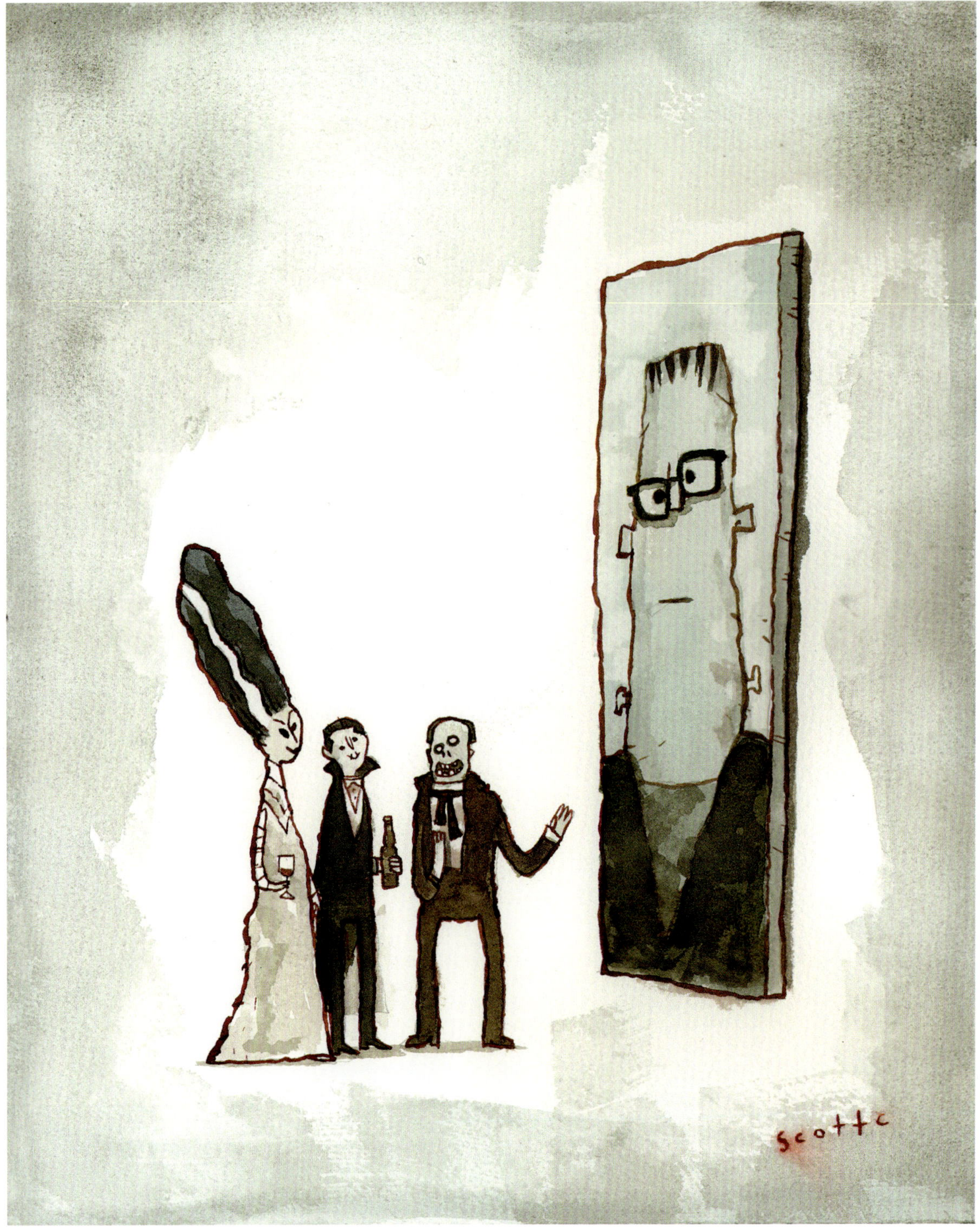

PHANTOM'S OPENING
watercolor
8" x 10"
2010

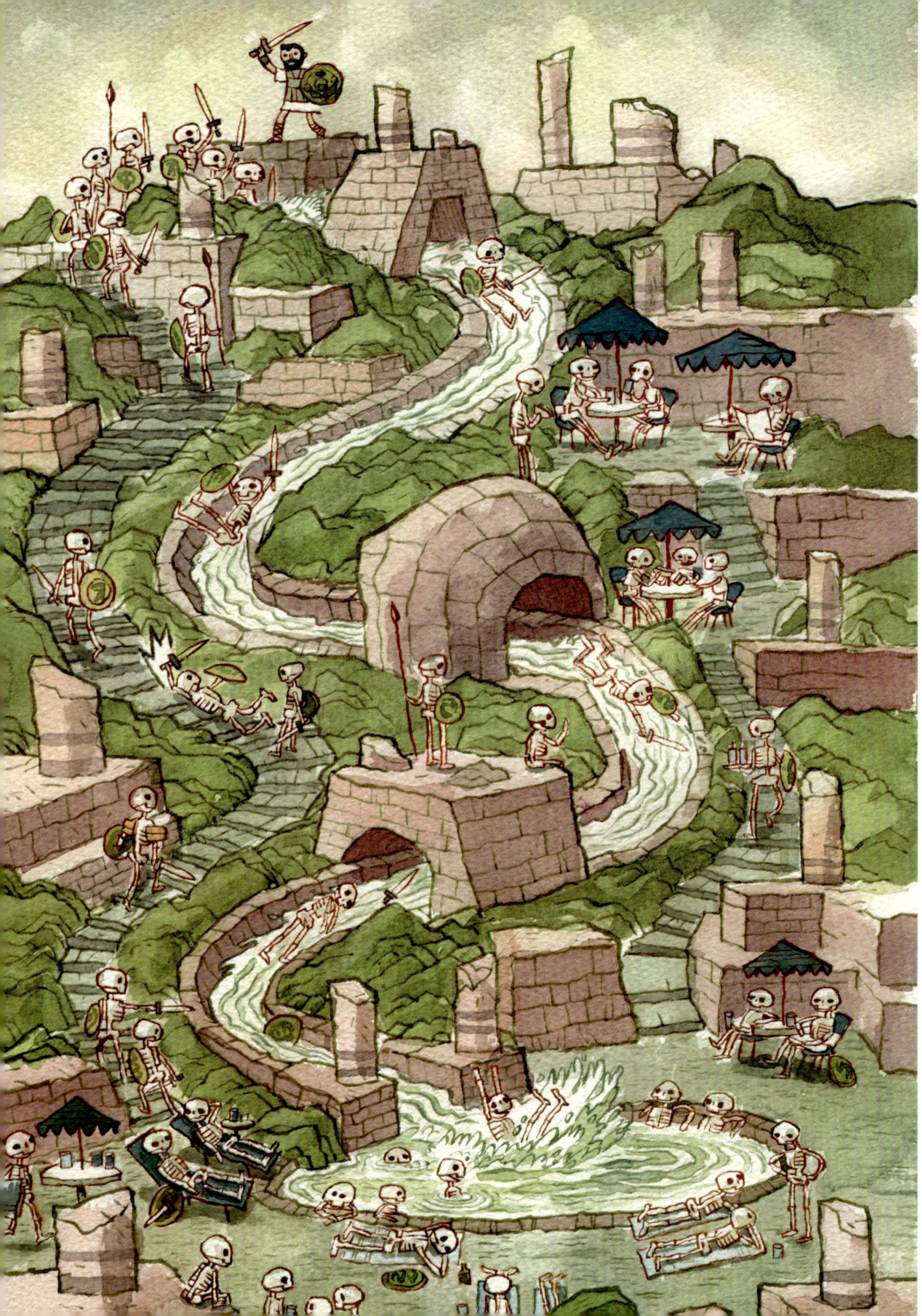

Skeleton Warriors are hard-working fighters, for sure. But they also get very serious about their recreation. The waterpark is a place where they may come fight a bit and relax a bit. They may take a dip after a particularly good sword battle. Some skeletons may not even get on the waterslide. Some prefer to lay out and take in the rays from the sun or read the paper. There are no rules to confine the skeleton warriors at the waterpark.

SKELETON WARRIOR WATERPARK
watercolor
11" x 17"
2010

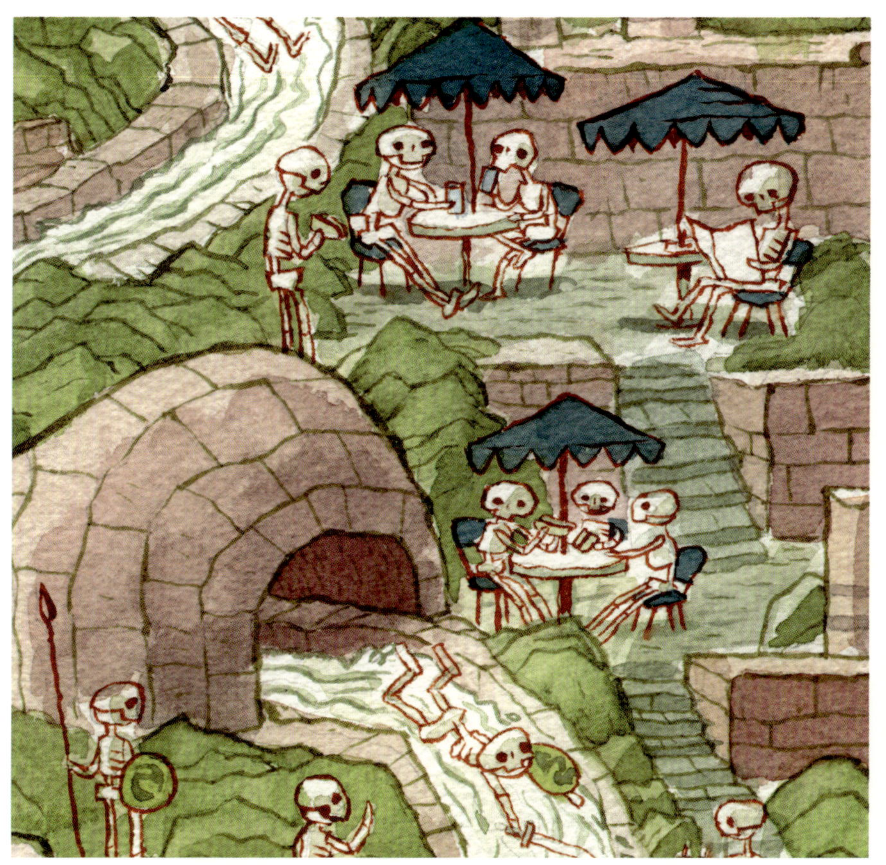

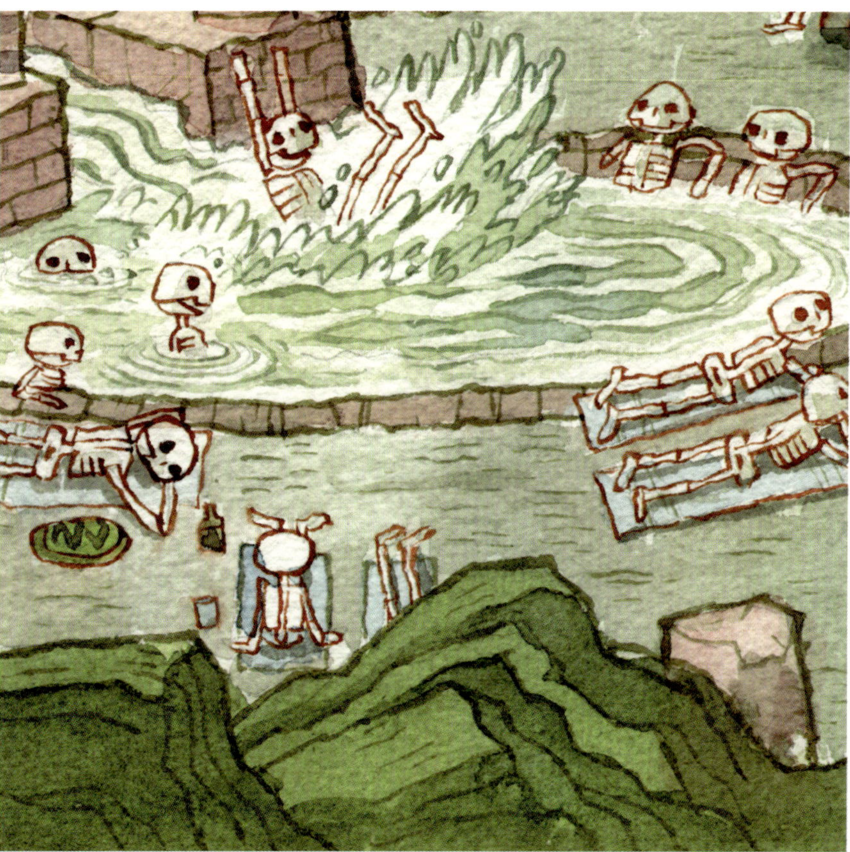

lumberjacks

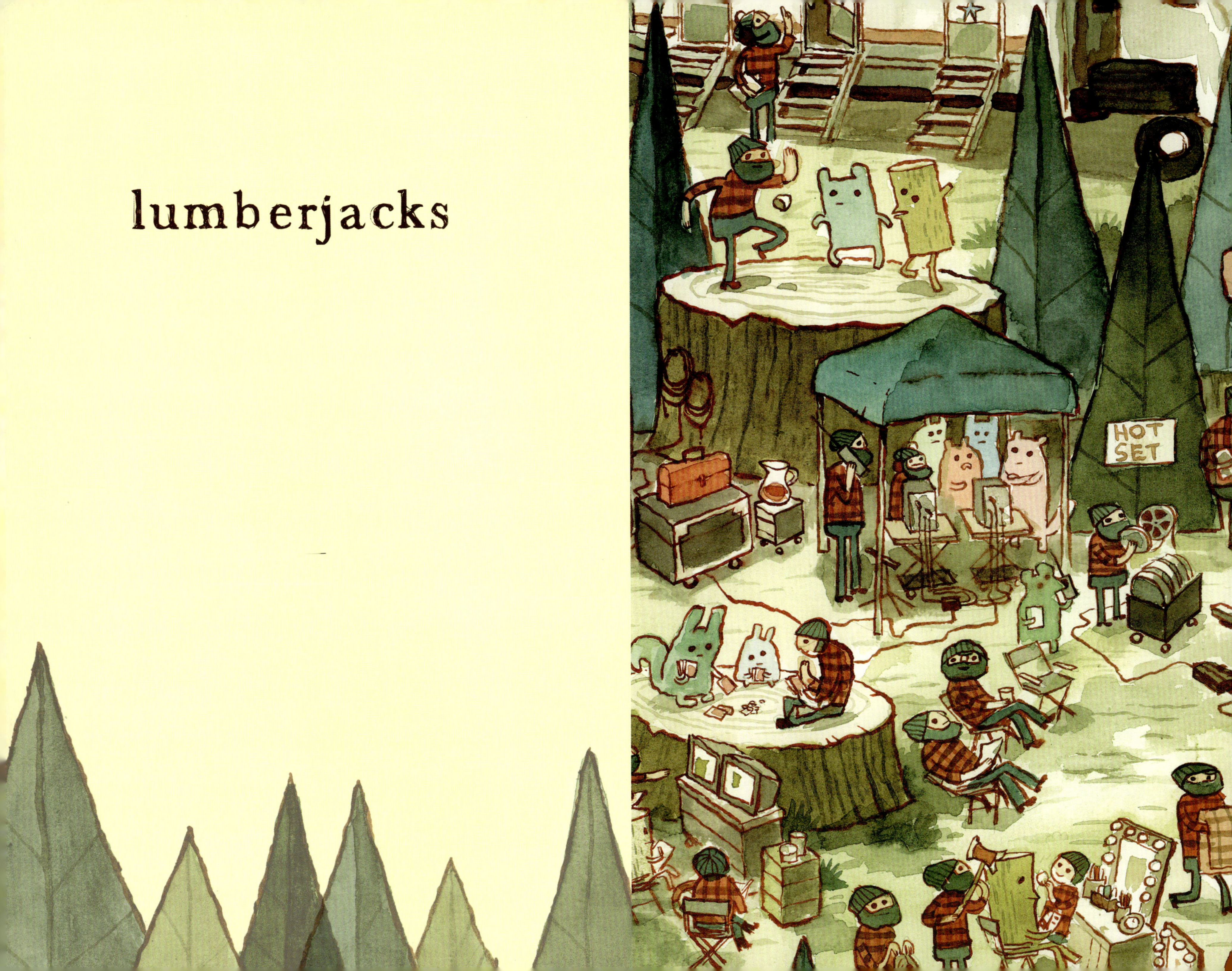

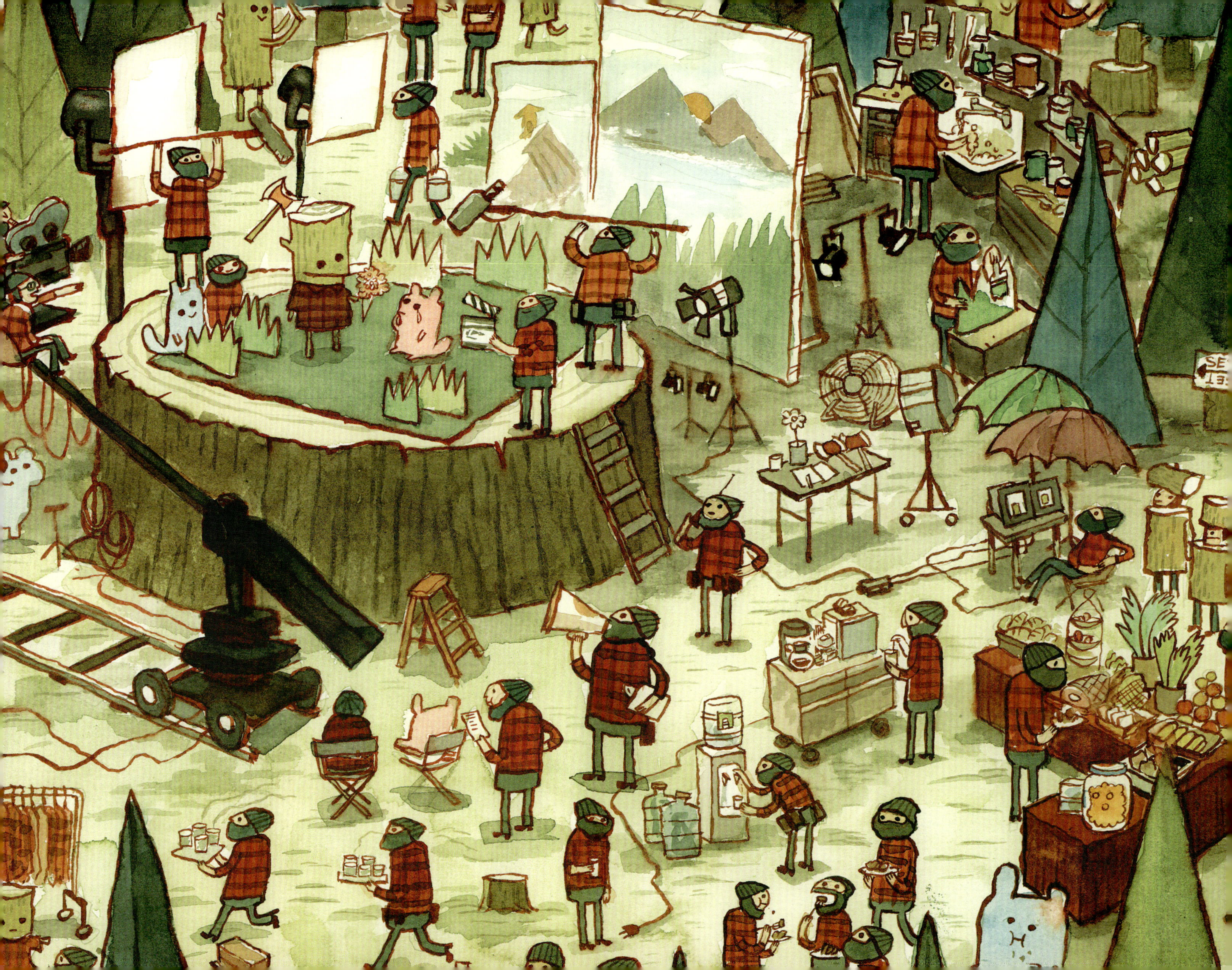

<< [section opener] LUMBERJACKS AT WORK | watercolor | 30" x 15" | 2010

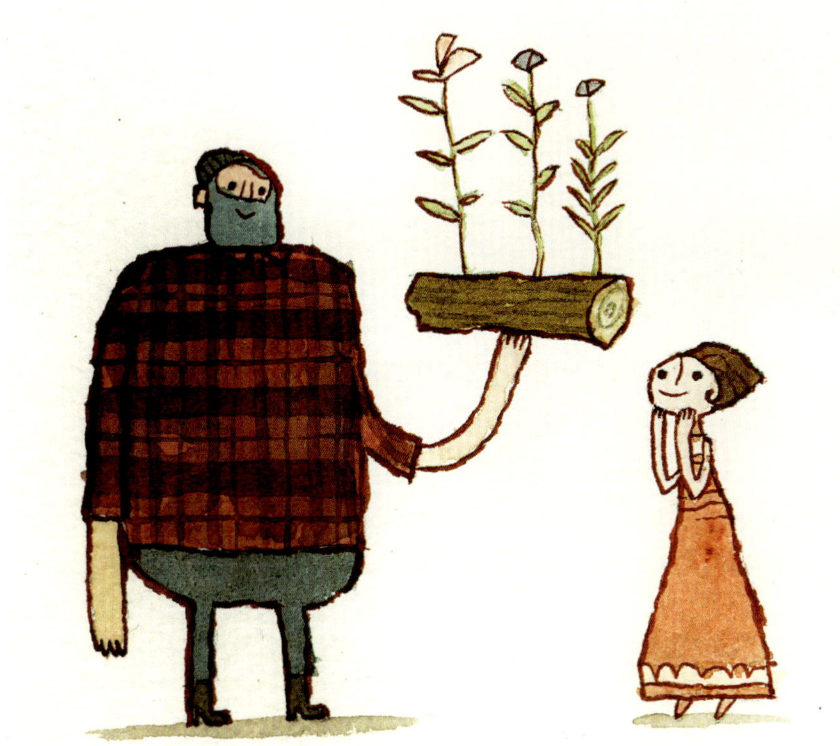

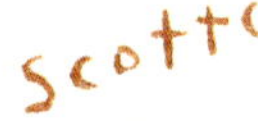

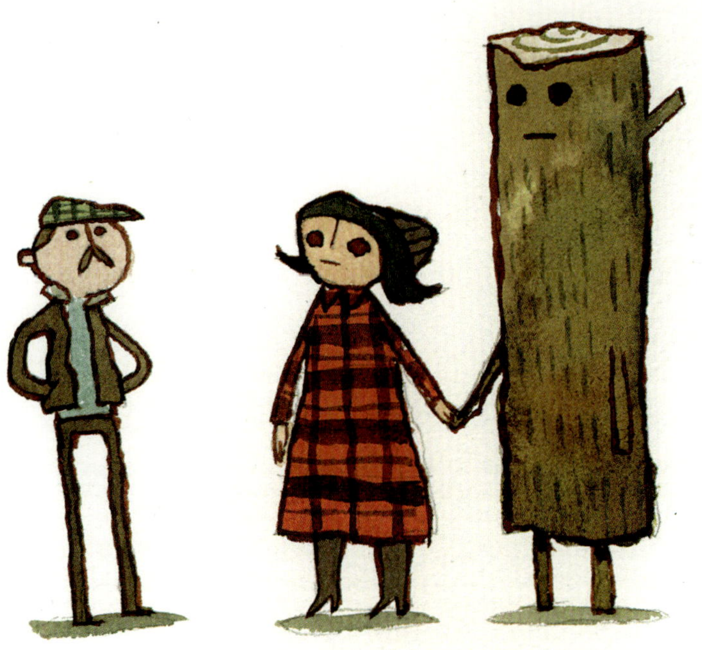

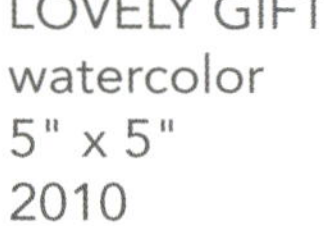

LOVELY GIFT
watercolor
5" x 5"
2010

THE OTHER
watercolor
5" x 5"
2010

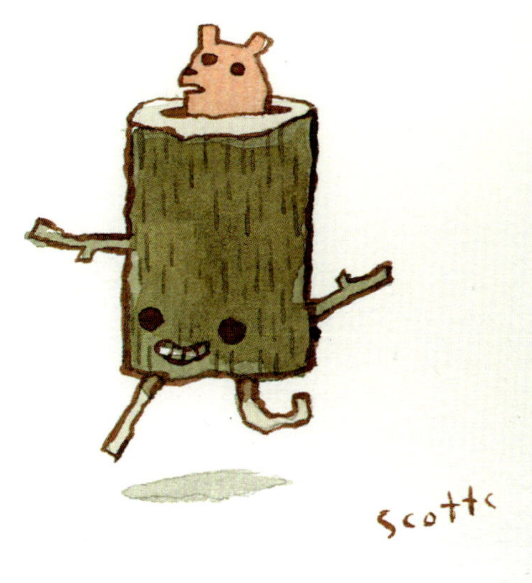

NO WOES
watercolor
3.5" x 3.5"
2010

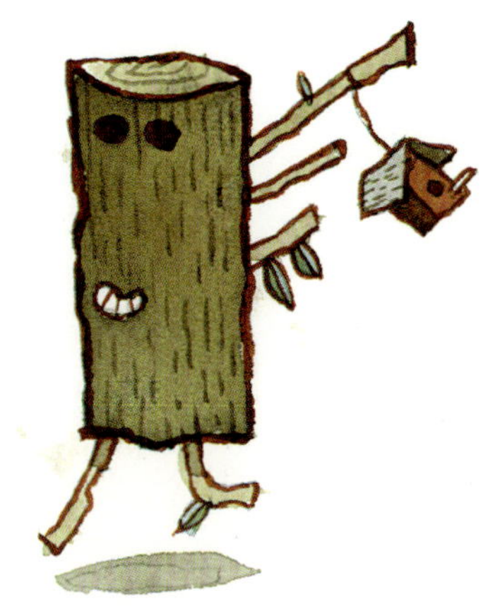
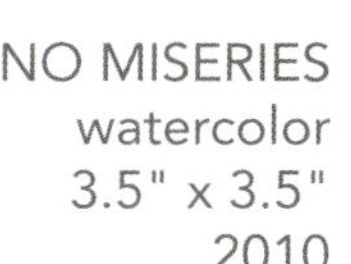

NO MISERIES
watercolor
3.5" x 3.5"
2010

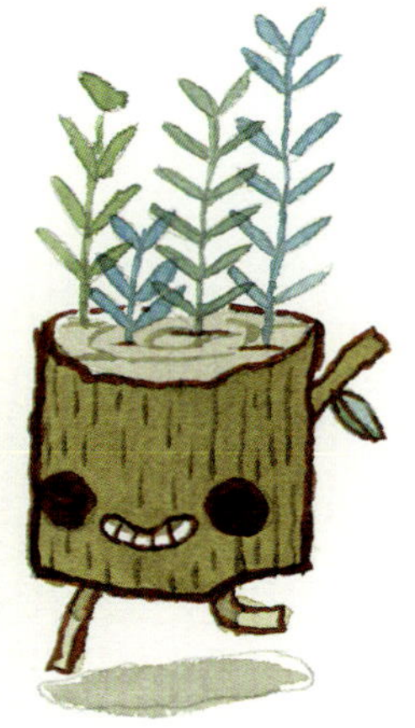

NO BAD FEELINGS
watercolor
3.5" x 3.5"
2010

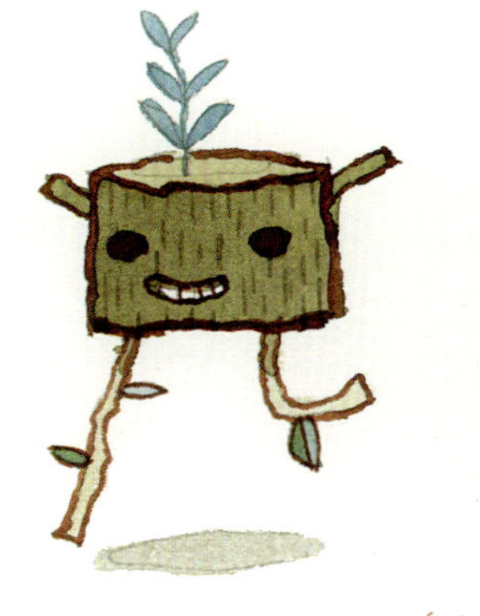

NO CONCERNS
watercolor
3.5" x 3.5"
2010

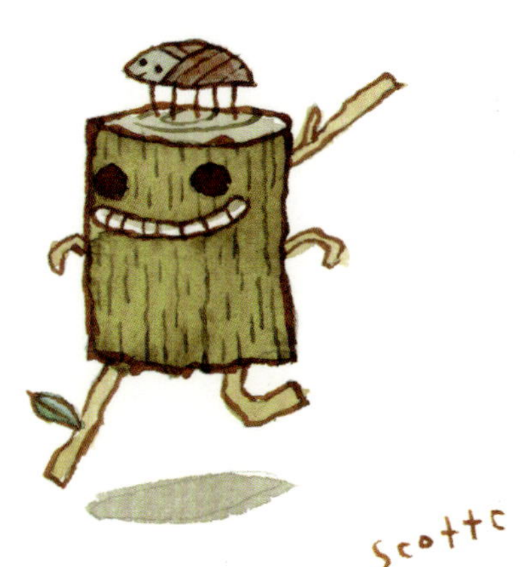

NO HASSLES
watercolor
3.5" x 3.5"
2010

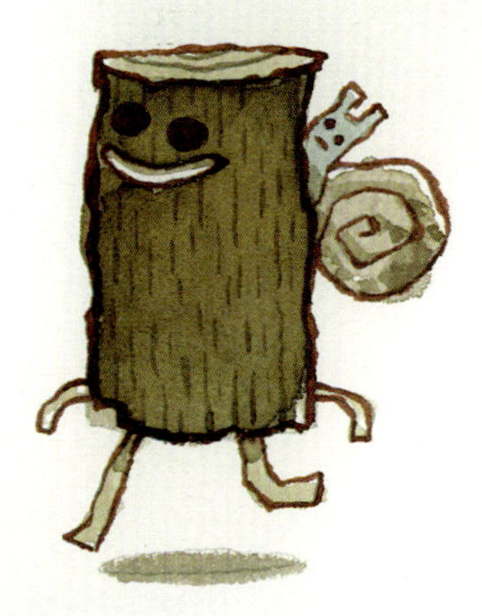

NO HARD TIMES
watercolor
3.5" x 3.5"
2010

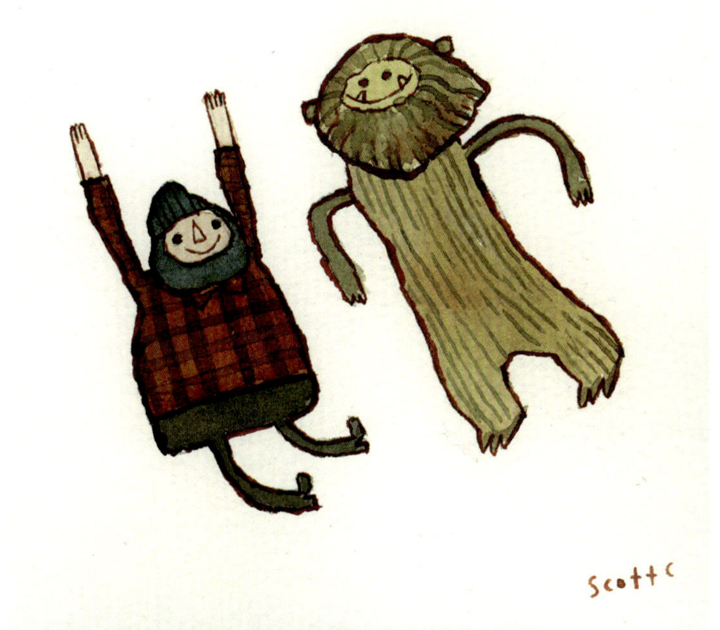

FEELIN' IT
watercolor
5" x 5"
2009

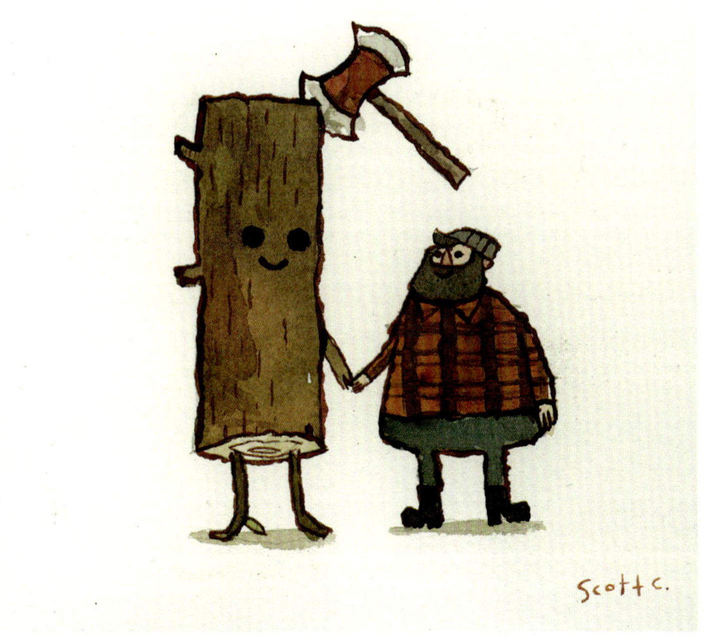

FRIEND OF LOG
watercolor
3.5" x 3.5"
2010

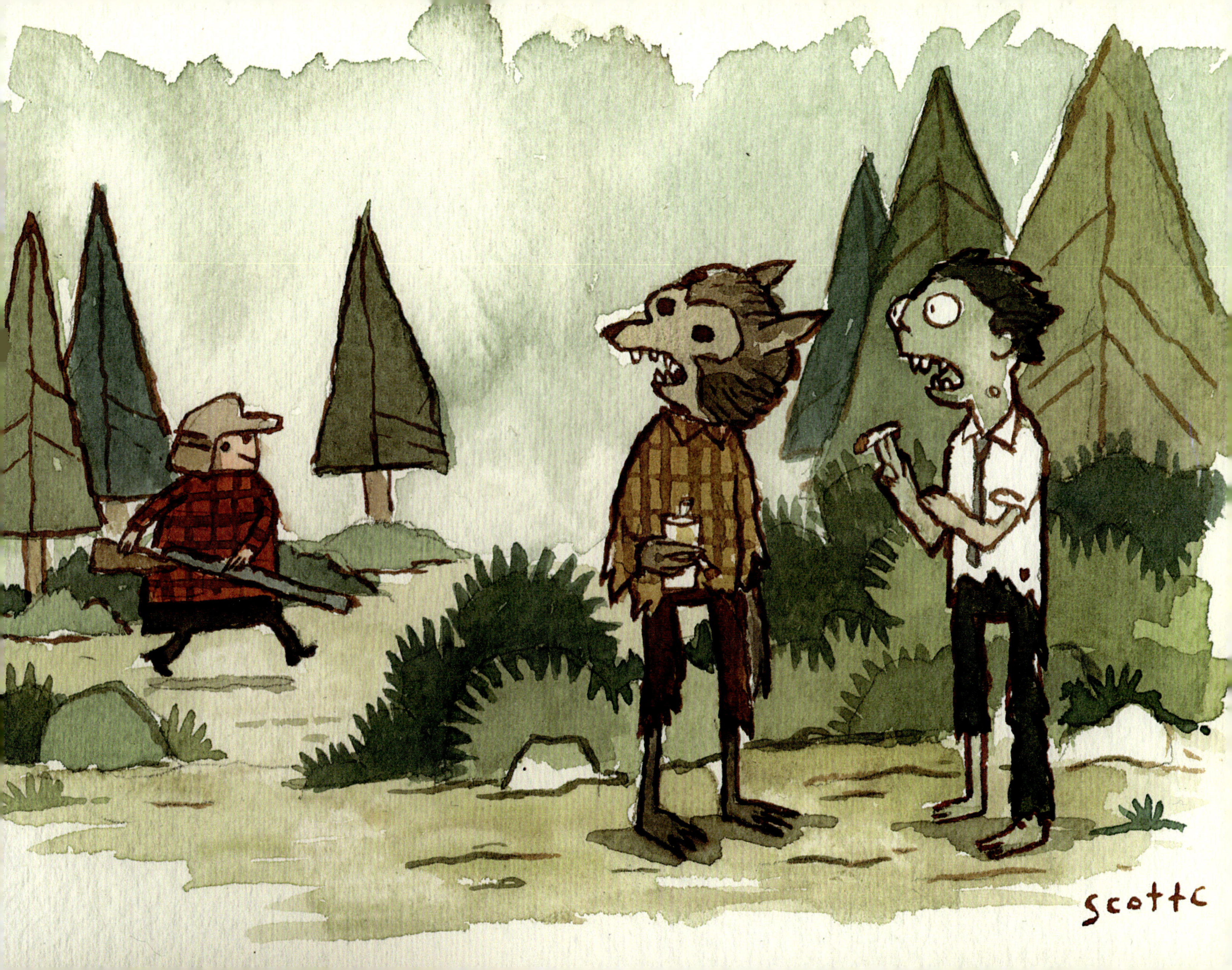
scottc

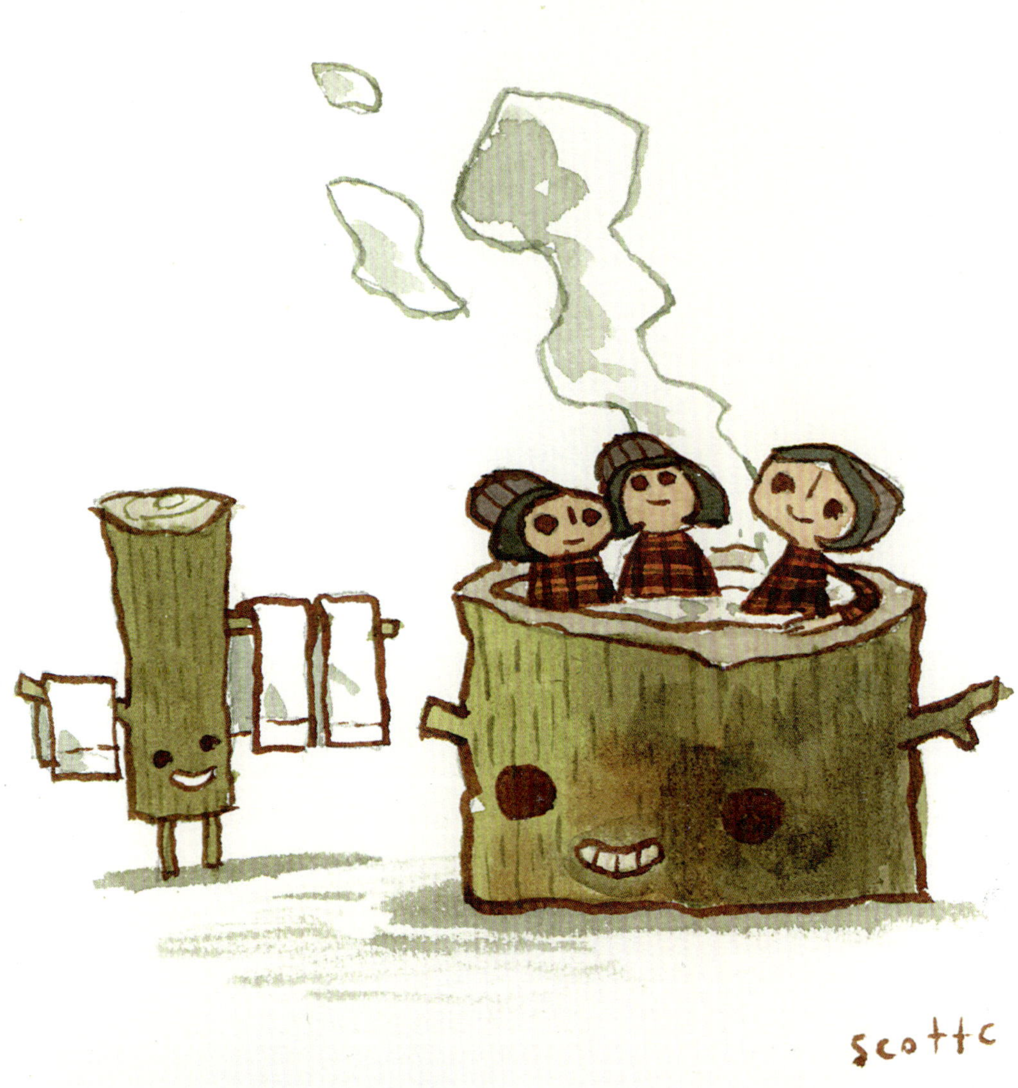

TUB
watercolor
5" x 5"
2010

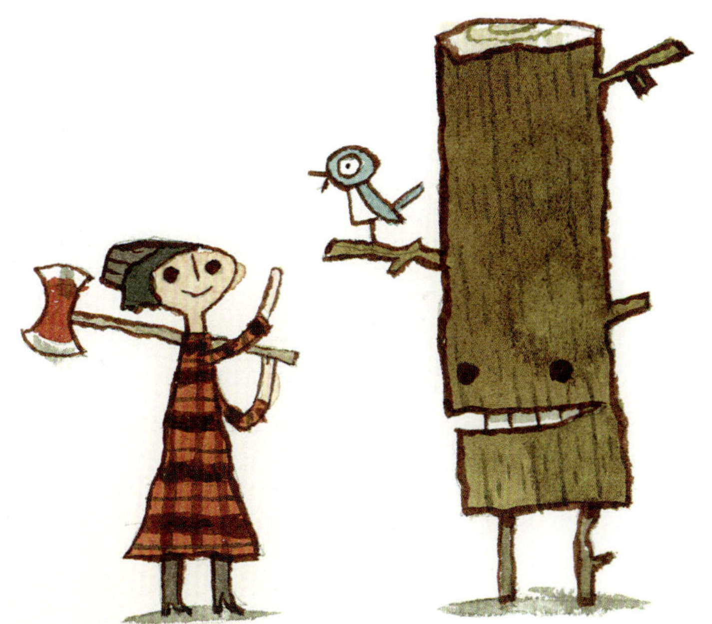

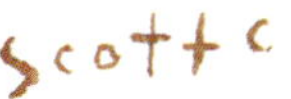

BIRD ON MY BRANCH
watercolor
5" x 5"
2010

DIARY
watercolor
5" x 5"
2010

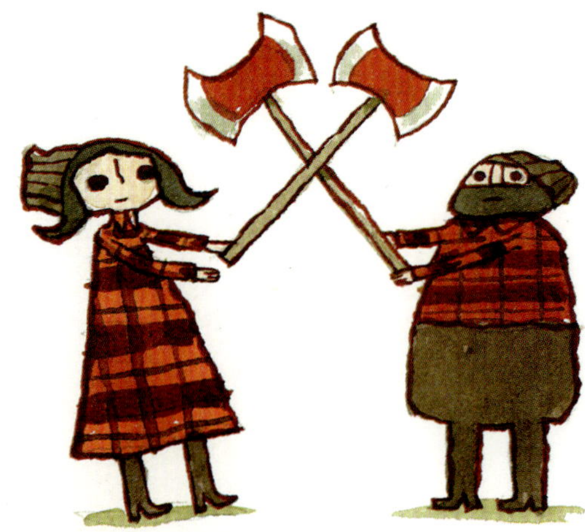

THE CLASH
watercolor
5" x 5"
2009

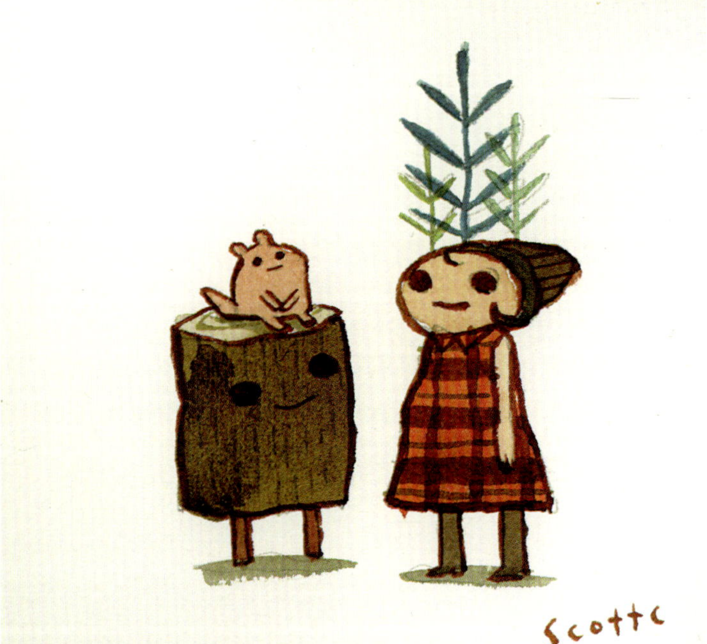

JUST TALKING
watercolor
3.5" x 3.5"
2009

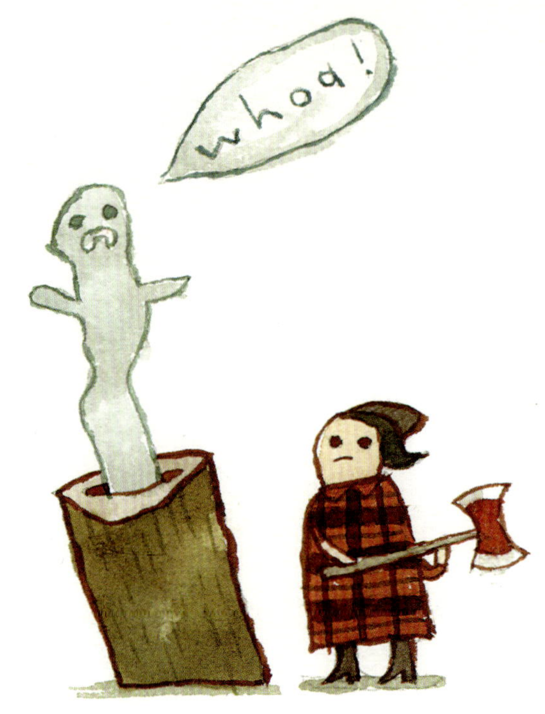

GHOST INSIDE
watercolor
5" x 5"
2009

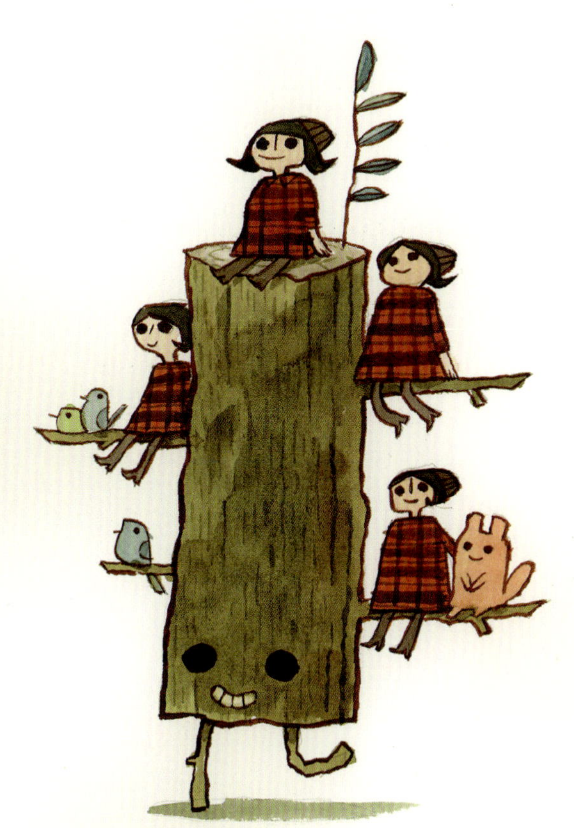

LADIES ON MY BRANCHES
watercolor
8" x 10"
2009

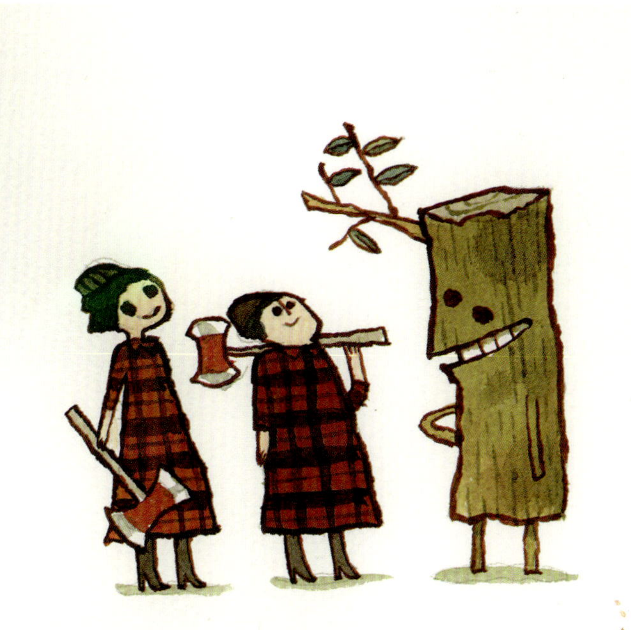

IT'S A BRANCH (NO BIGGIE)
watercolor
5" x 5"
2009

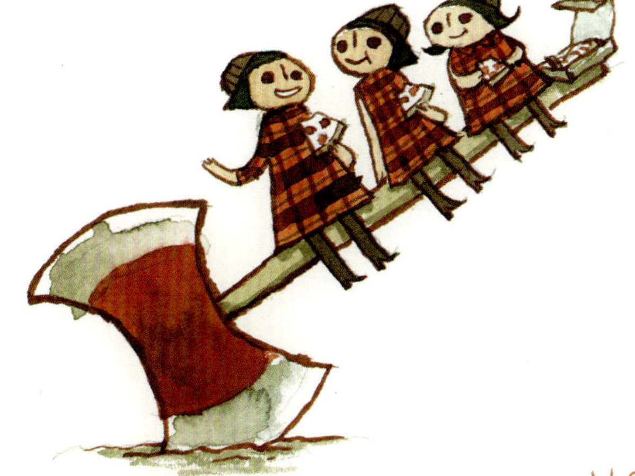

LUNCH ON THE AXE
watercolor
5" x 5"
2010

illustrations

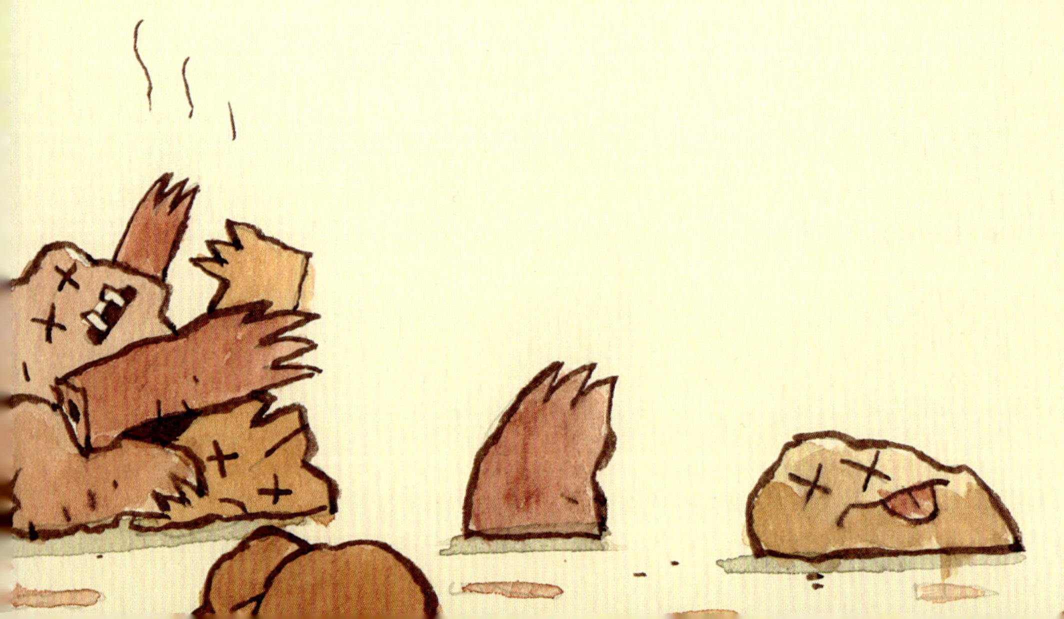

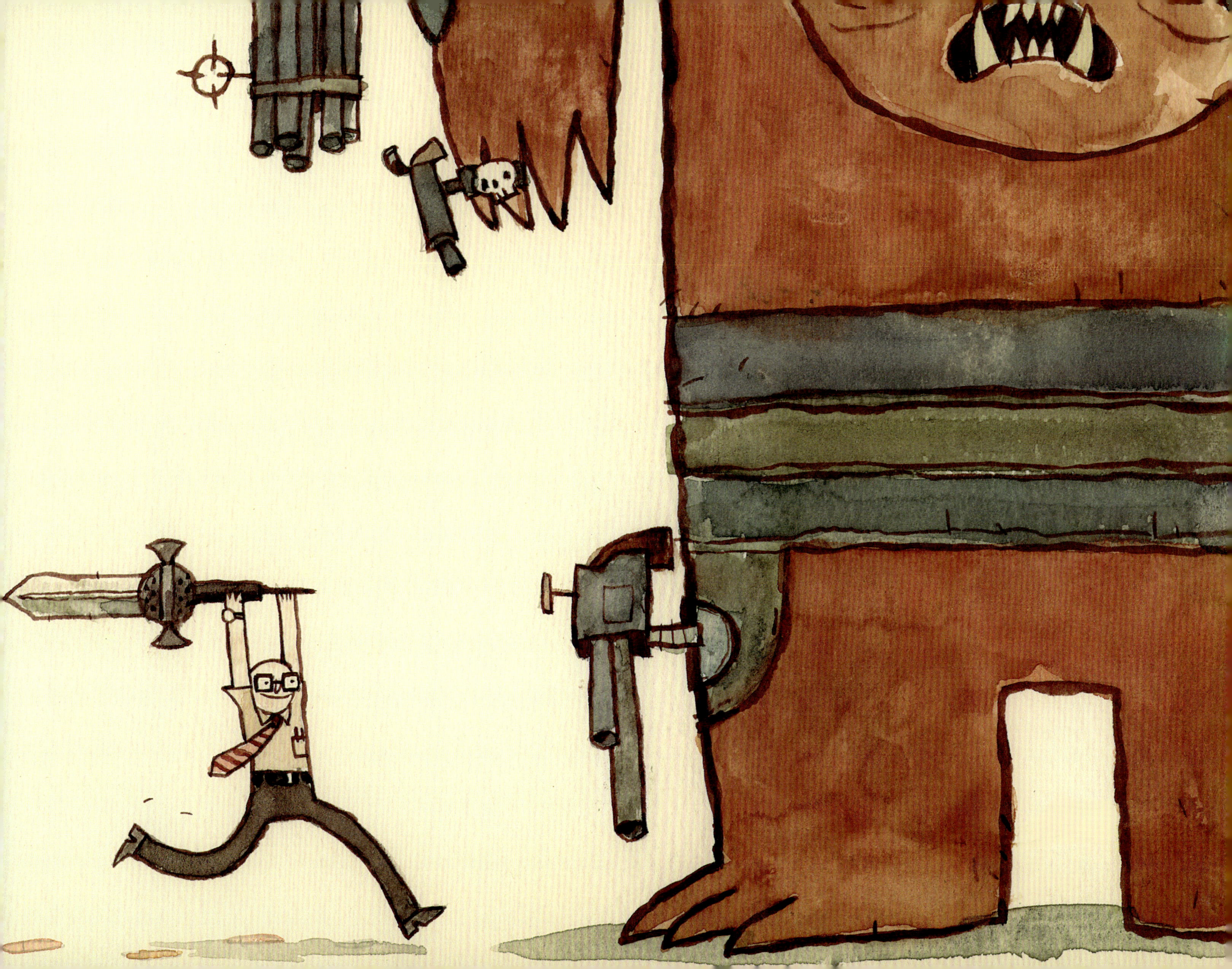

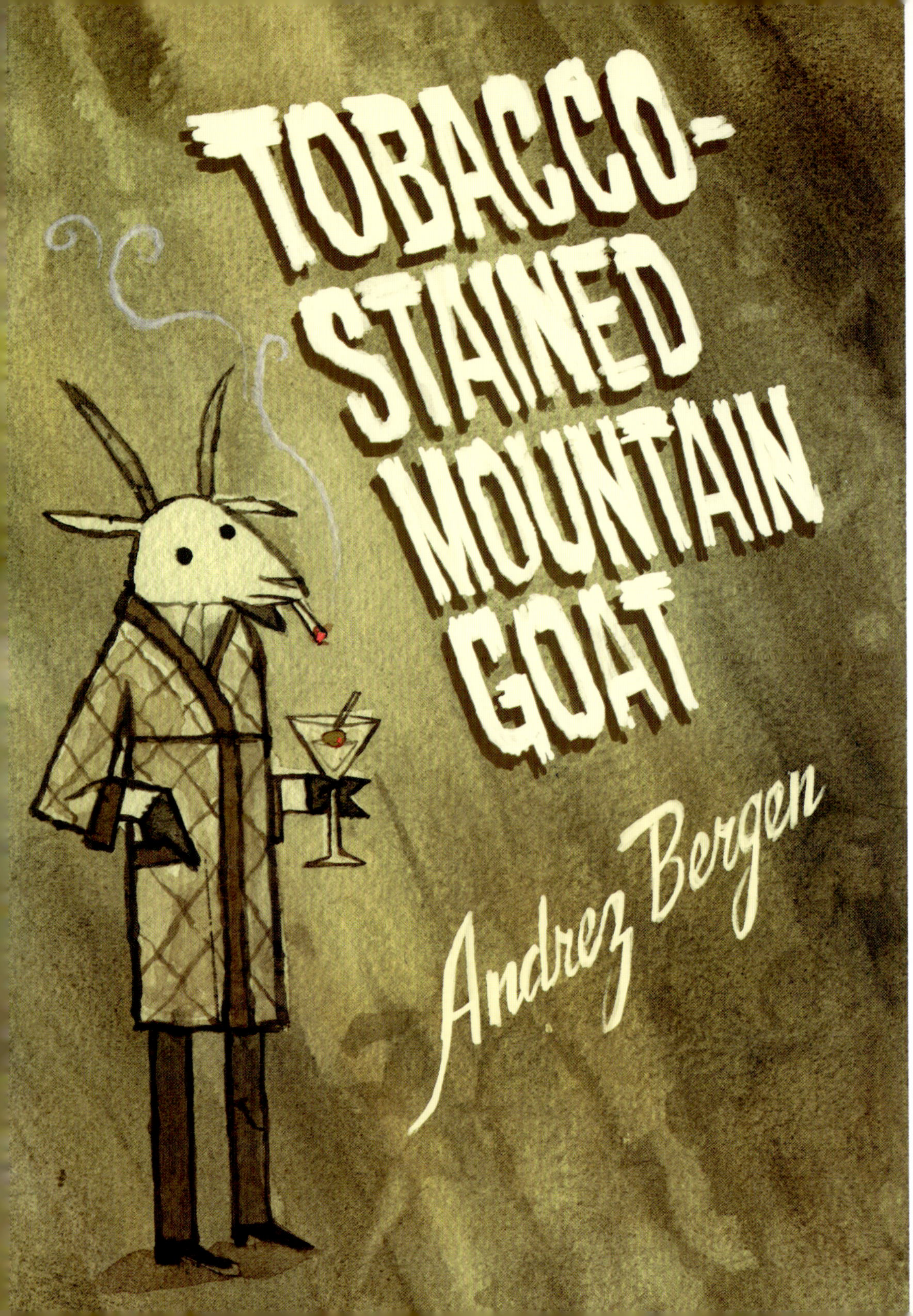

TOBACCO-STAINED MOUNTAIN GOAT

Andrez Bergen

<< [section opener] FINAL BOSS | album cover: MC Frontalot | watercolor | 16" x 8" | 2008

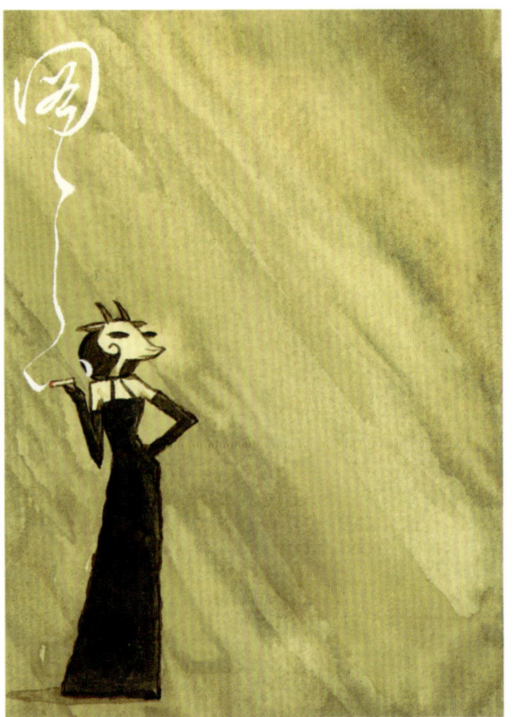

TOBACCO-STAINED MOUNTAIN GOAT
back cover: another sky press
watercolor
6" x 8"
2010

TOBACCO-STAINED MOUNTAIN GOAT
book cover: another sky press
watercolor
6" x 8"
2009

I like monsters and cars. I used to watch *Wacky Races* a whole lot on Saturday mornings. The monsters in this painting drive cars that make a whole lot of sense to them. The only one that gave me trouble conceptually was Wolfman's car. It was suggested the Wolfman drive a dog dish, but that felt too obvious. I chose a branch not so much because he could "fetch" it, but because the 1941 film *Wolfman,* starring Lon Chaney Jr., had a lot of shots in a foggy wooded area. I still don't know if it makes a ton of sense, but that was the thought process, you guys.

THE COMIC BOOK
cover insert: nickelodeon magazine
watercolor
8" x 10.5"
2006

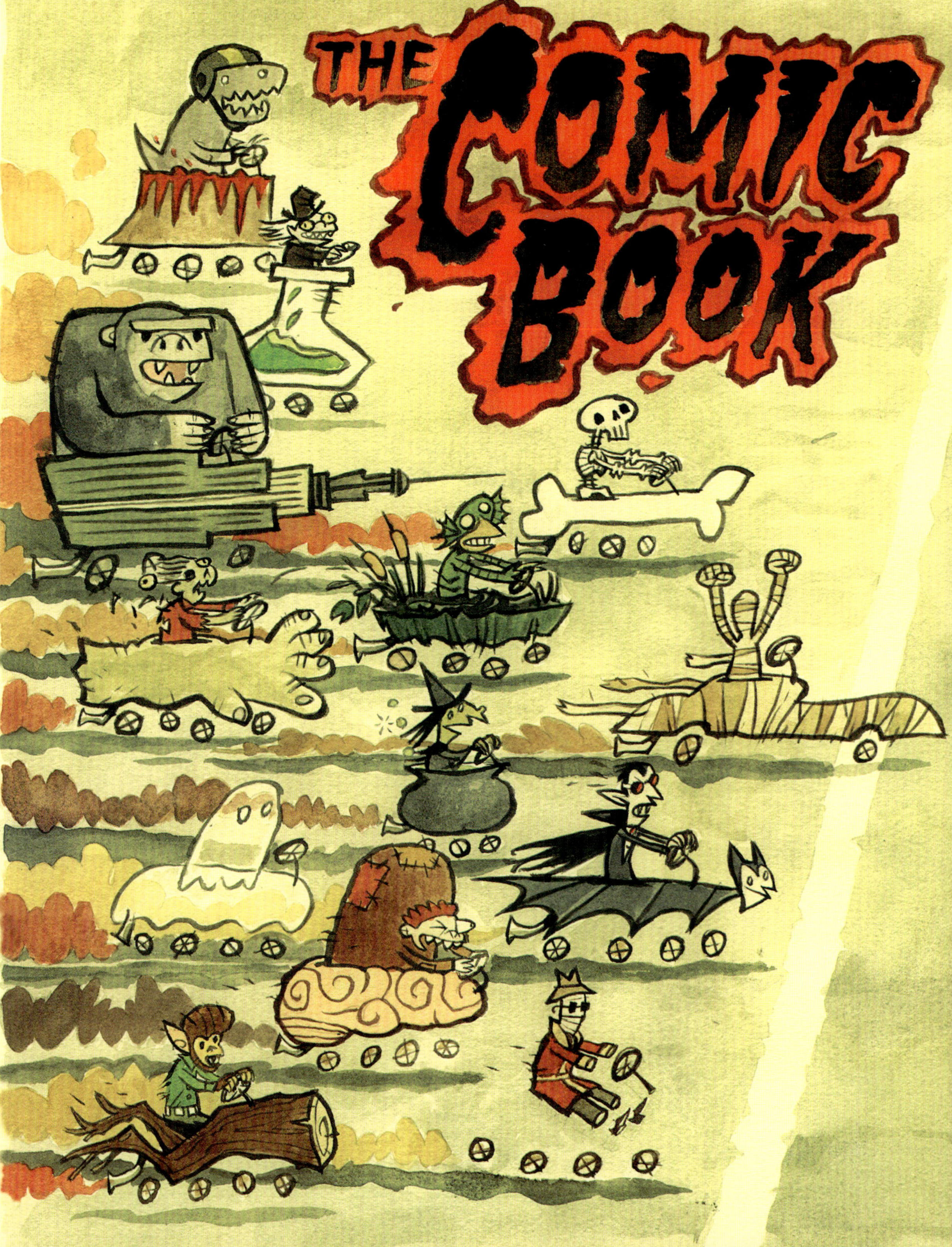

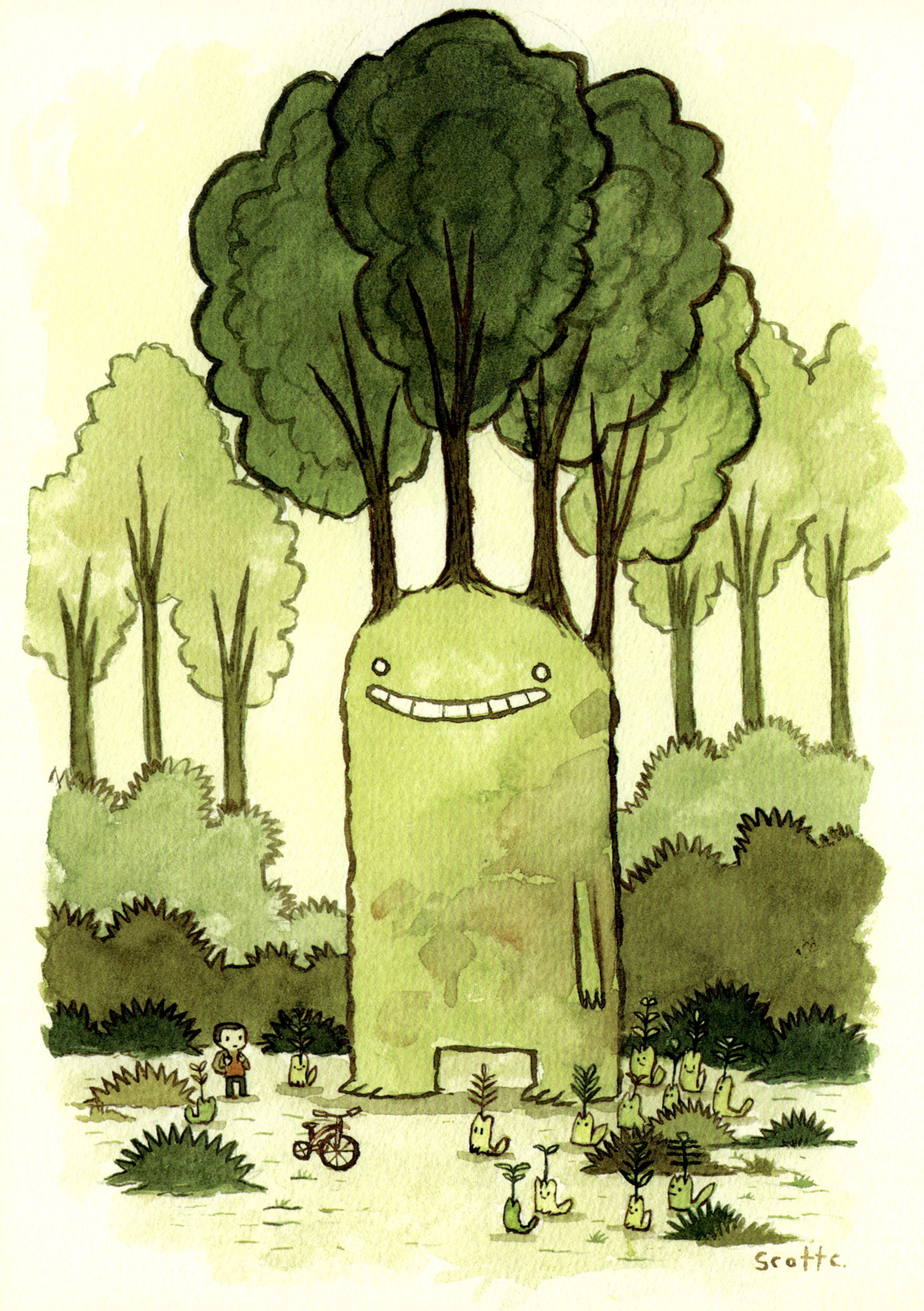

FOREST SPIRIT WITH BIKE
totoro forest project
watercolor
8" x 10"
2008

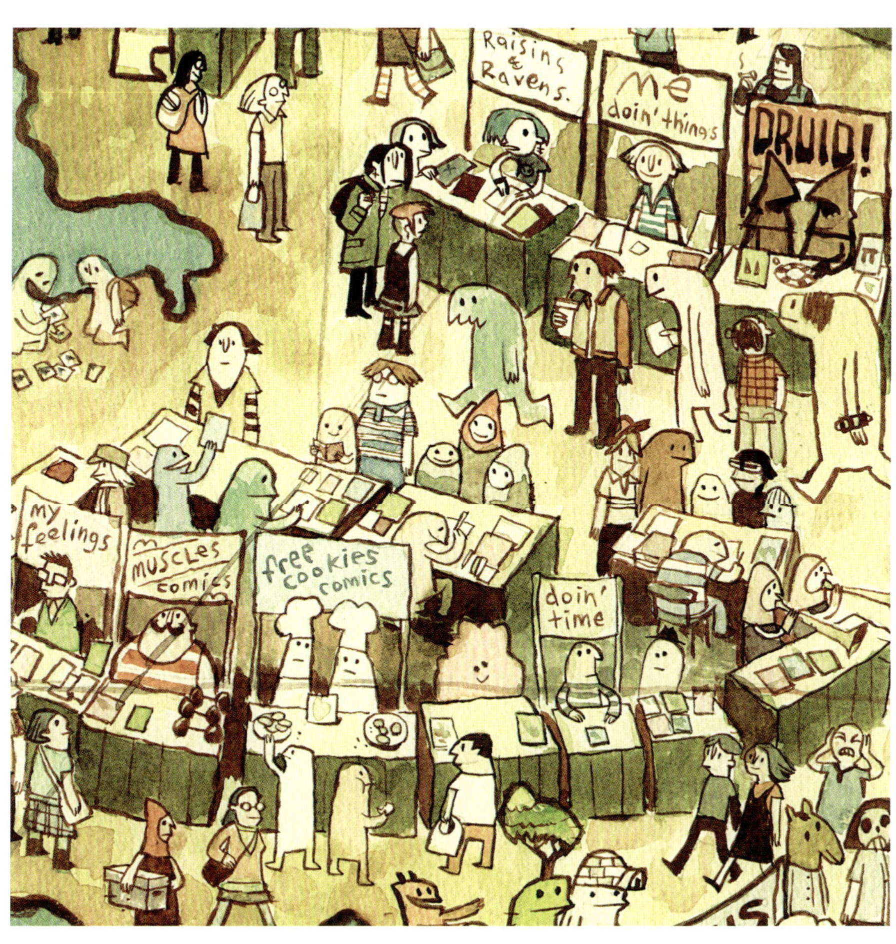

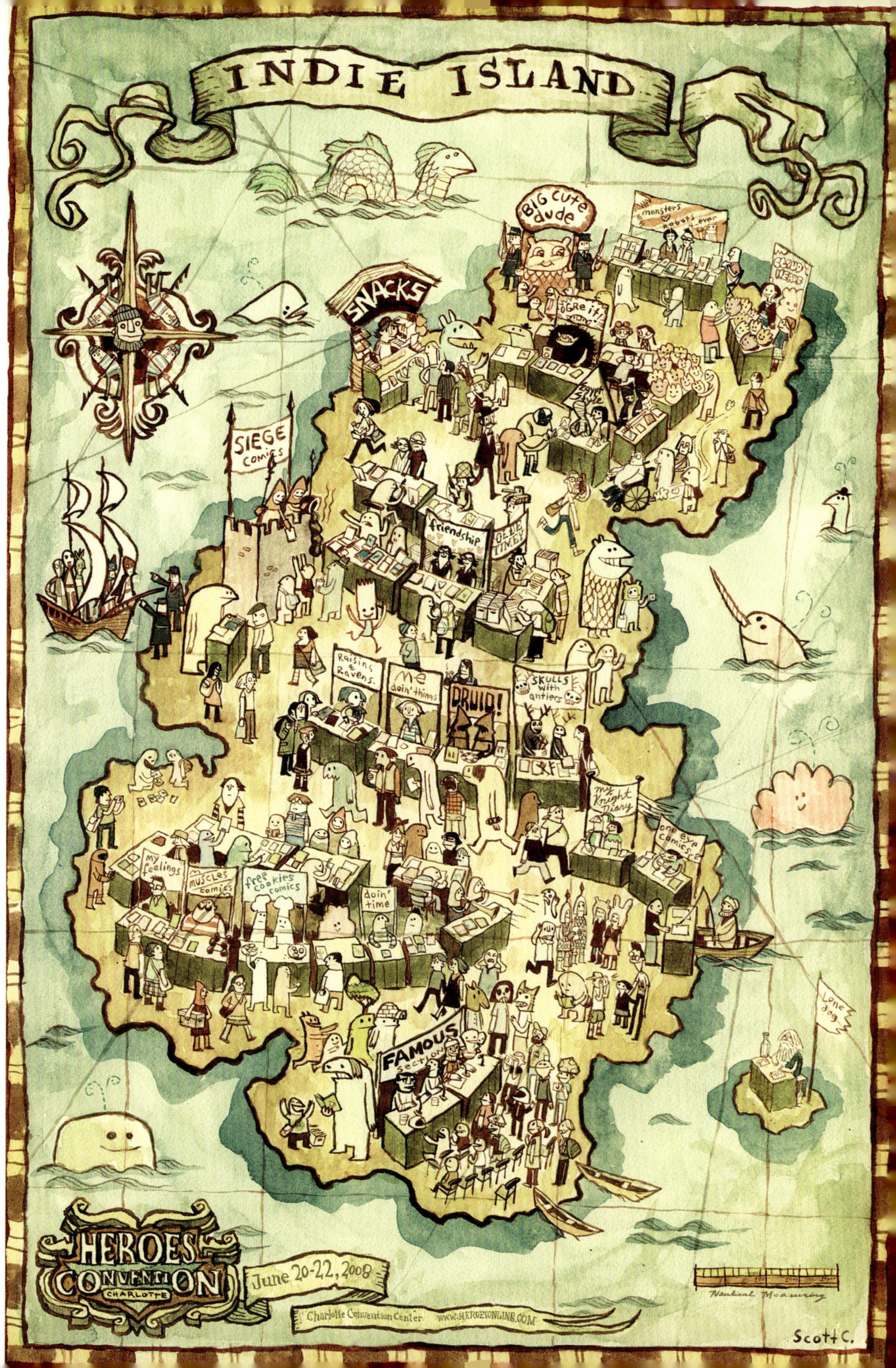

INDIE ISLAND
poster: heroes convention
watercolor
16" x 24"
2008

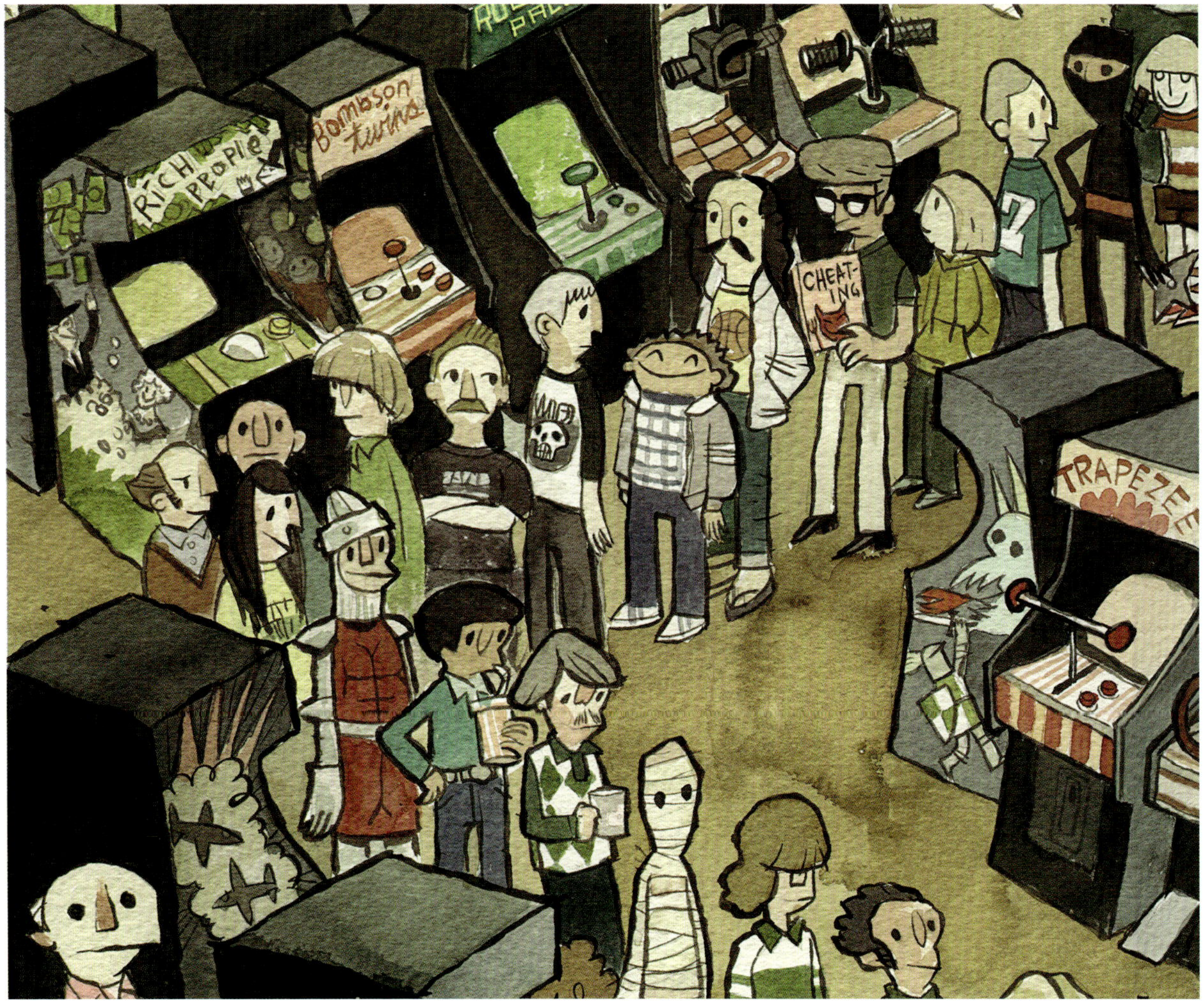

Doing the *King of Kong* cover was a dream come true for me, because my brother and I used to draw fantastical arcades all the time when we were little. We used to line up all of our Atari 2600 games and do drawings of the ultimate arcade incorporating each of our games. This way we could pretend we were in the arcade when we were playing them on our crummy TV. My favorite part of doing this painting was brainstorming the arcade titles. I would still very much like to see these games made in real life. I think *Raking* would be particularly successful.

KING OF KONG: A FISTFUL OF QUARTERS
DVD flip cover: new line cinema
watercolor
37" x 25"
2008

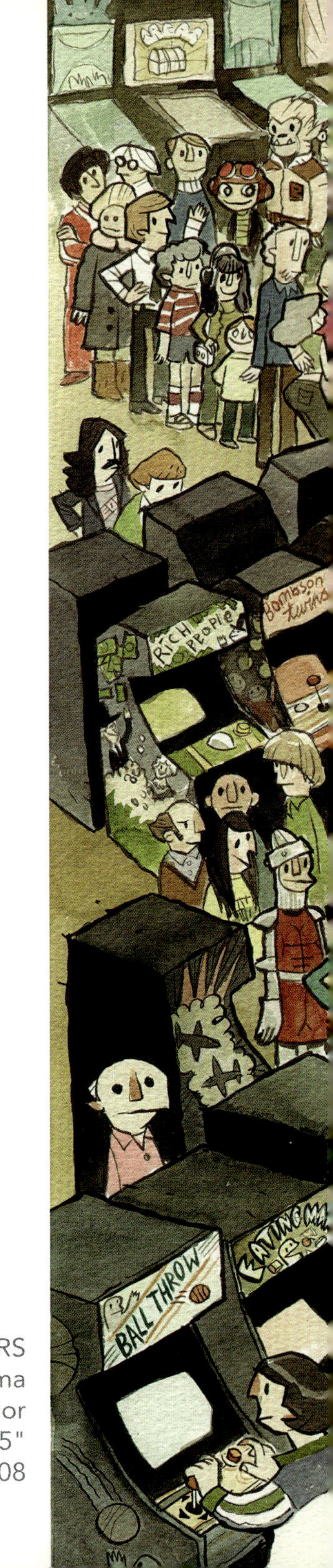

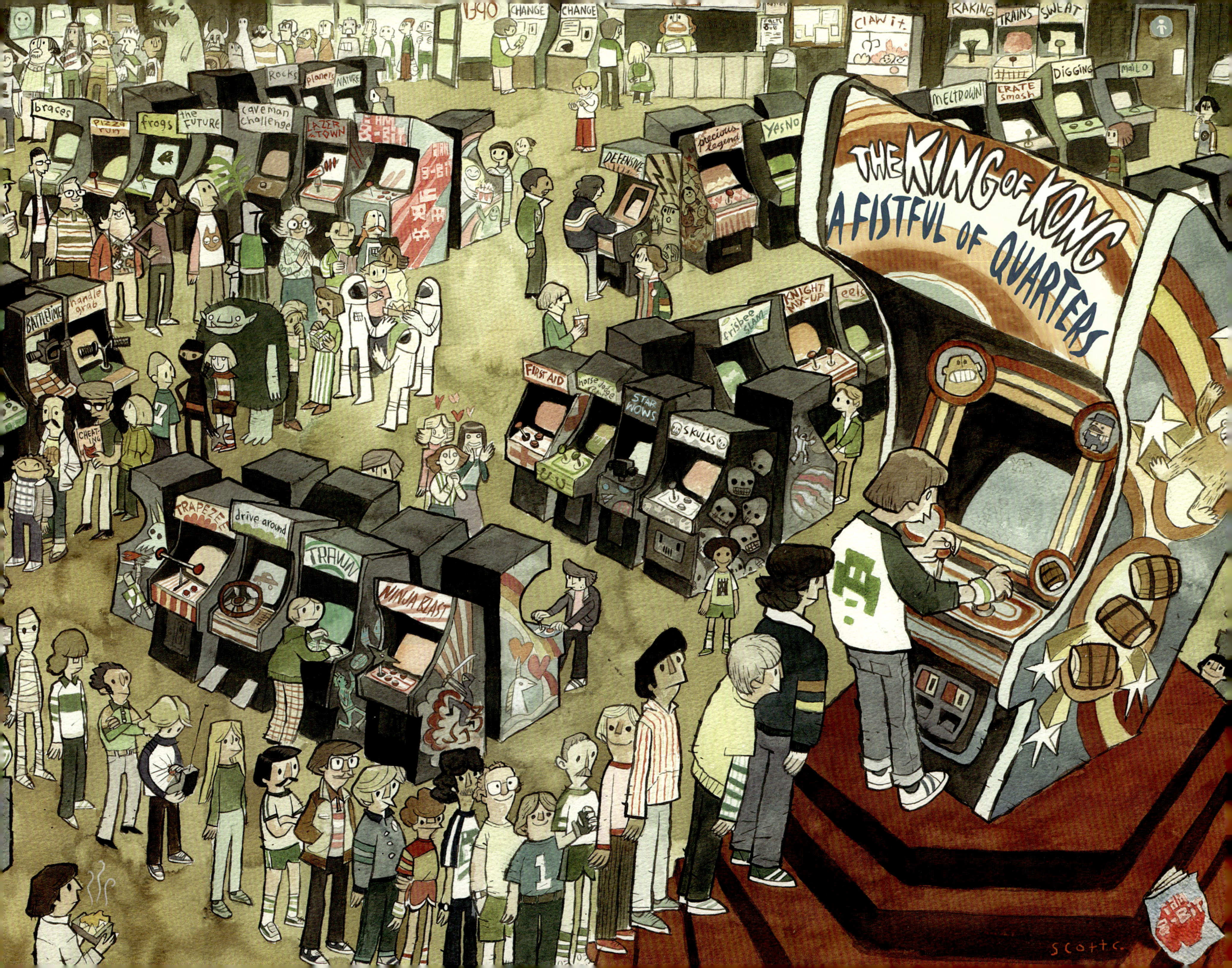
THE KING OF KONG
A FISTFUL OF QUARTERS
CHANGE
CHANGE
CLAW it
RAKING
TRAINS
SWEAT
DIGGING
MELTDOWN
CRATE smash
braces
frogs
the FUTURE
caveman challenge
Rocks
planets
NATURE
DEFENSIVE
precious legend
Yes No
handle grab
FIRST AID
SKULLS
KNIGHT MIX-UP
frisbee SLAM
TRAPEZE
drive around
NINJA BLAST
scott c.

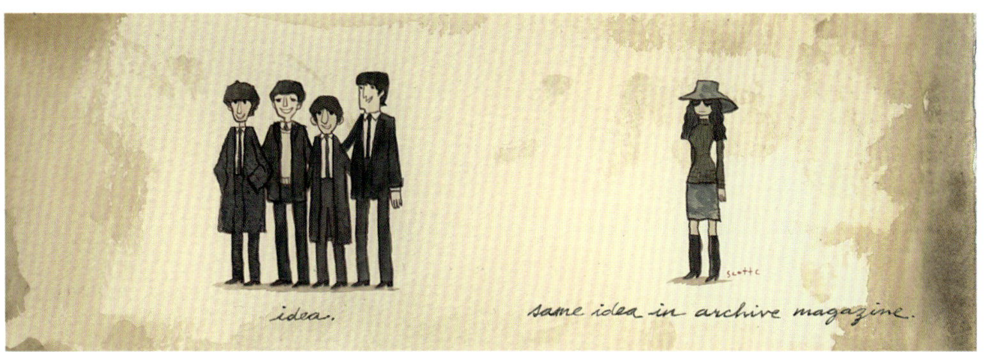

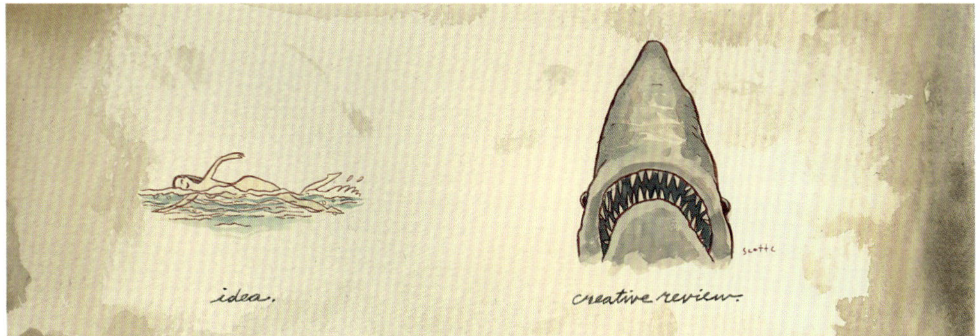

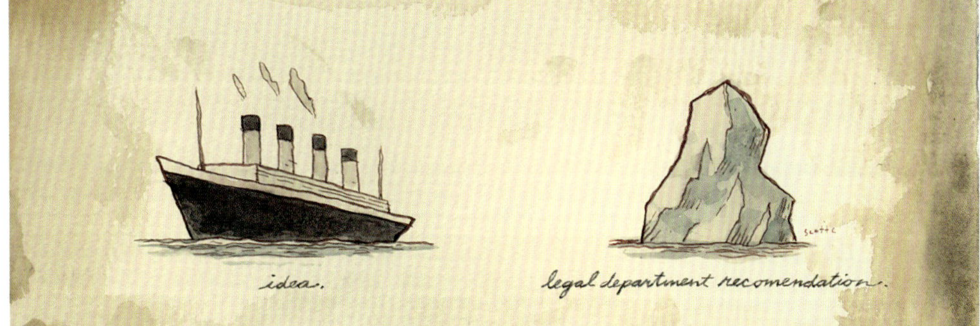

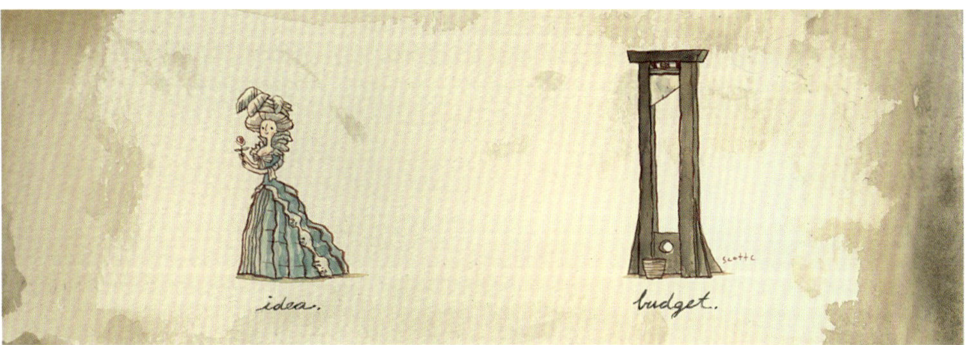

The "How to Kill an Idea" campaign ran in Portugal papers a few years back. They were meant to show the innocence and purity of the idea and the opposing forces that would bring them crashing down. The campaign was used to show the difficulties in getting creative ideas made and the red tape that the ideas have to go through. Like that poor girl who just wanted to do some swimming that one time. Sometimes the world works against your swimming.

HOW TO KILL AN IDEA
ad campaign: fuel
9" x 4"
2008

HOW TO KILL AN IDEA
ad campaign: fuel
9" x 4"
2008

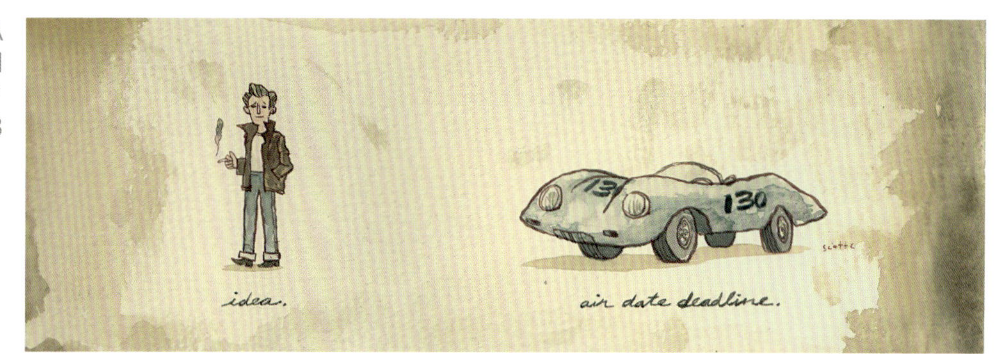

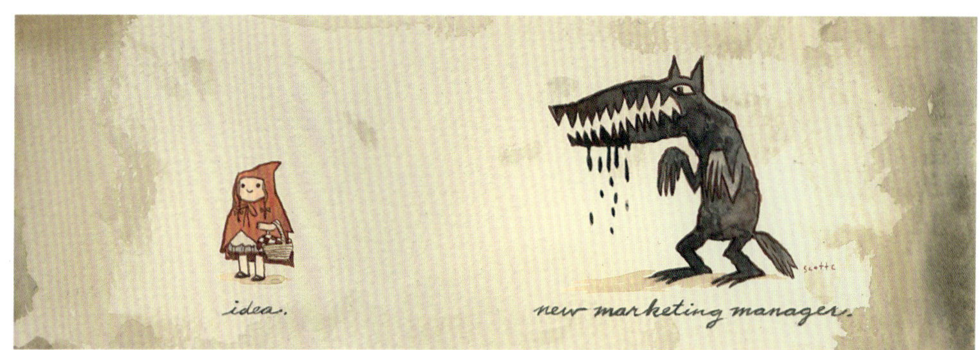

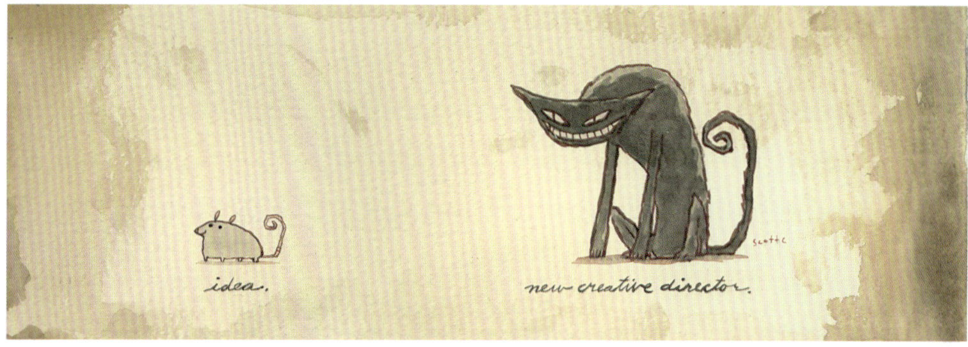

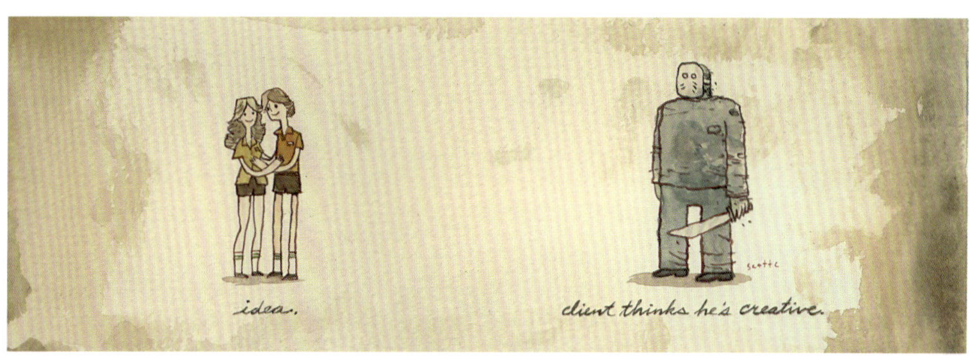

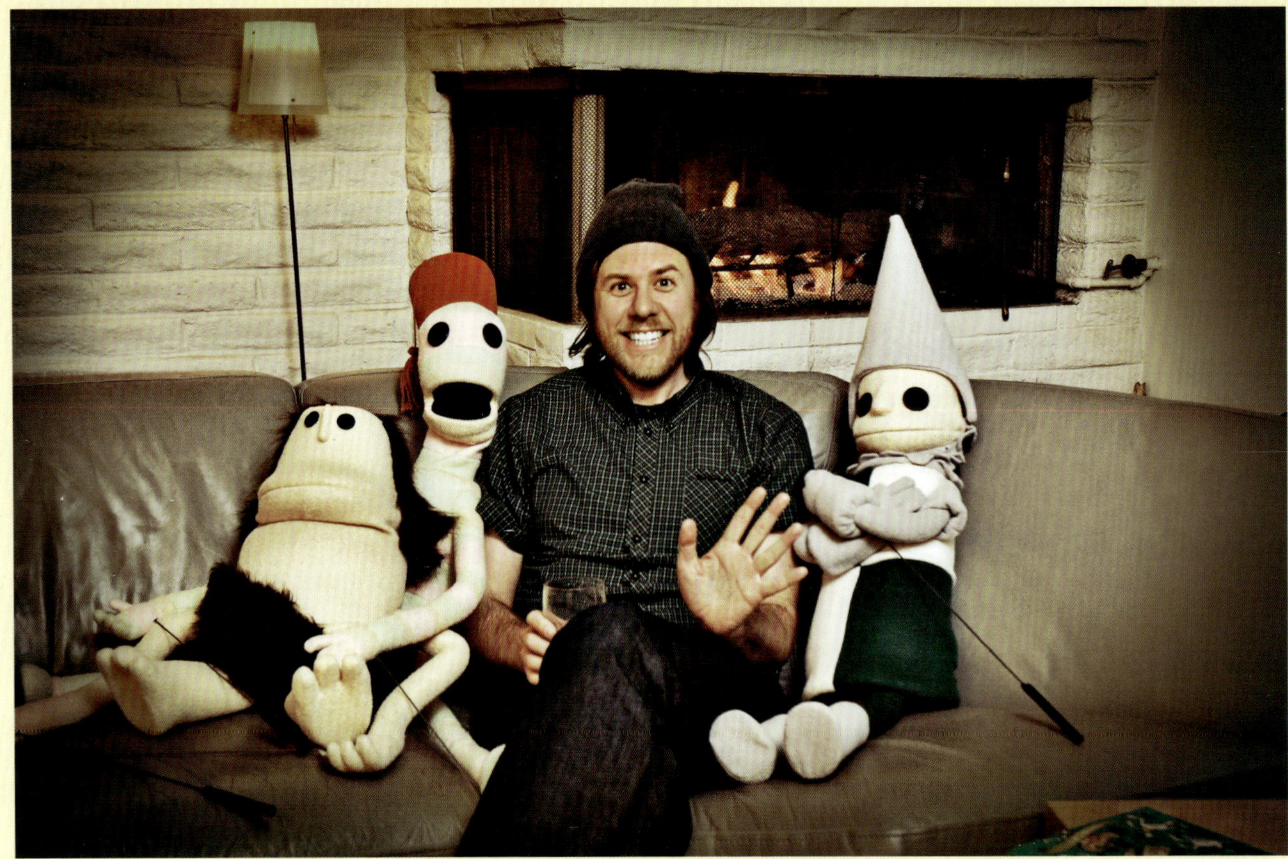

acknowledgments

Special thanks to Mom, Dad, Brian, Paul Allan, Michelle Schlachta, Micke Tong, Greg Morantz, Nate Simmons, Jon Klassen, Chris Appelhans, Jim Mahfood, Graham Annable, Joe White, Razmig Mavlian, Kazu Kibuishi, Judy Hansen, Nathan Stapley, Ian Berry, Alan Harris, Dan Felmlee, Victor Shih, Kate Beaton, Gallery Nucleus, Gallery 1988, MyPlasticHeart, London Miles, Poster Cabaret, Thinkspace Gallery, Bear & Bird Gallery, Redbird Gallery, Secret Headquarters, Katie Cromwell, Jensen Karp, Ben Zhu, Wade Buchanan, Russ Walko, Jon Gibson, i am 8-bit, Nerdcore, Derek Puleston, Tina Ziegler, Aristides Pinedo-Burns, MC Frontalot, Andrez Bergen, Diasuke Tsutsumi, Amanda Visell, Tara McPherson, Jesse Reklaw, Pedro Bexiga, Marcelo Lourenco, Hiro Kawahara, the Crook Family, Dustin Harbin, Gabe Miller, Tim Schafer, Sanjay Patel, and Kevin Toyama.

biographies

Scott Campbell (Scott C.) is a maker of paintings, illustrations, comics, children's books, and video games. At Double Fine Productions, he art directed the critically acclaimed video games *Brütal Legend* and *Psychonauts*. His paintings have been featured in galleries around the world, including Gallery 1988 in Los Angeles, Galerie Arludik in Paris, and the London Miles Gallery. He lives in New York City. Please visit him at pyramidcar.com and greatshowdowns.com.

Jack Black is a comedian, actor, and musician who has starred in films, including *School of Rock*, *Tropic Thunder*, and *High Fidelity*. He is also a founding member of the band Tenacious D and has had roles on such television shows as *The Office* and *Mr. Show*. He lives in Los Angeles.

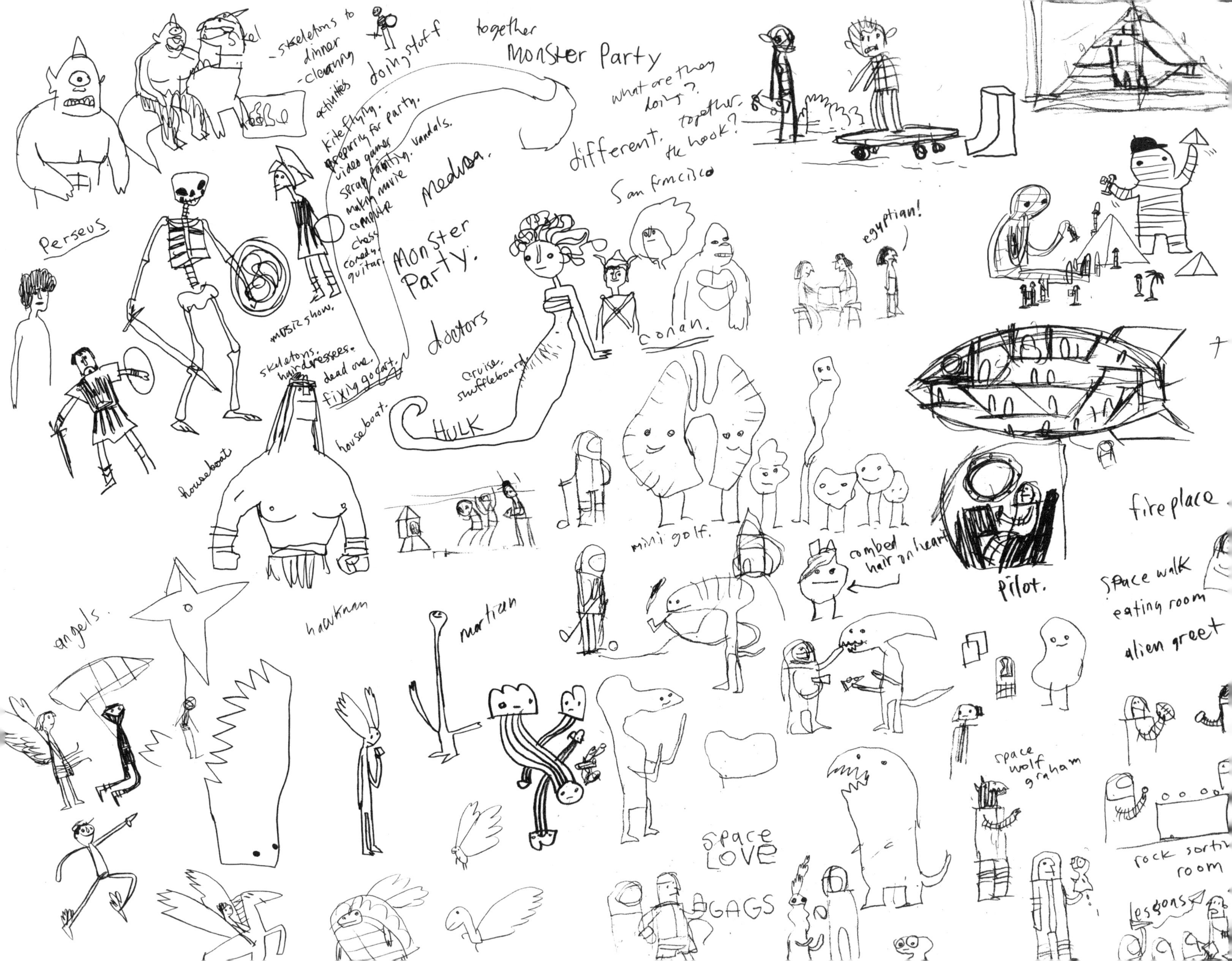

skel
- skeletons to dinner
- cleaning
activities
doing stuff
together
MONSTER Party
what are they doing?
different.
together.
the hook?
San francisco
Perseus
kite flying.
preparing for party.
video games
scrap painting. vandals.
makin movie
computer
chess
comedy.
guitar.
medusa.
MONSTER Party.
music show.
skeletons. hairdressers.
dead one.
fixing go cart.
doctors
cruise. shuffleboard.
HULK
houseboat.
houseboat
conan.
egyptian!
mini golf.
combed hair on heart
fireplace.
pilot.
space walk
eating room
alien greet
angels.
hawkman
martian
space wolf graham
space LOVE
GAGS
rock sorti
room
lessons